FAMILIES IN AMERICA

A Reference Handbook

Other Titles in ABC-CLIO's
**CONTEMPORARY
WORLD ISSUES**
Series

Books in the Contemporary World Issues series address vital issues in today's society such as genetic engineering, pollution, and biodiversity. Written by professional writers, scholars, and nonacademic experts, these books are authoritative, clearly written, up-to-date, and objective. They provide a good starting point for research by high school and college students, scholars, and general readers as well as by legislators, businesspeople, activists, and others.

Each book, carefully organized and easy to use, contains an overview of the subject, a detailed chronology, biographical sketches, facts and data and/or documents and other primary-source material, a directory of organizations and agencies, annotated lists of print and nonprint resources, and an index.

Readers of books in the Contemporary World Issues series will find the information they need in order to have a better understanding of the social, political, environmental, and economic issues facing the world today.

FAMILIES IN AMERICA

A Reference Handbook

Jeffrey Scott Turner

CONTEMPORARY WORLD ISSUES

A B C CLIO

Santa Barbara, California
Denver, Colorado
Oxford, England

Library of Congress Cataloging-in-Publication Data
Turner, Jeffrey Scott
   Families in America : a reference handbook / Jeffrey Scott Turner.
      p.   cm — (Contemporary world issues)
   Includes bibliographical references and index.
   ISBN 1-57607-628-8 (hardcover : alk. paper)
   1. Family—United States—Handbooks, manuals, etc.   I. Title.   II.
Series.
HQ536 .T798   2002
306.85'0973—dc21

                                                        2002002832

06 05 04 03 02   10 9 8 7 6 5 4 3 2 1

This book is also available on the World Wide Web as an e-book. Visit abc-clio.com for details.

ABC-CLIO, Inc.
130 Cremona Drive, P.O. Box 1911
Santa Barbara, California 93116–1911

This book is printed on acid-free paper ∞.
Manufactured in the United States of America

To my brother Gregg,
Who taught me the meaning of courage
as only an older brother can.

Contents

Preface

Families in America: A Reference Handbook is an in-depth and multi-faceted examination of the contemporary American family. The volume is designed for a wide range of readers in college, high school, and public library settings. It supplies a solid conceptual foundation of basic terms, concepts, and policies related to the topic as well as detailed coverage of important issues and controversies facing the modern family. The manual offers readers a useful combination of accumulated family studies knowledge as well as new research frontiers. Throughout the book, a particular emphasis is placed on exposing readers to historical, multicultural, and international perspectives. The result is a reference manual that is current, complete, and thorough in its coverage of the topic. The volume is especially valuable to students seeking information in such areas as marriage and family, intimate relationships, human sexuality, family planning, gender issues, parenthood, education, human development, psychology, and sociology.

This reference handbook offers readers an opportunity to explore and better understand the diverse, fluctuating needs of the contemporary family. As our family structures shift seemingly at the speed of technology, we must embrace our past in order to live through our present and prepare for our future. The new century brings challenging and complex issues to the forefront: soaring divorce rates, blended families of all races and religions, single-parent households, caring for aging parents, and reproductive technologies, to name but a few. *Families in America: A Reference Handbook* speaks to such topics while simultaneously responding to the family challenges readers have faced, or will face, as they are daughters and sons, wives and husbands, mothers and fathers, and grandparents. The study of family life is thus approached both scientifically and humanely; there are data to be conveyed and understanding to be sought.

The approach of *Families in America: A Reference Handbook* is twofold, both empirical and pragmatic. The volume offers an academically solid and comprehensive overview of family life, carefully integrating both the classic studies and contemporary areas of marriage and family research. But while the volume draws from highly regarded and respected family research journals and books, deliberate steps will be taken to avoid creating a complex and confusing experience for the reader. The writing style is engaging, concise, and politically sensitive.

The organizational framework of *Families in America: A Reference Handbook* consists of nine separate, but interrelated chapters. The first chapter provides readers with a historical overview of the family while the second chapter explores the diversity that exists in family life today. Chapter three probes an assortment of important family issues and controversies. The fourth chapter contains a detailed chronology of major trends and events shaping American family life, including the issues and controversies covered in the preceding chapter. The fifth chapter, biographical in design, offers a look at contributions of noteworthy family life and social science researchers. The sixth chapter, consisting of graphic material, offers the reader important statistical portraits of modern family life. The seventh chapter includes a diverse and comprehensive listing of family life agencies and organizations. The eighth chapter provides readers with a listing of recent and important books on family life as well as representative research journals from the field of family studies. Chapter nine includes a listing of educational videotapes on family life in America and a number of web resources for further study. For the dual purpose of convenience and organization, the resources contained in chapters seven, eight, and nine are organized according to the sequence of issues and controversies covered in chapter three. A glossary and complete bibliography conclude the volume.

Acknowledgments

Although authors bear the primary responsibility for the works they create, many other individuals and organizations play a part in a book's development, preparation, and eventual publication. Researching and writing can be lonely pursuits, and I would like to thank those who made the journey easier with their timely advice and spirited encouragement. Dr. Catherine Wright, my friend and teaching colleague, supplied professional insight on a wide variety of topics, and the research skills of Assistant Professor Jennifer Mauro proved invaluable in locating needed references and resources. I thank Mitchell College President Dr. Mary Ellen Jukoski and Vice President of Academic Affairs Dr. Jane Friederichs for their support of this research project. I also extend special appreciation to the United States Census Bureau and the Population Reference Bureau for granting us permission to reproduce important graphic materials.

I would also like to thank those persons associated with ABC-CLIO who contributed their expertise to this book. Acquisitions editor Mim Vasan saw the early promise of this work and convinced me to push the project forward with ABC-CLIO. Alicia Merritt supplied important guidance and direction during the early stages of development, and production editor Carla Roberts oversaw the book's evolution from conception to publication. Her knowledge, timely advice, and unbridled enthusiasm proved invaluable. Her many positive suggestions and creative changes were instrumental in transforming a raw manuscript into a cohesive and coherent reference handbook.

1

History and Scope of American Families

Family life, as it exists in modern-day America, is fully comprehended and appreciated when it is traced to its historical roots. Past social, cultural, legal, and political forces have helped to shape present-day family forms and variations. Understanding previous family lifestyles and practices puts us in a better position to understand today's changes and to appreciate contemporary family perspectives and theories. And, for today's family advocates, a walk backward through time will enable us to critically evaluate past efforts to better understand and improve family life. Our present-day vantage point will hopefully enable us to look at the past and avoid past mistakes, borrow what was good, and better plan for the future. Let's begin this historical narrative with a look at family life during colonial America.

Colonial America

The colonists who voyaged to America were in search of a better life in the New World. The early colonies were divided into three geographical groups: the northern colonies, now the several states of New England; the middle colonies, consisting of New York, New Jersey, Delaware, and Pennsylvania; and the southern colonies, stretching from Maryland to Georgia. The colonial period began with the settlement of Jamestown, Virginia, in 1607 and ended with the start of the Revolutionary War in 1775. During this relatively short amount of time, a wilderness was conquered and a new nation was established.

Many of the colonists were Puritans, a group of Protestants who broke away from the Church of England, and wanted to purify their churches and focused on such things as eliminating priestly vestments and elaborate ceremonies. Many Puritans were guided by the thinking of John Calvin. In England, the Puritans were subjected to religious persecution, so they journeyed to America with the hope of discovering religious liberty.

The Puritans were governed by strong clerical leadership and driven by a compelling work ethic. They brought a number of European customs and beliefs to the New World. Early marriages and the creation of large families were encouraged so that the family could function as an economic unit and reap productive harvests. Failure to marry was viewed as impractical since it resulted in a loss of harvest and a failure to cultivate important farmland. Throughout colonial history, bachelors were viewed with suspicion and in some instances, mistrust. In several colonies, such as Plymouth, single men had to pay special taxes because of their unmarried status. In Hartford, Connecticut, for example, the penalty for remaining single was twenty shillings a week.

Unlike marriages in the Old World, most Puritan marriages were not arranged by a couple's parents. However, it was expected that the prospective bridegroom would secure the father's permission for the bride's hand in marriage. In general, the courtship period was short and often romance was not a part of the bonding process.

The Puritan marriage structure was male dominated, and the husband controlled all domestic matters. Men were expected to provide for their families and to be faithful to their wives. Puritan women occupied a clearly subordinate position to men. Their place was in the home, tending to household responsibilities and caring for children. The woman's property belonged to her husband, and she did not have the right to vote in public matters. Men were permitted to punish their wives and children physically if they wished.

The Puritans practiced considerable sexual restraint and a strict moral code prevailed. Even the clothing worn by the Puritans reflected sexual repression. Believing that bright colors incited lust, they wore only black, gray, and white. Any pleasure derived from sex was frowned upon. Sex was for the purpose of procreation, and only married partners would engage in it. Sex was also forbidden on the Sabbath, a day devoted to religious

activities. Premarital sex, viewed as succumbing to the tempta-
tions of the flesh, was not tolerated, and *both* women and men
were expected to be chaste before marriage.

Adultery was a serious offense, punishable by death. However, adulterers more often than not received lesser penalties
such as imprisonment, whipping, banishment from the community, or the stigma of having to wear the letter "A" on one's clothing (as Hester Prynne did in Hawthorne's *The Scarlet Letter*).
Some adulterers were even branded on the forehead with the letter "A." As far as other sexual behaviors were concerned, masturbation and oral- and anal-genital sex were viewed as sinful
and prohibited.

The Industrial Revolution

Those living in late-nineteenth-century North America witnessed
a nation beginning a transformation. The Industrial Revolution,
as it came to be known, began to change the predominantly
agrarian (farming) society of America into an urban and industrialized one. Instead of functioning together as a productive
agrarian unit, families now seldom worked together physically.
In the growing number of nonfarm families, the husband and
father went off to work in an industrial setting while the wife and
mother remained at home with the children. Women, once labor
partners in farming families, were exclusively assigned to the
home and the hearth. Employment outside of the home and
away from the family became the province of men. It can be said,
then, that as the Industrial Revolution brought about significant
technological change, it also introduced a new dimension to sex-
role behaviors and expectations.

In time, the need for female workers in the labor force
would become evident, but there would be resistance as well.
Due to gender-role stereotyping, women who worked outside of
the home were often regarded as unfeminine or as negligent in
their wifely and mothering responsibilities. However, the
increased number of women joining the labor force helped to
change these attitudes and, in turn, to encourage more women to
seek employment outside the home.

The frequent need to search for employment prospects during the Industrial Revolution also made the family unit more
mobile, thus tending to isolate it from relatives. At one time chil-

dren were regarded as needed hands on the farm and were expected to make worthwhile and productive contributions. At least in the middle classes, children now became economic liabilities as parents had more mouths to feed in their daily struggles to carve out an existence in this new state of American history. Work and family life thus became separate enterprises; families still consumed as a unit but no longer produced as a unit.

For these reasons, smaller families became a desirable goal and birth control an important concern. During the 1920s and 1930s, Margaret Sanger led the birth control movement in the United States. Sanger, a nurse, wrote and distributed booklets on birth control and opened clinics to advise people on methods and techniques. Because it was illegal to distribute birth control information, Sanger, who was responsible for founding the Planned Parenthood Federation of America, met with considerable resistance from law enforcement officials. However, she ultimately succeeded in promoting the concepts of safe and responsible methods of birth control.

Fertility rates in North America declined significantly both during and after the Industrial Revolution. The percentage of families with six or more members was 51.8 in 1790, 32.8 in 1900, and 20.1 in 1930. Meanwhile, the percentage of childless marriages increased. This trend provides an interesting contrast to the high premium placed on having many children during earlier historical periods.

The path to marriage also changed, including new patterns of courtship. The "Roaring Twenties" heralded new levels of autonomy and freedom, as America experienced a wave of prosperity and self-indulgence. Daring young "flappers" shocked their elders with short skirts and the free use of cosmetics and cigarettes, and many drank illegal liquor in clubs called "speakeasies." The invention of the automobile made it possible for young couples to be alone together and to engage in much more sexual activity than was possible within the home. The sexual needs and sexual rights of women were being increasingly recognized. The notion of the shy, passive female was being eroded.

Parental control over courtship lessened considerably, and arranged marriages for the majority of couples became a thing of the past. Women experienced much more freedom in selecting a mate, and for most partners of both sexes, love and affection became pivotal features of the relationship. The concept of romantic love was reborn and became increasingly popular.

Also at this time, the family became targeted by a wide range of social scientists. For example, child-care experts began to offer a wide range of advice and guidance regarding the upbringing of youngsters, including disciplinary strategies (see Chapter 3, "Contemporary Parenthood"). Books, magazine articles, and newspaper columns focused on the best way to raise children. Also, marriage and family counseling services began to emerge, offering professional therapeutic services to those experiencing domestic problems.

The Sexual Revolution

Thus far we have focused our attention on family life in colonial America and the Industrial Revolution. As we have seen, the family as a social institution was distinctly shaped by these historical eras. For example, the colonists regarded marriage as the proper and only place for sexual relations, and sex served primarily a procreative function. Large families were needed to fulfill the various roles associated with an agrarian society. Although the Industrial Revolution began to introduce change, the most sweeping and extensive changes in gender-roles, gender-role behavior, and sexual activity occurred in the latter part of the twentieth century, beginning in the 1960s. Many researchers have referred to these changes as the *sexual revolution* and cite a number of important developments: more tolerant attitudes toward certain sexual behaviors, a shift in relations between men and women, the emergence of new political movements, and a greater emphasis on gender equality.

Many social scientists feel that the sexual revolution brought about more relaxed, tolerant, and flexible attitudes toward sexual morality. Some hold that it brought about greater equality, both general and sexual, between men and women. However, as far as equality of the sexes in other aspects of life is concerned, some researchers hold that the liberation of women as defined by the sexual revolution was largely a myth. Although many women today hold managerial and leadership positions, most remain trapped in low-paying jobs, have few career opportunities, and, in addition, shoulder the burden of child care.

From a historical standpoint, the conservatism of the 1950s appears to have been a springboard for the many changes that occurred during the sexual revolution. Attitudes toward such topics as birth control, divorce, abortion, premarital and extramarital sex, cohabitation, and homosexuality became more relaxed and tolerant. The sexual revolution also saw a great change in the openness with which sexual matters were discussed.

Gender-role attitudes and behaviors also began to change. During the sexual revolution, the women's liberation movement worked for the enforcement of laws and regulations promoting the equality of women in the workplace and in other areas of life, as well as greater rights for many other groups. Although this movement was prominent in North American society from the 1840s until the granting of women's suffrage in 1920, public interest in it declined until the 1960s. The National Organization for Women (NOW), founded in 1966, would become the largest formal organization in the women's movement and has been especially active in implementing reform in the educational and vocational arenas.

Because of the work of NOW and other similar organizations, and of growing levels of social consciousness as a whole, the belief in male superiority began to dim during the sexual revolution. Some relationships moved from a male-dominated structure to one based on equality, and a considerable number began to be characterized by changing activities within the household. Many couples began sharing domestic chores and chose to deemphasize traditional gender-role stereotyping. As a result, relationship dynamics became based on mutuality and reciprocity. The sexual revolution also ushered in more dual-earner households; that is, both husbands and wives began working outside the home. As we shall see throughout this book, the emergence of dual-earner households, including the balance to be struck between the workplace and the home, would forever change the complexion of American family life.

Contemporary Families

Since the exploration of family life as it exists in contemporary society is the primary concern of this reference manual, we will bring our historical narrative into the present by briefly examining some key trends and changes in family life. By so doing, we can make comparisons to earlier historical times and develop a foundation for the important family issues and controversies that follow in the next chapter.

Let's begin with the institution of marriage and its choice as a lifestyle in contemporary society. Similar to earlier historical periods, marriage continues to be a popular lifestyle for a significant portion of the American population. In 1999, for example, an estimated 56 percent of all American adults (111 million people) were married (U.S. Bureau of the Census, 2000). However, today's couples are waiting longer to get married, an interesting comparison to the early marriages encouraged years ago. In 1999, the median age at first marriage was 26.8 years for men and 25.1 years for women. These figures, which have steadily increased since the mid-1950s, were the highest levels recorded in more than a hundred years (U.S. Bureau of the Census, 2000a). For a historical comparison of the median age at first marriage, see Chapter 6 (Figure 6–1).

But while Americans still demonstrate a propensity to marry, other lifestyle options exist. Two of these, singlehood and cohabitation, are especially popular today and have met with increasing levels of societal acceptance. Regarding singlehood, figures gathered in 1999 revealed that about 34 percent of the adult population between 25 and 34 years of age were singles. The proportion of single adults has increased for whites, African Americans, and Hispanic Americans over the past thirty years. Among whites, the proportion rose to 21 percent, 39 percent for African American, and 30 percent for Hispanic Americans (U.S. Bureau of the Census, 2000a). For a statistical breakdown of the number of persons living alone by age, including projections to the year 2010, see Chapter 6 (Figure 6–2 and Table 6–1).

The increasing number of unmarried couples living together, or cohabiting, mirrors the more tolerant sexual attitudes ushered in by the sexual revolution. Cohabitation has grown from one-half million in 1970 to approximately 4.2 million in 1999. This represents a seven-fold increase. The majority of unmarried adult couples have never been married. Regarding age variables, about 62 percent of cohabitants are under age 35, approximately 32 percent are 35 to 64 years old, and about 5 percent are 65 years of age or older. About 35 percent of cohabiting couples have children under 15 years of age (U.S. Bureau of the Census, 2000b).

Another contemporary family trend deserving attention is the decrease in household size. Fifty years ago, the average size of family households in America was 3.54 persons. Since that time, this figure has steadily dropped, reaching 3.15 in 2000 (U.S. Bureau of the Census, 2000a). By the year 2010, the average family size is projected to drop even more to 3.05 (see Chapter 6, Table 6–2). There are many reasons for this decrease in family size. Among the reasons are the increasing numbers of single parents, persons living alone, and couples choosing not to have children.

Declining fertility rates (the number of births a woman could expect to have before the end of her childbearing years) have also contributed to today's smaller household size. American women averaged more than seven children each until the early decades of the nineteenth century. In 1920, the fertility rate was 3.3 but began to fall steadily until it bottomed out to 2.2 during the Great Depression. The fertility rate began to rise again until it reached a plateau of 3.7 during the post-war "baby boom," and then fell to its current level of 2.1 (Population Reference Bureau, 2000). (For fertility rates in the United States, see Chapter 6, Figure 6–3.)

Why are couples today choosing to have fewer children? First, the economic value of children to families has changed. Once an economic commodity, children today have become an economic liability. Although many children were an asset to families living in preindustrial societies, this is not the case with families of the industrial age. Children today must be loved and wanted for reasons other than the work they can perform.

Today, the costs of housing, feeding, clothing, and providing for other necessities for one child through the first 17 years of life are staggering. One source (U.S. Department of Commerce, 2000) estimates that for a baby born today in a middle-income, two-parent family, the costs for raising that child over the course of 17 years is $160,140. For those children attending college and graduate school, this figure sharply increases. In 1960, a middle-income family could expect to spend about $25,990 to raise a child through age 17.

As indicated, many modern-day couples are choosing not to have children. According to data recently gathered by the U.S. Census Bureau (2000b), 27 percent of all women between the ages of 30 to 34 had never given birth. In 1976, the corresponding proportion was 16 percent. Among women between the ages of 40 to 44 years, the proportion of those who were childless increased from 10 percent in 1976 to almost 20 percent in 1999 (U.S. Bureau of the Census, 2000b). In Chapter 6 (Figures 6–4 and 6–5), readers can statistically compare projections of families having children with those that do not.

We mentioned earlier that the economic complexion of families has changed. Beginning during the sexual revolution, the family became more dual-earner in scope, in the process no longer casting the male as the principal breadwinner. As we enter this new century, demographics reveal the widespread nature of working families, including record numbers of women employed in the workplace. Over the past fifty years, the proportion of wives in the labor force has nearly tripled, from 23 percent in 1950 to 62 percent in 2000. Of the nation's 3.7 million women with infants under the age of one, almost 60 percent were in the labor force. This was a record high and almost doubled the 30 percent participation rate of mothers twenty-five years ago. Of these 3.7 million women with infants, 36 percent were working full-time, 17 percent were working part-time, and 6 percent were actively seeking employment (U.S. Department of Commerce, 2001; U.S. Bureau of the Census, 2000).

The issue of who is going to care for the children of working parents is an important one today. Whereas the Industrial Revolution virtually dictated that mothers would remain at home to care for their young , today's dual-earner couples must turn to the outside for child-care assistance. For growing numbers of working parents, economic necessity forces the search for quality child care to begin early in the youngster's life.

Yesterday's family was a rather permanent, immobile unit. Of course, there were those who pushed West to explore the nation's territorial borders. Once settled, though, most new additions to the family were raised and died in pretty much the same geographical location. This physical permanence was due to a number of factors, among them the independent and self-sufficient nature of towns and villages, as well as the fact that many children were groomed to take over the family enterprise. If one did venture away, it was usually for only short distances to gain local employment.

The twin forces of industrialization and urbanization, in comparison, have created an increasingly mobile family unit today. The contemporary family is likely to change its residency as often as career and economic needs dictate. This in itself is a striking contrast to employment and economic situations in early American history. At one time, machines and jobs followed the population as the nation expanded. Now, the reverse appears to be the case. Our population usually follows the machines to gain employment. There are obvious implications here for all family members. Moving from location to location implies the repeated introduction of formidable challenges: adjusting to new career demands, adapting to new living environments, making financial adjustments, meeting new friends, and entering new school systems.

In light of rising divorce rates, our discussion of modern-day families would be incomplete without some mention of marital dissolution. Marital disharmony and collapse, historically speaking, did occur in the past but was not widespread. In comparison, consider today's divorce statistics. Divorce rates hit an all-time peak in 1946 and then declined steadily until the late 1950s. The approximate one million divorces granted in 1974 marked the first time in American history that more marriages ended in divorce than through death. Today, there are approximately 19.3 million divorced adults living in the United States. This represents about 10 percent of the adult population (U.S. Bureau of the Census, 2000a).

Why were divorce rates so low in earlier historical periods? Why did so many couples remain together, even in the wake of marital strife and disharmony? Several reasons can be cited. To begin with, many couples stayed together for purely economic reasons. The family functioned as a working unit and a divorce would cripple the household's overall operation and finances. In this sense, it was simply economically unfeasible to divorce. Other reasons to remain together included a concern for one's standing in the community as well as the expense of the actual divorce, not to mention the rather unpleasant and time-consuming chore of obtaining one.

Although these reasons for remaining together still exist for some, we are living in a society that more readily accepts divorce. As indicated, households today rarely produce as a total working unit and large numbers of women are no longer economically dependent on their husbands. Today, divorces are relatively easier to obtain, particularly since the inception of such legal mechanisms as the "no-fault" divorce concept. And while divorced parties do experience role readjustment, the sheer numbers of divorced parties in this country has lessened negative community reaction.

In the wake of high divorce rates, many individuals are exhibiting new attitudes about marital dissolution. Our society seems to be placing an increasingly high premium on individual choice and personal fulfillment. Divorce for many may reflect this attitude. Divorce is often not viewed as personal disorganization, but rather as a mechanism for individuals to improve their overall lives.

Of particular concern are the numbers of divorces involving children. It is estimated that over one million children each year will see their parents' marriage end in divorce. If current divorce rates continue, an individual faces a 50 percent probability of becoming a member of a blended family (stepfamily) as a child, parent, or stepparent (U.S. Bureau of the Census, 2000a; U.S. Department of Commerce, 2001).

Finally, the rapid increase of single-parent families in modern society should be recognized. The single-parent family has become one of the fastest growing family forms in America today, largely because of upswings in divorce, cohabitation, and out-of-wedlock childbearing. In 1999 there were almost 10 million one-parent families with children under age eighteen, compared to 1.5 million in 1950. The majority of children who lived with a single-parent in 1999 lived with their mother (about 85 percent). Approximately 40 percent of these children lived with mothers who had never been married. Children who lived with their father only were more likely to be living with a divorced father (44 percent) than with a never-married father (33 percent) (U.S. Bureau of the Census, 2000b).

Suffice it to say that the modern family lives in an age of near-overwhelming change. Today's family, faced with an assortment of challenges, has experienced transformation and alteration. This means that what is happening to the modern family represents a continuation of what has been happening to it over time. Today, as divorce rates have risen, as dual-earner households have become the norm rather than the exception, and as single-parenthood has become a way of life for many, we must seek to understand how the contemporary family has responded to challenge and change and how it can best prepare itself for the future. Exploring such issues lies at the conceptual foundation of this handbook.

Summary

In order to better understand the modern-day family, this chapter explored various historical periods in America. Family life in colonial America reflected beliefs practiced for centuries, including such customs as marriage at early ages, male-dominated households, and an emphasis on large families. The Industrial Revolution would change the complexion of society, including the family unit. Most families experienced an economic realignment, and gender-role behaviors and expectations changed. Employment away from the family became the province of the male while females remained behind at home. For the first time in history, work and family life became separate enterprises. Children were also viewed in a new light at this time. Rather than economic commodities, they now were regarded as liabilities. The sexual revolution of the 1960s also shaped marriage and the family. More specifically, this time period produced, among other developments, more tolerant attitudes toward certain sexual behaviors and attitudes and a greater emphasis on gender equality.

Marriage and family life in contemporary society have many different dimensions. Although marriage is still the choice for a clear-cut majority of the population, other lifestyle options have emerged, such as singlehood and cohabitation. Also, growing numbers of contemporary marriages are dual-earner in nature, more mobile, and smaller in size than yesteryear's households. Modern family life is also marked by high divorce rates and a sharp increase in single-parent households.

Any interpretation of history is selective and prone to oversimplification. Nevertheless, examining American family life as we've done in this chapter should enable you to see how structural and functional changes must be studied against a historical backdrop. Indeed, as customs and beliefs change or shift and as civilizations advance, family life also undergoes alterations and transformations. The contemporary family is no exception, and the remaining chapters of this reference manual explore important family life topics, including key issues and controversies. Hopefully by exploring the past we've piqued your curiosity about family life in this new century and about what the future holds.

References

Population Reference Bureau. 2000. *America's Diversity and Growth: Signposts for the 21 Century.* Washington, DC: Population Reference Bureau.

U.S. Bureau of the Census. 2000a. *Statistical Abstract of the United States.* 120th ed. Washington, DC: U.S. Government Printing Office.

———. 2000b. *Marital Status and Living Arrangements.* Washington, DC: U.S. Government Printing Office.

U.S. Department of Commerce. 2000. "Expenditures on Children by Families." http://www.usda.gov/cnpp. Accessed on 4 April 2000.

———. 2001. *United States Department of Commerce News.* Washington, DC: U.S. Government Printing Office.

2

Exploring the Diversity of Family Life

L iving in a modern age grows more complex each day, with each new event and with each technological innovation. Never before in history has the world experienced such up-heaval, change, and transformation. The family, much like other facets of society, experiences these changes and interfaces in complex and diverse ways with other social organizations, such as economic and educational structures.

In order to fully comprehend the nature of family life, one must capture an accurate picture of it, including its many dimensions and facets. The family is not as simple as it appears on the surface, nor does it reflect the singular, traditional, idealized image many have of it. Rather, it is a complex social institution marked more by diversity, not uniformity. Not only is there wide variation in today's family forms and structures, but considerable cultural variation as well.

This chapter will explore the more important differences that exist in modern-day families by first exploring various structural and organizational variations of marriage and family life and then utilizing a cross-cultural examination of marriage and family to sharpen perceptions of cultural diversity.

Variations in Family Structure and Composition

Variations in family structure and form can be identified according to a number of criteria. One criterion is the number of partners involved in a marriage. *Monogamy* is the marriage of one man to one woman. This is the characteristic form of marriage in the United States, and the only type that is legal. However, because of escalating divorce rates, some researchers feel that serial monogamy is the more accurate title for marriage in this country. *Serial monogamy* is a succession of partners through the process of marriage, divorce, remarriage, and so on.

It might seem that all societies would regard monogamy as the preferable marital arrangement, but this is not the case. Rather, a significant number of societies practice what is called *polygamy*, or plural marriage. The word polygamy comes from two Greek words meaning "many marriages." There are two basic forms of polygamy: polygyny and polyandry.

Polygyny is the marriage of one man to two or more women. Of the two forms of polygamy, polygyny is the more prevalent. Many societies have practiced polygyny at one time or another and many still do, particularly in regions of Asia and Africa. However, while a given society may permit polygyny, a monogamous relationship is usually the preferred arrangement.

Polyandry is the marriage of one woman to two or more men. Polyandry has been an extremely rare occurrence throughout history. It is practiced, though, among some Buddhist Tibetans, some groups in Nigeria, and the Toda in Southern India. In the Himalayas, some polyandrous households involve a number of brothers who share a wife, thus preventing the dissolution of family wealth or property.

A second criterion used in categorizing variations in family structure is the generations composing the household. The *nuclear family* consists of the mother, father, and children living in a home or residence of their own. Sometimes called the *conjugal family*, the nuclear family is two-generations; that is, it includes parents and offspring. Most individuals can expect to live in two nuclear families during their lives—the one into which they are born, called the *family of orientation*, and the one that is established through marriage and parenthood, known as the *family of procreation*.

The *extended family* consists of parents and children as well as other relatives such as grandparents, aunts, and uncles living in a single residence. Also called the *consanguine family* or the *family of kinship*, the extended family is thus multigenerational. *Modified extended families* are families that have a nuclear structure, but live in geographically dispersed locations. They are a modified version of the extended family because they maintain an ongoing network of interaction.

A *blended family* results when a divorced parent with custody of children remarries. Also called the *compound* or *reconstituted family*, this household consists of parent, children, and stepparent. However, more complex arrangements are possible. For example, both parents may have children from previous marriages, or they may choose to conceive their own offspring.

Finally, a *single-parent family* is one in which one parent assumes the responsibility for raising biological or adopted children. As discussed in the last chapter, the blended family and the single-parent family have become more common because of the increase in the divorce rate, the popularity of cohabitation, and the number of children born out of wedlock.

A third criterion to categorize variations in family structure is rules of descent, or how family members are related to one another. Patterns of descent, important for the tracing of one's lineage as well as for inheritance and other purposes, can be traced in three ways. *Patrilineal descent* traces lineage on the husband's side of the family. *Matrilineal descent* places the importance on the wife's side. In the United States today, though, *bilateral descent* is the more prevalent pattern. Bilateral descent places equal importance on the families of both the husband and wife. Power, property, and the like are transferred from both the husband's and the wife's side of the family to their offspring.

Where a family chooses to reside is a fourth way to categorize household variations. *Patrilocal residency* means that the couple lives with or near the husband's relatives. *Matrilocal residency*, on the other hand, places the couple with or near the wife's relatives. Although these two patterns of residency can apply to some couples in the United States, another is more apparent: *neolocal residency*. Neolocal residency occurs when the couple establishes its own separate living arrangement. Their geographical location is not based on ties originating from either the husband's or the wife's family.

A fifth criterion used to categorize family structure is patterns of authority, or who influences and dominates decision-making within the household. A *patriarchal power structure* places the husband in this dominating position, while in a *matriarchal power structure* the wife is more influential. To date, there have been no truly matriarchal societies. An *egalitarian power structure* is emerging in the United States and other industrialized nations. The egalitarian system, which has been increasing in popularity in recent years, emphasizes the sharing of marital power between husband and wife. Spouses are regarded as equals and decisions are reached mutually.

Finally, the practices of *endogamy* or *exogamy* are other ways to categorize variations in family structure. Endogamy encourages potential partners to marry within their own social group. In other words, an African American marries an African American, or a Catholic marries a Catholic. Marrying outside one's particular social group is called exogamy; for example, a Native American might marry an Asian American (called an interracial marriage), or a Catholic might marry a Protestant (called an interfaith marriage).

Miscegenation is the technical name given to interracial marriages. As late as 1966, seventeen states had formal prohibitions against one or more forms of interracial marriage. The United States Supreme Court overturned the sixteen existing state antimiscegenation statutes (laws prohibiting mixed marriage) with a decision rendered June 12, 1967. The seventeenth state's statute (Virginia) was overturned in 1967, at which time the United States Supreme Court toppled the antimiscegenation laws. In making its decision, the Court said that distinctions between citizens solely because of their ancestry was "odious to a free people whose institutions are founded upon the doctrine of equality" (*Loving v. Virginia*). At one point or another, 40 of the 50 states have had laws that prohibited blacks and whites from intermarrying. Pennsylvania, in 1780, was the first state to repeal its antimiscegenation law, while Indiana and Wyoming took this action as recently as 1965.

Interracial marriages amounted to only 5 percent of all marriages in 2000, a total of about 1.5 million couples. Although this is a small percentage, it represents a tenfold increase since 1960. Within racial and ethnic groups, mixed marriages vary widely. Hispanic Americans and Asian Americans, the nation's fastest-growing minority groups, marry partners of different races at about three times the rate of African Americans and five times the rate of whites. Asian American women and African American men are more than twice as likely to marry outside their groups as are Asian American men and African American women (U.S. Department of Commerce, 2000a).

Studies exploring the stability of interracial marriages and the adjustment of children have produced uneven findings. Although some researchers have found a higher rate of divorce among interracial marriages, it should be recognized that other factors beyond race converge to create marital dissolution: age, educational level, and religious beliefs, to name but a few. The adjustment of children transcends skin color and depends more on such factors as the quality of the parent-child relationship.

It is estimated that 15 to 20 percent of all marriages are of the interfaith variety. As far as intermarriages in general are concerned, interfaith marriages are more common than interracial marriages. This is probably because of a decline in religious prejudice over the years and more societal tolerance of ethnic and cultural differences. Also, interfaith marriages, unlike interracial marriages, present no visible signs of intermarriage, like skin color.

Much like the findings about interracial marriages, efforts to assess the stability of interfaith marriages have yielded mixed results. Some researchers have found that couples of the same denominational affiliation are more apt to have stable marriages than those whose religions are different. However, other investigators have found minimal, if any, differences in the marital happiness of homogamous couples when compared to interfaith unions. There is also no evidence that interfaith marriages have negative effects on children, including a secularization effect.

Interestingly, interfaith marriages have unique demographic variations. For instance, in New York, where there are large Catholic and Jewish populations, there is a high incidence of Catholic-Jewish marriages. In Iowa, Minnesota, and Pennsylvania, where the religious makeup is about fifty-fifty Catholic and Lutheran, a higher than average rate of intermarriage exists between those two faiths.

Although today's clergy does not encourage interfaith marriages, they have a greater acceptance of them. In some states, such as Louisiana, Mississippi, New York, and California, an agreement exists between the Roman Catholic and Episcopal churches dispensing with the requirement of obtaining written permission from a bishop before allowing an interfaith couple to be married in the church. The agreement also encourages the couple to continue worship in their respective faiths. A number of congregations have also devised activities and programs to reach out to intermarried couples. For example, many synagogues now offer workshops on Jewish holidays and the life cycle. The Roman Catholic Church also offers a marriage preparation course that includes special counseling for intermarried couples.

Multicultural Family Variations

One needs to examine differences that exist across cultures to fully appreciate the diversity that exists in today's families. *Culture* refers to everything individuals do or have as members of society. Culture serves to identify, organize, and unify people who share a common way of life. Culture is never static; rather, it is constantly changing. When studying modern family life, it is imperative to include the concept of culture to help explain the wide variations that exist among groups of people.

Multiculturalism recognizes the cultural diversity that exists in the United States and seeks to promote the equality of all cultural traditions. From a multicultural perspective, there is no universal standard of good or bad when evaluating differences, such as those that exist within different racial and ethnic groups. Rather, this perspective maintains that an aspect of any given culture can be judged only within the context of that culture. Multiculturalism encourages a sensitive and tolerant perspective of cultural ways and the promotion of mutual harmony and respect.

The racial and ethnic composition of the United States has changed dramatically in the last twenty years. Although whites of European background are still the largest U.S. population segment (about 76 percent), minority populations are rapidly increasing. Today, it is estimated that one in four families is a family of color: African American, Hispanic American, Asian American, or Native American (U.S. Bureau of the Census, 2000). For a statistical analysis of racial and ethnic composition in the United States, including projections to the year 2025, see Chapter 6 (Figure 6–6).

African American Families

African Americans are the largest racial minority in the United States, numbering about 35.4 million. Overall, African Americans constitute about 12 percent of the total U.S. population. Over the course of the last fifteen years, this population has grown by 13 percent, more than double the growth rate of the white population. There are approximately 9 million African American households in the United States today. Although African Americans are the most widely dispersed minority group, they are still highly concentrated in southern states (U.S. Department of Commerce, 2000a).

Any discussion of close relationships among African Americans must take into account the social status and living arrangements of blacks today. More specifically, there have been growing numbers of poor, female-headed African American families. African American families are three times as likely as white families to be poor, and black unemployment is more than twice as high as it is among whites (see Figure 6–7 in Chapter 6). Although the significant majority of the 9 million African American households are family households (that is, the household members are related by birth, marriage, or adoption), only one-half are headed by a married couple. More than one-fourth of all African American children live with mothers who have never married (U.S. Bureau of the Census, 2000). For a statistical portrayal of African American households, including family size by type and income, see Chapter 6 (Figures 6–8 and 6–9).

Many experts believe that in the face of such stresses, African American families have developed unique coping skills. In particular, a hallmark of African American families is strong family ties. Through these family ties, African Americans find strength and support within their own families and kin networks. To deal with day-to-day struggles, black families turn within, in the process providing each other with gratification, help, and assistance. Older African American females, particularly widows, are noted for taking into their homes grandchildren, nieces, nephews, and other relatives to combine the resources of the extended family and provide familial assistance and support. According to many contemporary scholars, the end result of such support is that African American families tend to be stable and functional, not problematic and deviant. Indeed, most African Americans report a strong sense of family solidarity and cohesion.

Flexibility of family roles is another strength of African American families. African American families tend to be egalitarian with both husband and wife sharing in the authority to make decisions and other family responsibilities. Additionally, working mothers are not viewed as a threat to their husbands' egos; rather, their contributions to their households are regarded as a matter of economic necessity. Also, research does not support the stereotypic view that African American fathers are invisible and uninvolved with their children. Rather, African American fathers are more likely to share child care and domestic chores than Euro-American men. And, research shows that the greater the economic security of African American fathers, the more active they become in child care.

African American fertility rates are higher than those of whites. The total number of lifetime births per African American women is about 2.4 children compared to 1.8 for whites. About one-half of African American children are born to single mothers, and 4 out of 5 will live in a female-headed household at some point in their childhood (Spraggins, 2000; U.S. Bureau of the Census, 2000). However, as mentioned, many African American single mothers are more apt to live in an extended family with their own mother or grandmother. In such domestic arrangements, child care becomes shared, thus enabling the mother to improve her situation through work or education. The extended family framework helps many African American mothers cope with adverse social conditions and economic impoverishment.

African American parents view youngsters as essential for family continuity. As a result, considerable emphasis is placed on their achievement and fulfillment. Spirituality and a strong religious orientation are dominant cultural values taught to children. The child-rearing practices of African American parents are found to be similar to other groups in a number of respects. For example, when compared to Hispanic Americans, blacks tend to encourage early independence and autonomy of youngsters, practice authoritative modes of discipline, and encourage egalitarian family roles. The importance of educational achievement as a means to better one's quality of life is a frequent child-rearing theme. And, similar to other minority parents, most African American parents make active efforts to ensure that their children develop a positive ethnic group identity.

African American children and adolescents, like those of other races, discover that peer relationships, outside of the family, are an important facet of socialization. They learn that in many schools, peer groups are often segregated according to ethnicity and social class. Much like other minority youths, the peer group provides African Americans with an important sense of brotherhood or sisterhood within the majority culture. In this sense, the peer group and other socialization agents within the wider community mirror parental socialization values. Additionally, the peer group helps forge a sense of identity and feelings of self-worth. Some researchers believe that African American youths often rely on peer groups more than white adolescents.

African Americans are more willing than white families to take relatives into their households. Additionally, the family figures prominently in the social support of aging relatives. Both young and old family members interact frequently and nurture close affective bonds. With the rapid increase of the elderly population in America today, such social support becomes increasingly important (see Chapter 6, Figures 6–10 and 6–11). Having an adult child and relatives nearby tends to facilitate the emotional and social integration of older African Americans in family networks. Such intergenerational relations are particularly important in later life because they serve to reduce the negative effects of aging. A norm of reciprocity between generations is also evident in African American families. Child-care services, transportation, household tasks, and care when someone is ill are often exchanged between grandparents, parents, and adult children. Similar to trends observed with white caregivers, it is the adult daughter who typically provides the most support to aging parents.

Hispanic American Families

Hispanic Americans are the nation's largest minority group, after African Americans. The Hispanic American population includes people who trace their ancestry to Spanish-speaking countries throughout Latin America, as well as some with links to Spain, Africa, and southwestern regions of the United States (see Chapter 6, Figure 6–12). An estimated 35.3 million Hispanics live in the United States today, which represents about 12 percent of the total population. It is projected that between the year 2000 and 2050, Hispanics will account for the majority (51 percent) of the nation's population growth. The Hispanic American population is highly concentrated in southwestern regions of the United States (U.S. Department of Commerce, 2000b).

Hispanic American families, much like African American families, tend to experience high levels of poverty. This is because Hispanic Americans are apt to have less education, lower incomes, and higher rates of unemployment than the general population. They have also faced discrimination in housing, in schools, and in obtaining jobs and promotions. Although the proportion of Hispanic Americans in white-collar occupations has grown in recent years, they still tend to work in low-paying, semi-skilled jobs. Moreover, many are employed in economic sectors vulnerable to cyclical unemployment. Hispanic American women, and Puerto Ricans in particular, are less likely to be working than other women. Within Hispanic American groups, poverty rates tend to be higher for Puerto Rican families, followed by Mexican American and Cuban American families (U.S. Department of Commerce, 2000b).

In recent years there has been an upswing in the number of households maintained by women, a trend that has greatly increased the economic vulnerability of Hispanic Americans. Hispanic American families are more likely to be single parent, female headed than are white families. About 24 percent of Hispanic American families are female headed, which is almost double the percentage for whites and Asian Americans, but about one-half the rate for African Americans (see Chapter 6, Figure 6–13). Female-headed households are often associated with lower economic status and related problems. To illustrate, the potential earning power for this kind of household is less than that for a household with two working parents. Of all Hispanic American groups, Puerto Rican families have the highest concentration of female-headed households (U.S. Bureau of the Census, 2000).

Economic disadvantage among Hispanic Americans has been linked to a retreat from marriage, premarital childbearing, and marital dissolution, each of which contributes to female family headship. Moreover, children who grow up in mother-only families are at an increased risk of poverty during childhood. This, in turn, heightens the risk of health problems, often delays intellectual development, and creates poor school performance. Hispanic American children living in mother-only families are also less likely to complete high school and more likely to have low adult earnings than are children from intact families.

The average Hispanic American woman will have 2.7 children, about one child more per woman than the rate for non-Hispanic whites. Hispanic American women will also have their first child at a younger age than non-Hispanic white women, and there is a greater likelihood that the mother will be unmarried.

Teenagers account for about 17 percent of all births among Hispanic Americans (Spraggins, 2000; Bachu and O'Connell, 1999).

Researchers studying close relationships among Hispanic Americans have long emphasized the importance of family life. Hispanic Americans are characterized by their strong sense of family; indeed, most regard *la familia* (the family) as the center of their life. The family is a treasured entity and close kinship ties are forged between the nuclear family, its relatives, and even entire neighborhoods. Kin relationships are marked by mutual support, assistance, and cooperation. It is also not uncommon for "fictive kin," people who are not related to a family but who will informally adopt children during periods of family stress or crisis, to emerge and offer support, particularly in the Puerto Rican community.

The parent-child relationship in Hispanic American families is warm and nurturing. Children are regarded as important members of the overall family system, and at early ages they are taught the importance of loyalty, respect, and politeness. Important cultural values stressed by Hispanic American parents are avoidance of interpersonal conflict, deference and respect for authority systems, and educational achievement. Within the family system, mutual support and attachment are apparent among siblings, particularly those who are close together in age. None of the foregoing family dynamics appears to be altered by social or economic status.

At one time, gender-roles in the Hispanic American family were portrayed as being traditional and rigid. The concept of *machismo,* a type of traditional gender-role behavior apparent in many Latin American countries, was used to explain family functioning. Machismo viewed the Hispanic American male as a standoffish, swaggering authoritarian, the undisputed master of the household. The female, on the other hand, was seen as submissive and weak. Today, these gender-role behaviors are seen as inaccurate and misrepresentative of typical Hispanic American families. Rather, most homes tend to reflect a decline in machismo and an upswing in egalitarianism, the latter being a sharing of gender-roles and family decision-making. Although traditional masculine authority still exists today, it is characterized more by fairness and respect for others than machismo-like behavior. A number of explanations are given for this shift in gender-role behaviors, including increased urbanization and the feminist movement in both the United States and Latin America.

About 70 percent of all Hispanic American family households consist of married couples. This compares to about 80 percent of non-Hispanic families. Although the rate of intermarriage is several times higher than that of African Americans, intermarriages account for only about one-sixth of all Hispanic American marriages. When interpreting these and other marital trends, differences in Hispanic American groups must again be taken into account. For example, while marriage rates are lower among Puerto Ricans than Mexican Americans or Cuban Americans, this may be due to the popularity of nonmarital cohabitation within the Puerto Rican culture (U.S. Department of Commerce, 2000a; U.S. Bureau of the Census, 2000).

Finally, given the strong and extended kinship network among Hispanic American families, aging family members are provided with considerable care and attention. The elderly are held in high esteem, and extending intergenerational support reflects the deep sense of family obligation characteristic of Hispanic Americans. Affective support, such as the provision of love and companionship, as well as instrumental support, such as transportation or the provision of food or housekeeping services, are commonplace. Many adult children live within close proximity of their parents, thus enabling frequent contact and interaction. As with other racial and ethnic minorities, a high level of reciprocity exists between older and younger Hispanic American generations. And, more often than not, females are more instrumental than males in the provision of intergenerational care. For a statistical portrait of aging among Hispanic Americans, see Chapter 6, Figure 6–14.

Asian American Families

Asian Americans, a category that includes both Asians and Pacific Islanders, represent the fastest-growing minority group in the United States today. Asian Americans may be the most diverse of America's minority groups. They come from more than two dozen countries and do not share a common language, a common religion, or a common cultural background. Asian Americans number approximately 11.6 million, about 4.5 percent of the total population. About 85 percent of all Asian Americans are in six groups: Chinese, Filipino, Japanese, Asian-Indian, Korean, and Vietnamese. Of these, Chinese, Filipino, and Japan-

ese represent the largest groups. Asian Americans tend to be concentrated in the western areas of the United States, particularly
California (U.S. Department of Commerce, 2000c).

Given the fact that Asian Americans come from many different countries and are such diverse people, many differences
exist between groups. However, Asian Americans are as likely as
non-Hispanic whites to have graduated from high school, and
more likely to have graduated from college. Compared to other
minority groups, they are more apt to work in professional and
white-collar occupations. The median family income of Asian
Americans is slightly higher than that of non-Hispanic whites.
However, a mixed picture of achievement often accompanies the
socioeconomic status of Asian Americans. For example, many
Asian immigrants earn low salaries and are hampered by their
inability to speak English when they first arrive in the United
States. This is especially true for recent refugees from Southeast
Asia, many of whom are poor and uneducated (U.S. Department
of Commerce, 2000c).

Asian Americans tend to marry later and experience less
marital dissolution. Regarding the latter, whites between the ages
of 30 and 44 are almost twice as likely as Asian Americans to be
divorced or separated. About 17 percent of all Asian American
marriages are of an interracial nature, with Japanese American
women and white men, and Filipino American women and
white men being the most common marital arrangements. The
interracial marriage rate among Asian Americans is about the
same as it is for Hispanic Americans (U.S. Department of Commerce, 2000c).

More than three-quarters of Asian Americans live in married-couple families, and female-headed families account for
about 7 percent of all Asian American households. Asian Americans are more than twice as likely as non-Hispanic whites to live
in extended families. The probability of a parent and a grown
child living together is about five times higher among Asian
Americans than it is in the total population. Also, the probability
of an adult residing with a sibling is three times higher in the
Asian American community than in the non-Hispanic white population (U.S. Bureau of the Census, 2000c).

Asian Americans tend to have a lower fertility rate and consequently smaller families than other minorities. The total number of children an Asian American woman will have is about 2.3.

Asian American women tend to have their first child at later ages than do other minority groups, most during their thirties. This is a fertility trend that contributes not only to a smaller family size but also to greater levels of economic well-being. Delayed parenthood increases opportunities for higher education and usually leads to better-paying jobs. Also, adolescent pregnancy is not widespread among Asian Americans (Spraggins, 2000; Bachu and O'Connell, 1999).

Asian American parenting styles tend to be authoritarian rather than permissive, and disciplinary strategies are more verbal than physical. Child-rearing continually reflects the cultural emphasis placed on family loyalty and togetherness. Parents promote family honor as well as respect for elders. Children also learn that cooperation with others, pacifism, self-control, and self-discipline are desired character traits. These are all values linked to Confucianism, especially among Chinese, Korean, Vietnamese, and Japanese. Within the home, children are also taught traditional gender-roles, with the father being recognized as the undisputed head of the household. Such teachings are part of a social order in which there is a hierarchy of interpersonal relations; that is, parents are superior to children, and men are superior to women.

Other segments of the Asian American population offer unique parallels to the foregoing parenting styles. For example, a strong patriarchal structure characterizes the households of most Asian Indians, and such Hindu values as honor and family loyalty are used to guide children's development. Most Asian Indian boys and girls are taught traditional gender-roles and learn at an early age to defer to their parents' wishes. The importance of close sibling relationships is stressed in most Asian American homes and is particularly evident among Asian Indians, Pakistanis, and Cambodians. Finally, most Asian American children, including Filipino and Vietnamese youngsters, are taught the importance of determination and dedication, particularly if one expects to succeed and get ahead in the world.

The strong emphasis placed on family relationships among Asian Americans is reflected in the care given to elders. Because Asian Americans are influenced by Confucian ideology, which stresses children's moral obligation to care and respect aged family, their elderly receive considerable social support. Many Asian Americans live in close proximity to one another, so contact and assistance are regular. Given such frequent contact, many Asian American families are able to maintain the values deemed influential to family life. In so doing, the family remains the focus of an elderly person's life, an instrumental source of support, companionship, and satisfaction.

Native American Families

The terms Native American, American Indian, and Native Alaskan refer to a diverse minority population in North America (Alaska and the continental United States) that reflects many different histories and cultures. Native Americans were the original inhabitants of the Americas and today live mostly in the northwest and western sectors of the United States. They are composed of at least 124 federally recognized tribes and bands, with an approximate 450 or more subgroupings such as villages with distinct customs and traditions. The Cherokee, Navajo, Chippewa, and Sioux tribes are the largest Native American tribes. Combined, there are about 2.8 million Native Americans living in the United States today. Approximately one-third of this total live on reservations or other Indian areas (U.S. Department of Commerce, 2000d).

Like other minorities, Native Americans have historically experienced considerable hardship and discrimination. In the nineteenth century, the government enforced relocation policies against Native Americans. Today, Native Americans are one of the most disadvantaged minority groups in the United States. They have the highest rate of unemployment, the highest rate of high school dropouts, and the lowest median income of any racial or ethnic group. Over the past ten years, all racial and ethnic groups experienced an increase in median income with the exception of Native Americans. Compounding these economic problems is the fact that Native Americans live in some of the poorest rural areas in the United States. Among all minority groups, Native Americans also have the highest rates of substance abuse, particularly alcoholism. The general health status of Native Americans as a group is rated very poor, and their overall life expectancy is ten years below the national average (U.S. Department of Commerce, 2000d; U.S. Bureau of the Census, 2000).

Economic disadvantage resulting from poverty permeates Native American family life. Native American families have high

fertility rates, large numbers of illegitimate births, and a disproportionate number of female-headed households. Native American women tend to have their first child at a younger age than
non-Hispanic white women, and teenagers account for about 20
percent of all Native American births. As in all cultures, teenage
childbearing aggravates negative economic consequences for
mother and child, in addition to creating such health risks as pre-
maturity, infant mortality, and delivery complications (Spraggins, 2000; Bachu and O'Connell, 1999).

Children are greatly valued by Native Americans. Youngsters are taught a number of cultural values at early ages, including the importance of group cooperation, honesty, and independence. Many Native American parents regard competitiveness as
a lack of respect for and lack of loyalty to the group. Obedience is
also seen as a virtue, and children are trained to exhibit patience,
responsibility, and trustworthiness. A particular emphasis is also
placed on a harmony with and reverence for nature. Family loyalty and traditions have long been important to Native American
families, and youngsters are brought up to respect and care for
elderly family members.

Family difficulties place many Native American children
and adolescents at risk. For example, high rates of alcoholism
and homicide often create the loss of parents or siblings. Prema-
ture births by adolescent mothers often create developmental
lags in children, such as neurological problems or lowered intelligence. Economic deprivation may trigger disruptive and
aggressive behavior, both at home and at school. Running away
from home is not an uncommon occurrence among Native American youngsters. Given such problems, it should be fairly easy to
see why Native American youth represent a particularly vulnerable population segment, one that needs considerable social service intervention.

The extended family is an important source of care and
assistance for Native Americans. Kin form supportive bonds
with each other and traditionally promote the welfare and safety
of family members. Often, the extended family allows members
to combine their economic resources, thus serving an important
adaptive function. Given the extended family framework, children may also experience parenting from large numbers of relatives, especially in the face of domestic strain. Research has
shown that relationships with supportive and caring kin are
important modifiers of stress.

As noted, elderly family members are an integral feature of Native American families. Aged tribal members are respected for their wisdom and experience, and they serve as teachers and caregivers of the young. Elderly Native American family members are more involved in child care than their white or Hispanic American counterparts. And, marital dissolution, whether through widowhood, divorce, or separation, does not isolate aged family members from their children or grandchildren. Finally, because intergenerational relationships are characterized by mutuality and reciprocity, younger family members provide regular care to aging family members. The bulk of care, though, does not fall equally on all family members. Rather, the primary caregiver is almost always a woman.

Summary

Today's family is characterized by diversity, not uniformity. Variations in structure and form can be classified according to six criteria: number of partners, generation composition, lineage, residency, patterns of authority, and endogamous or exogamous social pressures. Given the importance of multiculturalism and the sharp increase in America's minority populations, an understanding of family diversity must take into account cross-cultural differences. This chapter explored four of the largest minority populations in the United States: African American, Hispanic American, Asian American, and Native American.

Recognizing the diversity that exists in American families is an important issue. Few can argue that efforts have not been made to better understand the variations that exist in families, including their various needs. This is expressed today by the sheer number of social scientists, institutions, social service organizations, publications, and government bodies involved in assisting the overall welfare and well-being of families in the United States. But while there has been progress, the task is not finished. Family policy programs must continually address the stress and difficulties arising from the turbulence of modern times, such as the pressures faced by low-income families, single-parent households, and elderly and minority families. From a multicultural perspective, we have yet to achieve the harmony, freedom, and equality essential for all families in this country to live and grow to their fullest potential.

References

Bachu, Amara, and Martin O'Connell. 1999. *Fertility of American Women.* Washington, DC: U.S. Government Printing Office.

Spraggins, R. E. 2000. *Women in the United States: A Profile.* Washington, DC: U.S. Government Printing Office.

U.S. Bureau of the Census. 2000. *Statistical Abstract of the United States.* 120th ed. Washington, DC: U.S. Government Printing Office.

U.S. Department of Commerce. 2000a. *Profile of the Country's African American Population.* Washington, DC: U.S. Government Printing Office.

————. 2000b. *Profile of the Country's Hispanic American Population.* Washington, DC: U.S. Government Printing Office.

————. 2000c. *Profile of the Country's Asian and Pacific Islander American Population.* Washington, DC: U.S. Government Printing Office.

————. 2000d. *Profile of the Country's Native American Population.* Washington, DC: U.S. Government Printing Office.

3

Family Issues and Controversies

What is happening to the family in America? The contemporary family is a far cry from what it used to be. Amid rapid social change—such as widespread divorce rates, vast increases in the numbers of latchkey children, or those couples choosing to remain childless—the "typical" American family has disappeared. Today's family exists in diverse styles and shapes: single parents, remarried families, dual-career couples, unmarried couples, and gay families, to name but a few.

Accompanying such dramatic shifts in family structure are many important issues and controversies. For example, reproductive technologies have provided the means for many infertile couples to conceive, but how far are we willing to let science go? Against the backdrop of America's elderly population explosion, what is it like for grown children to care for Mom and Dad? And why is it that so many men regard the marriage license as a license to hit?

In this chapter, ten important issues and controversies that are faced by today's families will be discussed. These topics have sparked considerable interest among family studies experts over the years.

Important background material will be presented including the various forces shaping the issues, important terminology, and implications for the families of tomorrow. Later chapters are designed to complement the material provided here, such as notable historical events (Chapter 4) and contributors to the field of family studies (Chapter 5).

Family Planning

What is 'the ideal family size? Is there a best time to have children? How widespread is infertility, and if it is experienced, where can couples turn for help? Is it socially acceptable *not* to have children? These are difficult questions, and in this opening section we will look for some answers. As we'll see, some couples may prefer to create a large family, while others are content to have only one child. Many couples choose to delay having children, while others prefer voluntary childlessness. And problems with infertility aren't as remote as we tend to think; yet modern medical science succeeds in bringing solutions to most couples.

The aforementioned areas illustrate the many sides to *family planning*. Broadly defined, family planning refers to the voluntary decision making about how many children couples want and when, or if they are wanted at all. Family planning embraces a number of important areas related to the reproductive lives of couples, such as conceiving children, the timing of parenthood, voluntary childlessness, and infertility.

Patterns of *fertility*, the number of births a woman will have during her reproductive life, have changed considerably in the United States. Prior to the nineteenth century, American women averaged between 6 and 7 children each. After falling to a low of 2.2 during the 1930s, the fertility rate reached a peak of 3.7 during the 1950s and has been declining ever since. As this new century unfolds, the fertility rate is about 2.1 births per woman (U.S. Bureau of the Census, 2000a, 2000c; Population Reference Bureau, 2000).

Factors Affecting Fertility

This decline in fertility can be explained by a number of factors, including the widespread use of contraceptives and abortion, and delayed marriage and childbearing. Because couples are postponing marriage and childbearing until a later age, fertility rates have dropped. Many women have postponed marriage and childbearing so long that they will have only one child or no children at all. Other factors affecting fertility include race, ethnicity, and socioeconomic status.

Age. Women are able to conceive a pregnancy beginning in their early teens and ending in their late forties. Over this roughly thirty-year span, birthrates vary substantially by age.

Over the last twenty years, U.S. women ages 25 to 29 have had the highest birthrates, slightly higher than women ages 20 to 24, the previous leaders. Also, childbearing among women age 30 to 44 reversed its steep decline and increased over the course of the last fifteen years. Many of these older mothers began to have the children they had postponed earlier in life (McFalls, 1998).

The birthrates by the age of mother follow the same general pattern in most societies—rates are low in the teens, peak in the twenties, and decline thereafter. But comparisons of the age-specific rates in different countries reveal significant variations. For example, in Japan, where the average number of children in a family is 1.4, there is a remarkable concentration of childbearing among women 25 to 29 years of age. These women produce more than 40 percent of all Japanese births. In the United States, birthrates also are highest for women 25 to 29 years of age, but they account for just under 30 percent of all births. In the southern African county of Zambia, where the average number of children in a family is 6.1, birthrates rise very gradually from the teens to a peak in the late twenties and then decline slowly into the forties. At every age, Zambian women have higher birthrates than American and Japanese women (McFalls, 1998; Haupt and Kane, 1998).

Race and Ethnicity. In many countries, racial and ethnic minorities have higher fertility than majority groups. Often these differences arise from religious beliefs and cultural traditions, but, they also are linked to the lower economic status of minority groups and the number of years they have lived in their adopted country. As immigrant groups assimilate socially and economically they tend to adopt the fertility patterns of the majority. In the United States, for example, fertility differences among white ethnic groups (e.g., Irish, German, or Italian Americans) are becoming less distinguishable over time. Groups not fully "assimilated" may maintain their distinctive fertility patterns. As seen in the last chapter, Hispanic Americans, African Americans, and Native Americans have higher fertility than the white, non-Hispanic majority. The average number of children in a family is about 1.8 for white women and 2.0 for African American women. The average number of children in a family for Hispanic American women is about 2.4. Asian Americans tend to have rates close to non-Hispanic whites (Pollard and O'Hare, 1999).

Socioeconomic Status. In nearly every contemporary society, the poor have more children than the rich. This is also true within all major racial and ethnic groups for the United States. In general, fertility goes down as the income and educational attainment of women increase. For example, today's women between the ages of 35 and 44 with five or more years of college average 1.4 births compared with 2.0 births for women who complete high school only, and 2.7 births for non–high school graduates (Population Reference Bureau, 1997).

Other Differentials. Numerous other social, religious, and cultural factors are associated with fertility differences. Most of these can be explained by the age, income, or educational differences among these groups. For example, in just about every culture, women who work outside the home have fewer children than those who do not, and rural women have more children than urbanites. People who actively practice a religion tend to have higher fertility rates than non-religious people. There are long-standing differences between major religious groups in many countries, but these often are intertwined with ethnic and socioeconomic differences (McFalls, 1998).

Cross-National Variations in Fertility

The current emphasis placed on overpopulation and deliberate family planning has created a shrinkage of family size in many developed nations, including the United States. Should present trends continue, the United States will reach zero population growth by the year 2020. Other developed nations such as Germany, Austria, Denmark, and Hungary have already reached zero population growth. In fact, fertility levels in these nations are dropping below the level of replacement, meaning that a population decrease is resulting. Nations such as Ireland, Poland, and the Soviet Union have fertility rates of above 2.1 lifetime births per woman. This is about the fertility level needed to balance a nation's births and deaths, thus maintaining a stable population (Population Reference Bureau, 1997).

But while zero population growth is considered to be a demographic ideal, a unique set of problems can develop when negative population growth is experienced. *Negative population growth* occurs when an actual decrease in a nation's population occurs. Spain, Hungary, Portugal, and Denmark are on the verge of zero population growth or at least nearer to it than the United States. One problem with zero population growth is that a population can age significantly, meaning the proportion of the population consisting of older adults rises dramatically. Aged persons consume a disproportionate share of medical and other costly public services. Labor force shortages also may occur. In an effort to prevent zero population growth, some nations offer housing, job benefits, or other incentives to couples if they have children (McFalls, 1998).

In other parts of the world, large families prevail. For example, in Rwanda, East Africa, the fertility rate is 8.1 children per woman. The average Rwandan woman is married before the age of 20 and has her first child before her second wedding anniversary. Kenyan women average 8 children each, causing the population increase of this Texas-size country to be 4.2 percent a year. Kenya's population is estimated to be 21 million and if current fertility rates hold, it will reach 63 million by 2025. In Haiti, women give birth to about 6 children, a total that parallels the fertility rate of Pakistani women. In Tunisia, women average about 5 children (Haupt and Kane, 1998).

Knowledge of family planning is an obvious prerequisite to lowering the birthrate in overpopulated countries. However, we must not lose sight of the fact that the number of children brought into the world is influenced by many factors. One of the most important is the economic role of children, particularly in developing nations. Larger families can typically be found in those agricultural areas where intensive labor is needed, such as Latin America. In India and Bangladesh, large families result from the desire for healthy male children. Boys represent economic security for the mother should she become widowed (Haupt and Kane, 1998; McFalls, 1998).

In some nations certain customs and practices contribute to high rates of fertility. For example, unlike in some other African countries, there is no taboo against postpartum intercourse in Rwanda. This postpartum abstinence can reduce the fertility level since it can last for as long as two years, or until the child is weaned. As another illustration, Muslim culture encourages large families and has a strong bias against birth control of any kind. A number of reasons can be cited for this bias, including fear of health-related problems, side effects, and the husband's opposition to birth control (Haupt and Kane, 1998).

No discussion of cross-cultural fertility rates is complete without some reference to the People's Republic of China, which boasts the largest population in the world. In the year 2000, the population in China reached almost 1.2 billion. (For comparison purposes, the population of the United States in 2000 stood at approximately 275 million.) Given its huge population, family planning in China is not a voluntary decision made by couples. Rather, it is the government that dictates family planning. In an effort to reduce overpopulation, couples in this nation are allowed to have only one child. The People's Republic of China is thus the first nation to ever restrict a couple's right to procreate. It has also raised the minimum age for marriage to 20 for women and 22 for men. Even marriages at a later age are encouraged to reduce the couple's risk of having more than one child.

The Chinese government imposes the one-child limit through incentives, peer pressure, and attempts to persuade newly married couples that their rational fertility decisions will mean a better future for their own families, their communities, and their nation. If the one-child limit is successful, it is estimated that the population will stabilize over the next five years. If unsuccessful and the population continues to grow, China's ability to feed its people is in jeopardy, among other consequences.

If Chinese couples follow government legislation, they are entitled to numerous benefits, including increased living space, pensions, free education, lower-cost health care, and better medical intervention. Eventually, the only child receives preferential treatment in the school system as well as in the labor force. Should couples give birth to a second child, the family forfeits all of these benefits. The fact that Chinese families have traditionally preferred male children complicates this fertility plan. Should a firstborn be female, couples may try to conceive again in an effort to bring a male into the world. This places couples at odds with the government, not to mention other consequences. Indeed, in one province of China, couples expecting a second child will have their wages docked if the woman decides not to have an abortion.

Delayed Parenthood

Delayed parenthood represents a deliberate effort on the part of a couple to postpone having children. Not only are the numbers of couples choosing delayed parenthood increasing, they are also having fewer children. Delaying parenthood provides couples with the opportunity to develop their personal, career, and marital lives before they take on the responsibilities of parenthood.

Demographers have supplied information regarding those couples choosing to delay parenthood. For example, education appears to be an important determining factor. The more education a woman has, the greater the likelihood that a couple will wait longer to have children. In addition, the closer a wife's earnings parallel her husband's, the more likely she is to delay parenthood. Also, women who grew up in cities, Catholic women, and those whose parents are well educated and whose fathers have relatively high-status occupations tend to be older when they have their first child. However, when the women's education level is held constant these associations lose their significance. Finally, the age at which a woman has her first child depends heavily on when she herself was born and when she married. Events such as wars and fluctuations in the business cycle caused by unemployment or recession explain some variation in the timing of a woman's first child.

There are a number of advantages and disadvantages associated with delayed parenthood. On the plus side, older women who have developed competence in the world before bearing children often bring to the mothering experience strengths different from those of their younger counterparts. Older mothers with established careers are often more accepting and less conflicted in the parenting role than younger professional women. They have a tendency to reveal strengths concomitant with their level of maturity that are generally advantageous for their children's development. Research has indicated that levels of marital satisfaction are higher among women postponing parenthood and childless women than among younger mothers.

It must also be acknowledged that there are forces that may work against the couple delaying parenthood. Perhaps the biggest risk is that a woman's fertility will decrease with age and health risks will increase. Mortality rates associated with pregnancy and childbirth are substantially higher for women in their thirties and forties than they are for women in their teens and twenties. The incidence of Down syndrome also rises sharply with the age of the mother. (Down syndrome is a chromosomal abnormality causing, among other characteristics, epicanthic eye folds, round heads, and usually developmental disability.) Another disadvantage associated with delayed parenthood is that older parents may not have the helping services of their aging parents. Finally, parents delaying parenthood may find the tasks associated with child care physically exhausting, maybe even more so than younger parents.

Voluntary Childlessness

Some couples today opt for *voluntary childlessness,* a conscious decision not to have children. Unlike couples wanting a family, voluntarily childless couples do not regard parenthood as a necessary ingredient for marital happiness or satisfaction.

About 20 percent of women will elect not to have children. This figure represents an increase over the approximate 10 percent reported in 1980. According to demographic experts (e.g., Bachu and O'Connell, 1999; Spraggins, 2000), women who had the highest levels of education, those engaged in managerial and professional occupations, and those with the highest family incomes experienced the highest levels of childlessness. For a historical and statistical comparison of childlessness, see Chapter 6 (Figure 6–15).

Voluntary childlessness is an interesting trend compared to the high premium placed on having children during early historical periods. Indeed, in the Old Testament God's directive to Noah was, "Be fruitful and multiply." Parents often faced certain consequences if they did not bear children and produce large families. In the classical age of Greece, barrenness was sufficient grounds for a man to divorce his wife. And remember that in colonial America, single men were viewed with suspicion and penalized with special taxes for not doing their share to increase the population.

The decision to remain childless is usually a difficult one for the couple. Organizations such as the National Alliance for Optional Parenthood are available today to help couples in their decision-making. The central theme of the National Alliance for Optional Parenthood is that parenthood is a life option for couples, not a duty. The organization seeks to promote the idea that it is perfectly acceptable not to have children.

Infertility

Not all couples can become biological parents. *Infertility* is the inability to achieve a pregnancy after at least one year of regular, unprotected intercourse. It is estimated that about 15 percent of the population—approximately one in seven couples—is infertile at any given time. However, patience is sometimes the answer for many of these couples. Pregnancy statistics tell us that for normal women who aren't using birth control and are sexually active, 25 percent will be pregnant in the first month, 63 percent will be in six months, and 80 percent will be in one year. An additional 5 to 10 percent will become pregnant the following year (Rosenthal and Khatamee, 2001).

About 40 percent of infertility problems can be traced to the male, 40 percent to the female, and 20 percent of the time, couples share the problem of infertility and the reasons are often unknown. Among the more common causes of male infertility are poor sperm quality, low sperm count, and poor sperm motility or movement. One of the causes of decreased sperm number and motility is varicocele, a condition that causes dilation of veins near the testicles. Other causes of decreased sperm number might include chronic fatigue and illness; poor nutrition; excessive use of caffeine, tobacco, or marijuana; too frequent intercourse; hot spas or saunas; nervous stress; fear of impotence; certain medications and treatments such as radiation to the testes; and possibly tight underwear and pants (Jequier, 2000).

The most common causes of female infertility are the blockage of fallopian tubes and the failure to ovulate. A number of causes may account for blockage, including tubal scarring from pelvic infections. Growing numbers of women develop pelvic inflammatory disease when sexually transmitted diseases such as chlamydia spread into the uterus and fallopian tubes, in the process affecting a woman's ability to conceive. Ovulatory defects include the inability of an ovary to develop or to release an egg or of the body to produce the proper amount or sequence of hormones. Another cause of infertility is the failure of the cervix at midcycle to secrete cervical mucus, a necessity for sperm survival. Or, the cervix may produce abnormal amounts of mucus, which impedes the movement of sperm (Treiser and Levinson, 2001).

Infertility can be related to aging processes. Women under age 25 have about a 7 percent chance of being infertile, but by the age of 40, one out of every three females is unable to have a child. A woman in her thirties does not have many fertile years left. Male infertility is also partly determined by age; a man of 50 generally has a lower sperm count than a man of 20, although the natural decrease in the 50-year-old's sperm count may not prevent him from having children if enough of his remaining sperm are healthy.

Other causes of infertility include sexual dysfunction, inappropriate timing of intercourse, and immunological factors. Also, stressful lifestyles, personal problems, vocational pressures, and general mental health may have physical effects on both male and female. And, environmental conditions such as exposure to pollutants, pesticides, or work hazards are other considerations (Bentley and Mascie-Taylor, 2001).

Today a number of medical interventions exist for infertility. The initial intervention for infertility usually includes a history and physical examination of both partners. The woman is often asked to chart her basal body temperature (lowest body temperature, usually taken in the morning before getting out of bed) so that the physician can assess the regularity of her menstrual cycle, when she is ovulating, and the optimum time for the couple to have intercourse. The man may also be instructed to abstain from sexual activity for several days before the woman's fertile period is expected, in the hope that his sperm count will rise. Sometimes special drugs are administered to the woman to induce ovulation (Williams, 2001).

For men, fertility is tested with a semen analysis, which assesses the number, quality, and motility of sperm. Should infertility be traced to the male, surgery might be in order to repair blockage in the testicles, such as varicocele or blocked sperm ducts. Other forms of intervention might include the medical management of hormonal abnormalities or infections. Hormone therapy for men has not consistently demonstrated an increase in sperm production and is still considered largely experimental (Burns and Covington, 2000).

For women, blood and urine tests are given to determine estrogen, gonadotrophin, and progesterone levels, and cervical mucus tests are used to assess whether sperm can penetrate and survive within the cervix. A physician might use microsurgical techniques to assess the reproductive system and any disease or blockage. Microsurgery is sometimes employed to correct blocked fallopian tubes, and laser surgery has recently been used to treat endometriosis.

In about 75 percent of infertility cases, the aforementioned procedures prove successful. Should such measures be unsuccessful, hope lies in several sophisticated *assisted reproductive technologies,* medical interventions used in helping women achieve pregnancy. Such interventions include in-vitro fertilization, artificial insemination, surrogate motherhood, and embryo transfer (Becker, 2000).

In-Vitro Fertilization. In in-vitro fertilization, sometimes referred to as test-tube fertilization, one or more ova are surgically removed from the mother, combined with the father's sperm, and placed into the uterus. The procedure is usually employed when the woman's fallopian tubes are blocked or diseased. Women with normal menstrual cycles and men with normal sperm counts are considered good candidates for this procedure, which is one of the most common forms of reproductive technology.

Although the pioneer successes with in-vitro fertilization used the woman's natural menstrual cycle for the procedure, clinics today experience higher success rates by hormonally stimulating ovulation with fertility drugs and "harvesting" three to five eggs, rather than just one naturally produced egg. When the eggs are mature, they are removed from her body by a surgical technique called laparoscopy. In this technique, under general anesthesia, a small incision is made adjacent to the navel and a small tube-like scope is inserted, enabling the physician to see inside. The eggs are retrieved with a hollow needle and placed in a petri dish where they are allowed to mature for several hours before they are fertilized with the father's sperm. The fertilized eggs are then placed in an incubator. About forty-eight hours later, when each egg has gone through the cell divisions necessary to produce a blastocyst, several are implanted in the woman's uterus.

Variations of in-vitro fertilization have been developed in recent years. For example, in *gamete intra-fallopian transfer,* ova are gathered in much the same way described above and mixed with the father's sperm. Then, both ova and sperm are placed into one or both fallopian tubes, the normal site of fertilization. Should fertilization occur, the zygote then travels to the uterus, where prenatal development proceeds. Another technique is *zygote intra-fallopian transfer.* Here, ova are retrieved and mixed with the father's sperm similar to in-vitro fertilization. However, the zygote is transferred back to the woman's body and placed in the fallopian tube at a much earlier stage of cell division.

Artificial Insemination. Artificial insemination involves artificially injecting sperm (fresh or frozen) into a woman's vagina, either on or near the cervix, at the time of ovulation. There are three types of artificial insemination. One type uses sperm from the husband, often when his sperm count is low or the wife has cervical mucus problems. When the husband's sperm count is too low, artificial insemination by donor is practiced, which utilizes sperm from an unrelated, usually anonymous donor. The donor is screened and matched as closely to the husband as possible for such characteristics as ethnic background, stature, complexion, and blood type. Special screening is also given to prevent genetic defects, sexually transmitted diseases, and other potential problems. A third type combines a mixture of sperm from a husband who has a low sperm count and sperm from an unrelated donor. In this case there can be some hope that the resulting child may be the husband's.

Surrogate Motherhood. Surrogate motherhood occurs when the father is fertile but the mother is unable to carry the child to term. In this technique, which is a variation of artificial insemination, a chosen surrogate mother is artificially inseminated with the husband's sperm. The surrogate mother carries and bears the child, which is then given back to the couple. The surrogacy center handles the screening of candidates, arranges medical, legal, and psychological services, and offers a standard contract to govern the transaction.

Embryo Transfer. Embryo transfer is somewhat related to surrogate motherhood, although it is much more experimental. Infertile women are usually the candidates for this technique, which involves impregnating another woman with the father's sperm. After several days, the fertilized ovum is removed from her uterus and placed within the wife's uterus, which has been hormonally prepared to accept it. This is done when the menstrual cycle of the wife indicates that she is prepared to accept a pregnancy. In some instances, the embryo is frozen and implanted at a later time.

Without question, these assisted reproductive technologies represent important medical breakthroughs. However, it must be mentioned that along with critical acclaim has come considerable controversy. Many object to such technologies on the basis of religious, moral, or ethical principles. Compounding the problem is that clear-cut or comprehensive laws regarding reproductive technologies are lacking. One source (Stephen, 1999) points to the legal complexities that exist in just identifying the parents. In some instances there may be as many as five people involved: a sperm donor, an egg donor, a gestational mother, and the contracting mother and father.

At the very least, reproductive technologies have radically altered the traditional transition to parenthood. They create a wide range of options in fertility and reproduction that need to be carefully studied. The most fundamental issue seems to be how far are we willing to let science go with reproductive technology—and where do we draw the line? Should this be resolved, another important issue immediately arises: *Who* should draw the line? The courts? The medical community? The infertile patients? Obviously, we will not find answers to such issues overnight. However, the complexities raised by such issues must nonetheless be addressed in the years to come.

Contemporary Parenthood

In many respects, parenthood represents the great unknown. Although the uninitiated often think about becoming parents someday, few are really prepared for it. As a result, important issues surface regarding parenthood's many sides. For example, many adults wonder how their lives will change with the addition of youngsters, including the potential rewards and sacrifices that child rearing brings. Others want to know more about the new role that goes along with parenthood and what kinds of expectations go along with it. Still others ponder whether or not there is a "best" way to rear children. Certainly, these are difficult issues. And since little formal preparation exists, such as required training programs, indoctrination into parenthood is often sudden and swift. Most learn to become a parent by becoming a parent.

Without question, the arrival of an infant changes parents' lives considerably. Indeed, parenthood may well be the most complex and dramatic change that most people will ever make in their lives. For instance, mothers and fathers must learn to adjust to loss of sleep and frequent physical fatigue. (The fatigue factor prompts the remark, "Those who claim they've slept like a baby obviously don't own one.") Many express increased worry over financial matters, and soon discover that the costs of rearing a child quickly escalate. Food, clothing, furniture, toys, and the like make parenthood an expensive venture. Most new parents also experience uneasiness about the unknown aspects of parenthood, particularly unfamiliar child-care routines and demands. Uncertainty often elevates parental anxiety and confusion, and many adults experience added pressure in the wake of mounting child-care chores (Jeffers, 2001).

In the midst of such adjustments, new parents often discover that it is difficult to enjoy each other's exclusive company. With the baby's arrival, patterns of intimacy and affection are changed and need to be redefined. Additionally, interactions and visits with friends become restricted. Parenthood may also mean that the child's needs compete with those of the spouse, causing some parents to feel angry, jealous, and resentful during stressful times (Beecham and Hillgartner, 2001).

There are many young mothers who report being overwhelmed by the constant flow of infant-oriented tasks to be carried out. Feeding and bathing of the baby and laundering clothing, added to the regular household routines of cleaning, cooking, and shopping, is a full day's work. Countless other chores can be added to this list. New mothers and fathers usually experience stress originating from the multiple demands of child care, work, and marriage. Many have difficulty adapting to unfamiliar child-care demands, such as infant soothing techniques, and marital conflict is common (Westman, 2001).

Many new mothers also report unmet violated expectations of the father with respect to the sharing of child-care responsibilities. Many investigators have found that mothers do much more of the housework and child care than they had expected, and many report less positive feelings about their husbands during the postpartum period than during pregnancy. Moreover, unmet expectations concerning division of labor are related to negative postpartum feelings concerning the overall marital relationship. Also, postpartum adjustment is more difficult when the mother's expectations exceed the actual support and assistance given from extended family.

The foregoing does not mean that parenthood is a gloomy, negative experience. Although it has its share of demands and strains, most parents are able to weather its difficulties. And even though some researchers find that the addition of children reduces marital happiness, most parents express overall satisfaction with their children and the parenting role in general. Such a perspective acknowledges the demands attached to parenthood but also emphasizes the bright side to raising children.

Experts believe that from the beginning, parents need to reject the idealistic myth of having the perfect family. Just like marriage, parenthood has its share of triumphs but also its share of ups and downs, heartaches, and headaches. Too many new parents strive for perfection, and in the process program themselves for failure. It is important for new parents to be flexible with their expectations and learn to take pride in their daily accomplishments. Fears and anxieties about child care tend to fade when parents learn that they do not have to do everything by the book. As a result of the experiences gained and lessons learned firsthand, parenthood begins to acquire a less tense and more realistic relaxed quality.

A critical component of effective parenting adjustment is the support partners give to one other, physical as well as psychological. For new parents, especially, openly discussing concerns and problems and working together as a team are instrumental in creating a favorable family climate. And, the availability of both informal and formal support beyond the home (e.g., assistance from family and friends, parenting support groups) eases the transition to parenthood. Parents also need to periodically get away from the baby and enjoy their own private space. Husband and wife need to maintain a loving, harmonious relationship so that they can better fill the roles of mother and father.

Adjusting to Motherhood

Many first-time mothers often feel inadequate to the task, mainly because they have had limited contact with children prior to their own. However, some type of formal or informal support system during the early weeks of motherhood is usually of great value. If a supportive relative or friend assists with child care and domestic chores, the new mother is usually able to adjust to infant demands and able to develop confidence and competency in her new role.

Often, the mother discovers that an infant is more work than she ever imagined. Unfortunately, society tends to paint an unrealistic image of motherhood, in some instances idealizing it beyond recognition. The truth of the matter is that mothers find their lives significantly altered with an ever-increasing workload. Many feel overwhelmed in the face of physical demands, not only those attached to caregiving, but also those related to the father's needs (Nee, 2000).

As we learned in Chapter 1, mothers in past historical eras were expected to remain at home and care for their children, particularly during their offspring's early years of development. Many felt that this was the only way a mother could love and properly rear her children during this important life stage. To venture away from the family in search of a paycheck was viewed as uncaring and unwise. Today, however, this image of womanhood is no longer true. A few statistics can shed light on the large numbers of working women in the United States today, as well as how the labor force has changed.

- The number of working women has grown from about 5.3 million in 1900 to about 65 million in 2000.
- Female labor force participation differs among racial and ethnic groups. In 2000, African American females had the highest labor force participation (64 percent), while Hispanic American females had the lowest (56 percent).
- Families in which both spouses work and have children now represent the majority (52 percent) of all married-couple families.
- Unlike earlier times, when mothers took years away from the labor force for childbearing, modern women return to the labor force rather quickly. In 2000, almost 60 percent were back on the job within one year, and one in four returned within three months.
- Approximately 75 percent of mothers with children from the ages of 6 to 17 are working (U.S. Department of Commerce, 2001; U.S. Bureau of the Census, 2000a; Population Reference Bureau, 2000).

Although the dual-earner family reaps its share of benefits and personal satisfaction, certain difficulties and adjustments are common in homes with younger children. The search for quality child care and the costs involved almost always head the list. In addition, the responsibilities of child rearing and tending to domestic chores are difficult obstacles for working women to hurdle. In most instances, the woman still carries the brunt of the household tasks, which intensify when employment outside of the home occurs. Consequently, the problem is that a two-career marriage is really a three-career marriage, with the woman typically holding down two careers (Hertz and Marshall, 2001).

Often, a mother's employment status has minimal effect on the husband's response. While many husbands may say that they prefer an equitable domestic arrangement, in actual practice domestic equality is the exception rather than the rule. Many mothers also report some anxiety about their child's well-being and wonder if they have made the right choice. Many who are full-time mothers, however, often want to go back into the labor force. Thus, a type of "Catch–22" situation exists. In other instances, working mothers are happy and satisfied with their chosen profession, but feel inadequate in the mothering role. Therefore, many working mothers feel conflicted about their role (Balswick and Balswick, 1999; Gill, 1998).

Adjusting to Fatherhood

Until recently the role and impact of the father in child care has been overlooked. Although the importance of the father in the household is generally recognized, part of the problem is that American society has been "mother-centered" in its philosophy of child care. With the rapidly increasing numbers of dual-earner households, the father's influence on various aspects of child growth and development is now being increasingly recognized.

Contemporary fathers represent an interesting comparison to their historical counterparts. In many ways, modern fathers want to avoid the mistakes that they feel their fathers made. They do not want to become overinvolved in their work or in their friendships and neglect their children. The modern father tends to make a conscious effort to spend more time with his children, perhaps in an effort to be the father he never had. The modern father also does not wait until his children are older before he gets to know them; he starts early. And, as much as he might not like it, he devotes more time to child-care responsibilities (Hertz and Marshall, 2001).

Adjusting to fatherhood may prove difficult for some men. Much of the problem is that many fathers are simply unprepared to assume active parental roles. This lack of preparation for fatherhood is often seen in fathers' not knowing developmentally appropriate parenting skills, understanding normal child development, and being sensitive to their youngsters' needs. Poor preparation usually originates from limited contact with paternal role models, restricted institutional support for the paternal role, and few opportunities to prepare for parenthood (Campbell, 2000).

Most experts agree that the key for new fathers is developing confidence—skills can usually be acquired later. Many fathers do not realize that most first-time mothers are just as ill prepared and unsure of themselves as they are. Possibly, the difference is that women are expected to know "how" to parent and cannot just withdraw from or more easily avoid the challenges involved. The role of mother embraces specific knowledge, ability, and motivation. Mothers who are uninformed often have to pretend that they know what they are doing, and then learn the necessary child-care skills as soon as they can. If a father has difficulty in dealing with an infant, he invariably turns to his wife for help. If the mother needs assistance, she is more likely to seek help from a relative, friend, or pediatrician.

Whether or not the father's influence becomes positive is an important issue. This influence hinges on a number of forces, including the father's involvement in child care and family activities, his upbringing, the quality of his other relationships, his personality characteristics (i. e., self-esteem and sensitivity), and the characteristics of his offspring. Although many fathers look forward to child care, there are some who resist the notion that they should be spending more time with their children. Many feel that they are poorly prepared already for the task of parenting, to say nothing of more child-care responsibilities.

Finally, it should be noted that greater paternal involvement does not always create domestic harmony. Increased involvement may trigger marital conflict and create lowered levels of marital satisfaction. When mothers are employed outside the home, some fathers may perceive their roles as being more restricted and their freedom as being reduced. Furthermore, many fathers are unaccustomed to the multiple role demands of being a parent and of working outside the home (Brubaker, 2000; Barnett and Rivers, 1998).

Child-Rearing Options and Strategies

One of the major responsibilities of parenthood is adopting child-rearing standards suitable for healthy growth and development. Beginning around the turn of the century, the United States experienced an unprecedented interest in this topic. Although child psychologists were scientifically exploring the foundations of behavior, child-care experts began to busily address themselves to the practical aspects of rearing children. In time, their guidance would find its way to books, magazines, professional journals, newspapers, and an assortment of parenting seminars and workshops.

The advice and guidance given by this country's child-care experts came in all shapes and sizes and focused on every conceivable aspect of child-rearing, from toilet training to temper tantrums. However, these experts did address themselves to parenthood's most persistent challenge: how best to raise children to become healthy, well-adjusted adults.

There is no question that this diverse assortment of child-rearing guidance has helped to better educate parents about children and their many needs. The range of differing opinions and philosophies has, however, produced its share of confusion, too. This is as evident today as it was when the child experts first began to present their opinions.

For example, consider the conflicting child-rearing advice that abounds regarding how much freedom to give a child. Historically, the swing of the pendulum on this particular issue has been extreme. The *restrictive parenting approach,* popular at the turn of the century, stressed strict parent-child relations. Considerable emphasis was placed on the development of self-control, respect, and disciplined character. Parental affection was generally discouraged, since it was believed that excessive amounts would create childhood immaturity and irresponsibility.

During the 1940s the *permissive parenting approach* to child rearing emerged. This approach emphasized greater levels of freedom with children and was popular among middle-class parents. Parents were advised to generate a loving attitude toward children, one that encompassed understanding, sensitivity, and affection. As for disciplining measures, parents were encouraged to move away from physical punishment and adopt more relaxed but firm measures. They were also urged to develop confidence in their roles as parents. The permissive approach is evident in many books, the most notable being Benjamin Spock's *Baby and Child Care,* first published in 1945. This is an enormously popular book on child rearing, still used by many parents today. For more information on Spock and his impact on child rearing, see his biography in Chapter 5.

These two contrasting child-rearing approaches are good illustrations of the range of advice available to parents. In the light of such advice, it must be emphasized that a scientifically proven means of child rearing has yet to emerge. Although suggestions are bountiful, clear-cut and precise answers are elusive. It seems likely that parents will continue to be swept into a crossfire of opinion, as they seek out the best way to raise their children.

Because of the numerous and diverse child-rearing strategies offered to past and present-day parents, it is helpful to categorize approaches according to their operating philosophy. This may help to develop a better understanding of the rationale behind a suggested guideline or opinion. Although it is impossible to cover all approaches, the following is representative of some of the more popular child-rearing strategies to emerge.

Developmental-Maturational Approach. The developmental-maturational approach was developed by Arnold Gesell (1940) and it is best known as an age-stage theory of child rearing. Gesell maintains that although individual variations exist, most children will pass through basic patterns of growth at fairly predictable ages. He expended considerable energy exploring this principle, leading him to devise numerous norms of infant and child development. Gesell stresses that parents should be aware of childhood's developmental sequences and should structure their expectations, demands, and child-rearing strategies accordingly.

Behavior-Modification Approach. Borrowing from B. F. Skinner (1953) and the theory of behaviorism, experts emphasizing the behavior-modification approach call attention to the child's surroundings. More specifically, it is maintained that the environment is capable of shaping a child's behavior. Practitioners advocate the use of positive reinforcement, or the rewarding of a desired behavior (a child is given a toy for good behavior), or negative reinforcement, giving children the opportunity to behave in a way that reduces or eliminates an aversive stimulus (children are sent to their rooms because of a temper tantrum, but can return when they calm down). Proponents claim that when consistently adhered to, these principles will enable parents to nurture desired behavioral patterns in their children.

Humanistic Approach. The focus of the humanistic approach, developed by Haim Ginott (1965), is the development of parental empathy, sensitivity, and insight into the needs of children. Parents are urged to improve their communication abilities so that they can better appreciate children's feelings and motivations. Among other suggestions, Ginott advocates the practice of preceding statements of advice with statements of understanding, the resolution of conflicts without attacks on personalities, and the abolishment of all threats and sarcasm.

Parent-Effectiveness Training. Developed by Thomas Gordon (1978), parent-effectiveness training (P.E.T.) seeks to teach parents how to enhance children's self-images as well as their potentials in life. Gordon's techniques include the practice of reflecting positive images back to the child, engaging in mutual negotiation when problems arise, and engaging in "active listening" or verbally feeding back to the youngster what they've expressed. Gordon proposes that this latter communication technique enables children to better understand what they have said and assists them in solving their own problems. Gordon also advocates the use of "I" rather than "you" messages ("I get upset when you disturb me like that," as opposed to "You're a rude child to bother your father like this."). He feels that "I" messages are more likely to impart facts, while "you" messages tend to attach blame, promote rebellion, and reduce the child's self-concept.

Democratic Approach. The democratic approach is popular in the writings of many child-rearing experts, the most notable being Rudolph Dreikurs (1964). He believes that the family unit is the primary force in shaping children's behavior. Therefore, parents should seek to integrate them as fully as possible into the family network, so that they can benefit from everyone's observations, feedback, and encouragement. Children are urged to take part in family decision-making processes, including the establishment of rules and expectations. By so doing, Dreikurs believes, they will learn "logical consequences" of their behavior, those expected behavioral standards that will ensure the fair treatment of all family members. The promotion of such a collective and cooperative atmosphere will promote security, trust, and a sense of belonging within the child.

Transactional-Analysis Approach. Popularized by Eric Berne (1964), the transactional-analysis approach stresses the importance of three "ego states" and their relation to effective communication. The three ego states are the "child" (source of spontaneity, but also the source of fear, helplessness, and intimidation); "adult" (source or reason, but also the source of emotionless responses); and "parent" (the source of nurturing, but also the source of emotional response). Berne suggests that the adult psyche is capable of expressing these three unique ego dimensions when communicating with others. The analysis of communication patterns (called transactions), therefore, reveals interesting and complex dynamics.

In connection with child rearing, parents may inappropriately respond to a youngster's problem by activating helplessness within their own child state. Or both parents may be striving to solve the same child-rearing issue, but are unproductive because their ego states are incompatible (the father may be utilizing the nurturing facet of his parent state, while the mother's communication embodies the oppressive-adult ego state). In his approach, Berne stresses the importance of ego-state recognition and compatibility of exchange patterns, as well as the parental nurturing of the adult ego state in children.

All of these theories provide a great deal of insight into the nature of child rearing. However, these theoretical positions do not have to be examined or weighed in an either/or manner. Several of them could be operating at different times or under different conditions. For example, the fact that a child may be at a specific norm of Gesell's developmental-maturational theory does not mean that principles of reinforcement are not operating or that the youngster's interaction with the family unit becomes nonexistent. Thus, while each theory is an effort to explain child-rearing techniques, it is not uncommon for two or more of them to be operating simultaneously.

This is the primary reason why many parents today choose to be eclectic when viewing child-rearing theories. They select theories that they can accept, and then develop their own strategies. Moreover, theories need to be adapted and modified to take each individual child into account. Generalized child-rearing theories without individual modification downplay the uniqueness of both child and parent.

It should be remembered, too, that a theory is really a perspective, one of several ways to view development. Although each of these theories has broadened our understanding and offers us new areas of exploration, we have not yet been able to answer all our questions about child rearing. As indicated earlier, no theory has yet to explain the "best" way to rear youngsters. This underscores the need to further investigate this field of study, as well as the need for reassessing the theories and viewpoints generated thus far.

Work and Family Life

Fifty years ago, the manner in which work and family life converged reflected a traditional image, one captured in such television shows as *Ozzie and Harriet* or *Father Knows Best*. The father was invariably cast as the sole breadwinner, busily engaged in a career away from the home, while the mother was portrayed as a homemaker in charge of the children and the day-to-day operation of the household.

Times have obviously changed. Today, the "traditional" family of working father, homemaker mother, and one or more children now accounts for only 13 percent of all married-couple households and only 7 percent of all households. Dual-earner families, in which both husband and wife are in the labor market, now outnumber traditional families two to one. Furthermore, the proportion of married women in the labor force has almost tripled over the last fifty years (Population Reference Bureau, 2000).

The modern, dual-earner family faces a number of unique challenges and adjustments, paramount among them is achieving a balance between work and family demands. This section of the book is designed to explore the interplay that exists between these two worlds and the resulting family dynamics. Some key issues and controversies will be addressed, including the advantages and drawbacks of dual-earner households, the negotiation of roles and a division of labor, the changing role of women in the workplace, and the arrangement of child care (Hertz and Marshall, 2001).

Work and family life involve a complex set of circumstances and relationships that we are only beginning to understand. Dual-earner couples face special challenges as they seek to balance vocational and domestic responsibilities, such as coping with inflexible work hours to searching for quality child care. Dual-earner couples also discover that work and family life are intertwined in many ways. For example, employment conditions may affect family life in a positive way, just as the household stability or instability can impact one's job performance. Or, the demands of a high-powered career may clash with the demands of being a good spouse or parent. In such instances, people may try to insulate their career from their household, hence the expression "leaving the job at the office."

Dual-earner families have the potential of promoting considerably high levels of happiness, satisfaction, and accomplishment. Many dual-earner families report stability in the household and contentment with career pursuits. Indeed, some say that the involvement and sacrifices required in a vocation make marriage and family life more meaningful. Working wives, especially, generally feel better about themselves and often feel "liberated" by their work. Thus, two time-consuming, bustling vocations may bring considerable enrichment and contentment, not to mention elevated levels of finance (Berne, 2001).

However, there are two sides to every coin. Because of its demands, a two-paycheck marriage may also snap the patience of even the most dedicated couples. Such a domestic arrangement has the potential of bringing headaches and sacrifices, the pressure of which often overwhelm marriage partners. It is not uncommon for dual-earner couples to report tension over such issues as caring for children or a decline in family time. Moreover, the decision of both partners to work is often due to sheer economic necessity. For most, financial pressures are a fact of life and two paychecks are needed just to make ends meet (Campbell, 2000).

The household division of labor among dual-earner couples also has the potential of posing problems. Although increasing numbers of women are employed outside the home, most of the traditional roles attached to them are still in place. It is true that many couples share the burden of domestic chores and responsibilities, but most do not. Instead, most homes in the United States reflect a conventional orientation to household chores. This means that in addition to vocational demands, working women still carry the brunt of household tasks and duties. This situation often worsens during parenthood when child-care responsibilities are added to the woman's domestic responsibilities.

All of this means many women face inequality on two fronts, the workplace and the household. Beyond the pay differential that exists in the labor force, which we'll visit in a few moments, women still shoulder most of the domestic chores, from cooking to cleaning. When we add other pressures typically shouldered by women into the domestic mix, such as changing child-care arrangements or caring for aging parents (see "Caring for Aging Family Members" in this chapter), the potential for dissatisfaction and tension increases. Even in these modern times, multitudes of mothers have children on their hips and their careers on hold. Consequently for many women, the alignment that exists between home and the workplace remains lopsided (Hochschild, 2000).

However, it needs to be pointed out that many women are comfortable with such responsibilities as well as traditional gender-roles, including divisions of labor. Some wives resist the assistance offered by their husbands because they feel that the home is their turf, and part of their identity is derived from this role. The same would hold true for those husbands who are reluctant to accept spousal assistance in their particular territories. What, then, for most seems like inequities in household chores and child-care responsibilities, may instead be mutually acceptable to the mother and father. Friction may instead result from other sources: a non-supportive spouse, a lack of appreciation for the other's contributions, or taking one's partner for granted.

Another problem associated with dual-earner marriages is the pressure and competition it often creates among traditional couples. The husband's psychological identity with his work is often the cause of this problem. When both partners work, some men feel threatened because traditional gender-role boundaries have been crossed. This feeling intensifies in dual-earner households where wives are earning close to, or even surpassing the incomes generated by their partners. This may intimidate traditional men because money often translates into power, authority, and control, and some males may resist the notion of yielding these elements to women. Furthermore, there are some men who support and encourage women's career successes, provided they do not challenge or surpass their own (Campbell, 2000).

Domestic harmony and marital stability are likely to increase when men learn how to accept their partner's achievement without feeling threatened. Competitive one-upmanship related to career accomplishments promotes self-centeredness and almost always produces disagreement, resentment, and hostility. On the other hand, marital happiness and fulfillment is often achieved when couples de-emphasize work-related competition and instead express mutual interest and support. There is no need to view each other's professional gain as a personal loss.

Working Women, Working Lives

As we've mentioned, increasingly large numbers of women are employed in the nation's labor force. A few statistics will illustrate how widespread female labor force participation is. In this new century, women now constitute about 47 percent of the total labor force, a stark contrast to the 18 percent recorded in 1900 and the 30 percent of 1950. In terms of numbers, today's female labor force is over 64 million, compared to 5.3 million in 1900 and 18.4 million in 1950. As far as future trends are concerned, it

is estimated that over 60 percent of all adult females will participate in the labor force by the year 2050 (U.S. Department of
Commerce, 2001; U.S. Bureau of Labor Statistics, 1999, 2000; U.S.
Bureau of the Census, 2000a). For more labor statistics regarding
women in the workforce, see Chapter 6, Figures 6–16 and Table
6–3.

What factors account for such increases in female labor
force involvement? Economic necessity is a big reason. A single
income is no longer enough for many couples. Also, growing
numbers of women are heading single-parent families. Higher
divorce or separation rates require more women to live on their
own incomes. Another motive is the need for achievement
beyond the home and family, particularly among college-educated women.

Today's working woman has transcended traditional gender-role barriers, not only by the work she does, but also by the
fact that she often operates from a set of carefully cultivated
career goals. Such careful planning was virtually unheard of in
previous generations because yesterday's females were not
expected to have career goals. And for some of today's traditional females, this societal expectation still lingers. There are
also those who feel that success in a career is something to fear
and even shy away from, since they have been taught that being
competitive and successful is unfeminine.

Today, there are more career options available than ever
before in this nation's history. Particularly impressive are the
growing numbers of women employed in such careers as health
services, banking, legal services, insurance, and retail trade.
Women are also making significant inroads in those jobs previously held down by their male counterparts: politicians and
high-ranking government officials, pilots and navigators, and
professional athletes, to name but a few.

But, despite gains made in certain occupational sectors,
women still face an uphill battle when in comes to employment
discrimination. *Employment discrimination* refers to the unfair and
unequal treatment of a person on the basis of her or his sex. Even
in these modern times, women encounter employment discrimination in various forms, such as job segregation or pay differentials. As far as job segregation is concerned, most secretaries,
nurses, schoolteachers, and librarians are women (see Chapter 6,
Table 6–4). The majority of women who work in office settings

today handle secretarial and clerical chores, and the more prestigious and better-paying executive positions are held mostly by men. This unequal treatment extends even to such areas as access to credit and obtaining insurance at reasonable rates.

In 2000, the federal government (U.S. Bureau of the Census, 2000c) confirmed that working women remained trapped in "female" jobs. Women were over represented in administrative support and service occupations and underrepresented in precision production, craft, repair occupations, and the transportation and material moving occupations. To illustrate, almost 80 percent of the 18.6 million people involved in administrative support (including clerical) were female, and about 95 percent of the nearly 860,000 people who were employed as service workers in private households were female.

Regarding pay differentials, it is estimated that women who work full-time, year-round earn 74 cents for every dollar earned by men. It is also estimated that retired female workers average 77 cents for every dollar paid to retired male workers. The following data from 2000 adds further evidence of the pay differential that exists between men and women:

- The median earnings of women 25 years of age and older who worked full-time, year-round were $26,711. This income was approximately 73 percent of their male counterparts' median earnings of $36,679.
- The median earnings of women with high school diplomas were $21,963, compared with $30,868 for their male counterparts.
- The median earnings of women with bachelor's degrees were $35,408, compared with $49,982 for their male counterparts.
- The median earnings of women with professional degrees were $55,460, compared with $90,653 for their male counterparts (U.S. Bureau of the Census, 2000c).

But the United States is not alone with its vocational inequalities. According to the World Health Organization (1999, 2000a, b), women all around the globe earn less than men, in developing as well as industrialized countries. Women also work more hours a week, including housework, than men in every part of the world except North America and Australia. They work the hardest in Africa: it is estimated that African women work sixty-seven hours a week compared to fifty-three for men. In Asia, women work sixty-two hours while men average forty-eight hours a week.

Australian women are at the top of the pay equality scale, with salaries nearly 88 percent to that of men's. Other nations at the top of the pay equality scale include Denmark and France, 82 percent; Britain, 76 percent; Belgium, 75 percent; and Germany, 74 percent. Unequal pay is also usually accompanied by other negative employment conditions. Compared to men, women are trapped in unskilled types of occupations. Additionally, their chances for advancements in all vocational areas are fewer around the globe, and they are usually the first ones fired during recessions. All things considered, it should therefore come as no surprise that women make up 45 percent of the world's workforce, yet women account for 70 percent of the world's population working in poverty (World Health Organization, 1999, 2000a, b).

What can be done to remove the inequality that exists in the workplace? In the United States in 1964, Title VII of the Civil Rights Act prohibited discrimination in private employment on the basis of sex as well as of race, color, religion, and national origin. And in 1971, the Supreme Court ruled that unequal treatment based on sex violated the Fourteenth Amendment to the U.S. Constitution, which mandates equal protection of all citizens.

Unfortunately, the most comprehensive statement of the equality of the sexes before the law, the Equal Rights Amendment (ERA), is still far from becoming a part of the Constitution. First introduced into Congress in 1923, this amendment was finally passed by both the Senate and the House of Representatives in 1972 and, with a seven-year deadline for ratification attached to it, was sent to the states for their action. As 1979 approached, an insufficient number of states had ratified the amendment, and an extension of time was granted in response to the lobbying efforts of women's groups. However, by the extended deadline of June 1982, only thirty-five of the required thirty-eight states (three quarters of all states must ratify a constitutional amendment) had ratified the ERA.

Thus we are back at square one. The ERA has been reintroduced into every session of Congress since 1982, no body of Congress has passed it for a second time. When both the Senate and the House have again voted in favor of the amendment, each by the required two-thirds majority, it will again go to the states for ratification. To date, the ERA has been mired in the legislative process for nearly eighty years.

Who's Minding the Kids?

Many working parents search almost immediately for quality child care, which tends to be scarce and quite expensive. Finding care for toddlers also tends to be difficult since such programming usually embraces a high teacher-child ratio, which maximizes the individual attention that children receive. Although a wide variety of early childhood educational programs exists for older preschoolers, too many are of low or mediocre quality. When the youngster enters elementary school, after-school programming is as limited as it is cost-prohibited. Regardless of the youngster's age, the need for quality child care in the United States tends to exceed the available resources.

The demand for affordable child care is especially apparent among single parents, particularly considering that one-half of the households headed by single mothers aged 25 to 45 are poor (U.S. Bureau of the Census, 2000a). Single parents are thus faced with the dual prospects of finding a job and locating child care. Within intact families, those couples usually able to take advantage of early childhood education programming are well educated, work full-time, and have a comfortable family income. Conversely, lower-income couples often turn to family members for child-care supervision.

Much of the foregoing is confirmed by statistics compiled by the federal government (U.S. Department of Commerce, 2001). Among parents of preschoolers, it was estimated that about one-half of the children were regularly cared for by a relative. Grandparents were the single most frequently mentioned care provider among relatives. Other relatives—such as aunts, uncles, and cousins—played a smaller role in providing child-care services. The other one-half of preschoolers were cared for by a nonrelative on a regular basis, with about 30 percent of this figure enrolled in an organized facility. Multiple child-care arrangements tended to be common. Almost one-half of the preschoolers regularly spent time in more than one type of child-care arrangement per week. A statistical portrait of child-care arrangements in the United States can be found in Chapter 6, Figure 6–17.

Although older children attend grade school for most of the time that their parents work, growing numbers return from school to empty houses and engage in "self care" (also called "latchkey" arrangements). It is estimated approximately 7 million youngsters between the ages of 5 and 14 were left unsupervised while their parents worked or were away for other reasons (U.S. Department of Commerce, 2001). Children engaging in self care spent an average of six hours per week doing so. Self care tended to be more prevalent among middle school–age children than those in elementary school. Also, children were more likely to care for themselves if they lived with a single father than a single mother (U.S. Department of Commerce, 2001; U.S. Bureau of the Census, 2000a).

Many segments of society are concerned about the safety and well-being of children receiving self care. Working parents may be forced to rely on self care because no other arrangement exists. After-school care may be hard to find, nonexistent, or financial prohibitive. Critics of self care argue that school-age youngsters should simply not be spending time at home, in school yards, or on the street without any kind of adult supervision. In the minds of many child advocates, spending time alone after school invites poor choices, from excessive amounts of television viewing or recreational computer time to entertaining uninvited friends. Proponents maintain that self care is acceptable when certain conditions are met, such as determining the safety of the neighborhood and developing a contingency plan should an emergency occur. Also, self care needs to be carefully structured, particularly in terms of ground rules and parental expectations (e.g., using appliances, completion of homework, answering the door or phone). When such conditions are met, self care has the potential of nurturing such positive traits as maturity, independence, and organization.

It is not uncommon for working parents to feel a wide range of emotions regarding child-care arrangements and the vocational arena. For example, few parents return to work guilt free and many report some anxiety about their child's well-being. Some may wonder if they've made the right choice regarding a selected program or a particular child-care practitioner. Others may find that they are satisfied with their workplace performance but feel inadequate in the parenting role, particularly the perceived disruption of parent-child attachment. A type of "Catch–22" situation exists among many working mothers.

Most experts agree that quality, affordability, and accessibility are the key components of a child-care system that works for families and children. Searching for these components can be a tedious chore, but one well worth the effort. Parents need to look for child-care programming with such positive features as low adult-to-child ratios, proper nutrition, excellent sanitation conditions, and adequate staff training.

Most experts add that a child's successful transition from the home to a child-care program often hinges on parents' satisfaction with their lives and the quality, rather than quantity, of parent-child interactions. Paternal and maternal employment per se are not the major issues in either a child's adjustment to child care or, for that matter, smooth marital relations. Rather, the circumstances and stability of the family, the climate of togetherness that it offers, the attitudes and expectations held by the parents, and the distribution of the time available for meaningful interaction shape the course of domestic harmony and happiness for all concerned.

Finally, we should note that growing numbers of employers are helping parents balance the responsibilities associated with work and domestic life by implementing "family friendly" benefits. For example, leave policies (e.g., parental, family, medical, or disability) enable employees to take time from work to respond to family needs without a loss in job security. Dependent care policies provide support (e.g., direct services, financial assistance policies) for the employee's extended family. "Flextime" allows employees to design their own work schedules so long as they are compatible with the company's production needs. The scheduling possibilities are numerous: workers can work day or night, weekdays or weekends, or even ten-hour days. A variation of flextime is "flexplace," which gives employees the option of work off-site, at home or in a satellite office, during all or part of their scheduled hours. All of these family friendly benefits are regarded as career anchors, because they seek to retain or hold on to quality working parents. Rather than losing workers because of pressures associated with family responsibilities, family friendly benefits seek to emphasize commitment by making jobs as attractive and flexible as possible.

Single-Parent Families

The "broken home" family—this derogatory label paints such an inaccurate and misleading picture of single parenthood. Today, too many people take this label and generate negative stereotypes or make hurtful remarks regarding single parents and their children. Some persist in clinging to myths that do nothing but attach doom and gloom to single parenthood, from financial devastation to household chaos. Regardless of the circumstances responsible for the creation of a single-parent household, whether it be the result of a divorce or a parental death, all segments of society must seek to better understand this lifestyle. We need to abandon the unfair myths and stereotypes that exist, sharpen our perceptions, and become more sensitive to the needs of single-parent families (Darnell, 2000).

Single parenthood is a widespread household arrangement, although its growth rate has stabilized in the recent past. In the United States today, there are approximately 13 million single parents. The number of single mothers in the United States—almost 10 million in 2000—has remained constant since 1995, after nearly tripling over the previous quarter century. In 2000, women were about five times more likely than men to be single parents, with their families constituting 24 percent of all parent-child arrangements. Father-only families, on the other hand, constituted just 4 percent of all families. However, this small percentage of father-only families is deceptive, particularly in terms of recent trends. While the number of single mothers has remained fairly constant over the past few years, the number of single fathers has grown by almost 25 percent. For a statistical analysis of single-parent households and two-parent households, see Chapter 6, Figure 6–18.

Regarding other demographics that focused on single parenthood in 2000, consider the following:

- Nearly 20 percent of single mothers were raising three or more of their own children; the corresponding figure for single fathers was 11 percent.
- The majority of single fathers (about 60 percent) were raising one child.
- The number of single-father households has increased over 60 percent in the last ten years.

- About 40 percent of single mothers and approximately 35 percent of single fathers had never married.
- Most single mothers (over 75 percent) and single fathers (about 85 percent) maintained their own households (U.S. Department of Commerce, 2001; U.S. Bureau of the Census, 2000a).

According to the Population Reference Bureau (2000), considerable racial and ethnic diversity exist in single-parent households. Except for Asian Americans, minority families are more likely than white families to be headed by a single parent (usually a woman) living with dependent children (see Chapter 6, Figure 6–19). For example, in 1999, almost 20 percent of both Hispanic American and Native American families, along with 33 percent of African American families, consisted of a single parent with dependent children. Such households comprised just 6 percent of Asian American families and 9 percent of white families.

Female-headed households with children were the most common family arrangement for African Americans. They represented about 30 percent of African American households in 1999. In the years to come, it is projected that a significant majority of all African American children will experience a single-parent household and will spend a majority of their childhood in such a living arrangement (U.S. Department of Commerce, 2001; U.S. Bureau of the Census, 2000a).

Single-parent households usually face an assortment of financial pressures. Not surprisingly, single mothers with dependent children have high rates of poverty. About 60 percent of children living in mother-only homes are impoverished, compared with about 11 percent of two-parent families. A statistical breakdown of family income in mother-only homes can be found in Chapter 6, Figure 6–20. The rate of poverty in African American single-parent homes headed by women is even higher, two out of every three children are poor. Certain statistics shed additional light on the pressures faced by single-parent households. In 1998, the median income for families maintained by a woman with no husband present ($22,163) was lower than for families maintained by a man with no wife present ($35,681), and substantially lower than for married-couple families ($54,180). And in that same year, the poverty rate for families maintained by a woman with no husband present was 29.9 percent, compared with 12.0 percent for families maintained by a man with no wife present, and just 5.3 percent for married-couple families (U.S. Bureau of the Census, 2000a).

Such economic difficulty reflects the problems associated with conflicts between employment and home responsibilities, job discrimination against women, inadequate public assistance and child-care subsidies, and a lack of enforced child support from nonresidential fathers. Related to the latter, court-ordered child support is not large and is frequently not paid. Moreover, it is time consuming and expensive for mothers to collect unpaid child support from their former husbands, and few are successful. The supervision and care of the children becomes an additional financial problem, not to mention the quest for reliable and affordable child care. This is difficult for couples and magnified for single parents, particularly if one considers the absorption costs, transportation, and the like. On average, a poor mother spends about 32 percent of her total weekly income on child care (U.S. Department of Commerce, 2001; U.S. Bureau of the Census, 2000a, 2000e).

Myths and Realities of Single-Parent Families

At first glance the single-parent family seems to reflect a relatively simple structure and a fairly predictable composition of family members. Although the single-parent household often consists of a divorced mother and her children, divorce does not represent the only reason for this domestic arrangement. Rather, single parents may also be widowed, separated, or never-married men or women. Others may have had their children naturally, through adoption, or through artificial means. A grandparent raising a child alone may also be considered a single parent. In addition to these variations in composition, many myths surround single parenthood and tend to distort our perceptions. According to Stephen Sugarman (1998), the following are some of the more prevalent myths:

All single-parent families are headed by women. On the contrary, growing numbers of single-parent families are headed by fathers. As we pointed out earlier, while the number of single mothers has remained fairly constant over the past few years, the number of single fathers has rapidly grown. Men now comprise about one-sixth of the nation's total 11.9 million single-parent households. Single fathers are about twice as common among whites as among African Americans.

The single-parent household can be clearly identified. We've already noted how single-parent households can reflect unique variations in composition. Other complexities arise when we examine those cohabitants having children. For instance, while the female cohabitant may be the single mother by law, in many respects the cohabitants resemble a married couple. And, a number of possible cohabitation arrangements can complicate household identification: two biological parents not married but living with their child, a single biological mother and child living with a man who is not the child's father, or a gay couple in which one of the partners is the legal parent. Thus, while the structural framework of single-parent families seems relatively simple in design compared to more complicated two-parent families (e.g., blended or extended families), a number of variations exist in single-parent households.

Women who head single-parent families have never been married to the father of their child. The fact of the matter is that there are more divorced (and separated) single mothers than there are unwed mothers. Furthermore, because of the predominance of divorced and widowed mothers, large numbers of women become single mothers, not at their child's birth, but later on in their child's life, often during their adolescence.

Most single mothers are not gainfully employed. A large proportion of single mothers are in the paid labor force. Indeed, earlier in this chapter we acknowledged that about three-quarters of *all* women with children are in the labor force. Studies have shown that divorced women work *more* than married women, and single mothers often feel compelled to work full-time even when their children are very young.

All single mothers are poor and on welfare. Although it is true that more than a third of family households headed by a single mother live below the poverty level, more than one-half of all single mothers are not on welfare. Those who escape poverty tend to do so primarily through earnings and secondarily through child support and government benefits (or through a combination of these sources)—although typically not by receiving welfare.

Single mothers are usually racial and ethnic minorities. Earlier we mentioned that minority families are more likely than white families to be headed by a single parent, usually a woman. However, this fact needs to be placed into a proper context. Although it is accurate that minority families are disproportionately represented given their share of the population, more single mothers are white than any other group.

Characteristics of the single parent have remained the same over time. In actuality, the demography of single parenting has changed considerably over the years. For example, in 1900 the typical single parent was a widow; becoming a single mother by becoming pregnant outside of marriage was not very common. Also during this time, divorce and cohabitation were not popular lifestyle choices.

Strengths of Single-Parent Families

Some people tend to view the single-parent family as a dysfunctional family unit, one that consists of an insurmountable assortment of problems and difficulties. However, while we have seen thus far that certain stresses do exist, this does not mean that all adults and children living in a single-parent household experience negative consequences. Indeed, Stephen Duncan (2000) points out that many single-parent families are quite resilient and successful, having taken this parenting challenge as an opportunity to develop strength and resourcefulness. More specifically, Duncan identifies the following strengths of single-parent families: interdependence, organization, resiliency, validation, and responsibility.

Because of its composition, the single-parent family often becomes more interdependent and tends to work closely together in its problem-solving strategies and daily living responsibilities. Single parents depend more heavily on the voluntary cooperation of their children, and as they get older, children often become directly involved in family decision making. Such escalating levels of involvement often prompt children to exhibit more dependability and reliability.

As far as organization is concerned, single-parent families tend to emphasize structure. Indeed the unique challenges of being a single parent, such as assuming sole responsibility for meeting multiple needs, requires careful scheduling and accountability from each family member. The organization that characterizes daily rituals and regular routines, such as eating dinner together each night or reading a book together, in turn helps to promote domestic stability and security.

Regarding resiliency, single-parent families tend to develop the resources necessary to surmount adversity. In the process of discovering ways to cope with difficulties, such as financial restraints, the single-parent family often becomes a stronger family unit. Rather than viewing themselves as powerless or vulnerable to negative forces, single-parent families often discover hidden resources and ways to regain stability.

Members of single-parent families tend to validate one another. Children, especially, often feel more needed and valued as contributing members of the household. In two-parent families, parents typically share the major household responsibilities. In single-parent families, each child's help is needed and considered vital to everyday functioning. Consequently, family members feel more valued.

Finally, single-parent families promote responsibility. From the parent's perspective, successful adjustment to everyday life and its problems is shaped considerably by the acceptance of the obligations and challenges associated with single parenting. Successful parents do not minimize nor exaggerate problems but instead seek solutions. They tend to acknowledge the difficulties inherent in this lifestyle and seek to develop coping strategies without self-pity or bitterness.

Combined, the potential strengths emerging from single-parent families help us to see this household arrangement in a more positive light. In so doing, a more accurate portrayal of single parenthood is created, one that hopefully lends itself to more positive acceptance. While single parenthood has the potential for adversity, it simultaneously offers challenging opportunities for positive growth.

Qualities of Successful Single Parents

While the single-parent family typically encounters an assortment of stresses and strains, it finds ways to adapt and thrive. It is incorrect to assume that children from single-parent households are a disadvantaged lot. However, Shellee Darnell (2000) points out that single parents must take active steps to help pave the way for healthy childhood adjustment. Commitment and dedication to the single-parent role is paramount to a youngster's chances of becoming a happy, productive, and successful adult. Furthermore, successful single parents are likely to share certain child-rearing qualities. Along these lines, Darnell identifies the following features of successful single parents:

Maintenance of Personal Health and Well-Being. Successful single parents take care of themselves physically as well as psychologically. They recognize that a child's well-being rests heavily on their own maintenance of well-being. The most successful single-parent homes are those adopting healthy life choices and placing a premium on wellness. For both parent and child alike, optimal well-being embraces such important elements as proper diet, exercise, and relaxation.

Employment of Successful Stress Management Skills. There is no mistaking the fact that single parenthood is hard work, a challenge often filled with unprecedented demands, restraints, and pressures. Effective single parents employ stress management strategies so that they do not feel overwhelmed with the responsibility, tasks, and emotional overload associated with raising children alone. They are mindful of the situations and events capable of triggering tension and are skillful at curbing its expression.

Creation of Realistic Expectations. Successful single parents do not distort their surroundings or create unrealistic expectations for themselves or their children. On the contrary, they are flexible with their aspirations, goals, and hopes. Successful single-parent families focus on achievements, not failures. When faced with a pressing challenge or need, they typically work together to establish realistic goals, including establishing priorities and mapping out alternative plans.

Recognition of Personal Limitations. Similar to the creation of realistic expectations, successful single parents have realistic self-perceptions. They do not distort or exaggerate their abilities or capabilities, and they are aware of their personal limitations. Regarding the latter, successful single parents know what they can and can't do. Furthermore, children are made aware of parental limitations and are encouraged to be flexible with their needs.

Creation of Domestic Stability. One of the most important chores facing all parents is the establishment of household stability and security. Successful single parents recognize that their children have experienced a loss of domestic stability and that they need to regain equilibrium. Successful single parents restore household stability and make their youngsters feel secure and protected in a loving, nurturing environment.

Development of Clear Family Rules and Boundaries. Households regulated by clear family rules and boundaries tend to produce harmony and accountability while discouraging irresponsibility and unruly behavior. By establishing clear, realistic rules and boundaries, children learn that there are limits to their behavior and consequences for whatever misdeeds that transpire. Furthermore, successful single parents make it a point to consistently uphold such household regulations.

Formation of a Social Support Network. Social support is an important resource to single parents and their children. Talking about one's situation with supportive friends, family members, or professionals usually proves invaluable, especially in times of need. Successful single parents have usually developed a wide network of people who provide emotional support, companionship, and assistance. Conversely, not having a social support network often isolates parents and intensifies existing pressures and tensions.

Families with Physical Disabilities and Chronic Illnesses

Good health is something that many of us simply take for granted. We often feel that we are immune and invincible, cloaked in a suit of armor that protects us from conditions threatening our health and well-being. Indeed, we never fully appreciate our health until we have to face the fact that we have a permanent condition or illness.

We need to be reminded that we are mortal beings and that we live in a world marked by potential risk and accident. One false step on a staircase, a heart attack, or an automobile accident can forever change our lives. Whether it be a baby born into the family with a developmental disability or an elderly parent suffering from a stroke, challenging health conditions not only alter family dynamics, but they often make family members dependent on others for the simplest tasks.

In this section, we will focus on physical disability and chronic illness and the impact they usually create on the person and the family. We do so because of the widespread nature of these health conditions in America, the special challenges that afflicted persons must face, and the various family adjustments that usually have to be made. Regarding the latter, disabilities and chronic illnesses exert an influence on a wide range of interactions, such as those between work and family, parent and child, brother and sister, and caregiver and elderly parents. We also include the topics of disabilities and chronic illnesses because of the huge challenges they pose for individuals, health-care professionals, and policy makers.

Before exploring the manner in which physical disability and chronic illness impacts on family life, the terms "physical disability" and "chronic illness" need to be clarified. A *physical disability,* such as cerebral palsy or a spinal cord injury, is an impairment of body structure and function, including mobility impairments, amputations, skeletal deformities, and disfigurements. An individual is considered to have a disability if she/he has difficulty executing certain activities (e.g., talking, walking, seeing, hearing), or has difficulty performing activities of daily living (e.g., bathing, toileting, eating), or has difficulty with certain social roles (e.g., working at a job). An individual who is unable to execute one or more activities, or who uses an assistive device to move from location to location, or who needs assistance from another individual to execute basic activities is considered to have a severe disability.

Disabilities are widespread in the United States (see Chapter 6, Figure 6–21 and Figure 6–22). It has been estimated that about 1 in 5 Americans have some kind of disability, a proportion translating into an estimated 50 million noninstitutionalized persons. About 1 in 10 Americans have a severe disability, which accounts for approximately 24 million persons. And, since the population is aging (see "Caring for Aging Family Members" in this chapter) and the likelihood of having a disability increases with age, the growth in the number of individuals with disabilities is expected to accelerate in the future. Consider these facts, gathered in 2000, regarding physical disabilities:

- Approximately 1 in 2 seniors 65 years of age and older has a physical disability.
- More than one-half of those Americans with a severe disability are between the ages of 22 and 64.
- Disabilities affect about 3 million children under the age of fifteen.
- Among the more common physical conditions causing disability are arthritis, back problems, cardiovascular disease, respiratory problems, and high blood pressure.
- The presence of a disability tends to be associated with lower earnings.

- Persons with disabilities are less likely to have private health insurance coverage (U.S. Bureau of the Census, 2000e; Administration on Aging, 2000).

A *chronic illness,* such as diabetes or arthritis, is a progressive disorder caused by a nonreversible condition that often leaves the person with some type of disability. Chronic illness is thus a long-term or permanent condition, one that often results in the need for rehabilitation or continuous care. Although chronic illness cannot be cured, it can often be controlled with carefully followed dietary, exercise, and medication regimens.

Similar to disabilities, chronic illnesses are prevalent in the United States. It is estimated that more than 90 million Americans live with chronic illnesses; of this figure, about 57 million have two or more chronic diseases. Chronic illnesses account for one-third of the years of potential life lost before age sixty-five. Approximately 90 percent of illnesses and 80 percent of deaths in the United States are related to chronic conditions. In addition:

- The medical care costs of people with chronic illnesses account for more than 60 percent of the nation's medical care costs.
- Persons with chronic illnesses account for about 85 percent of prescription drug use.
- Persons with chronic illness represent the highest-cost and fastest-growing service group in health care.
- More than 25 million family caregivers provide an estimated $196 billion annually in "free" caregiving services to disabled or elderly family members with chronic illnesses (National Chronic Care Consortium, 2001; Centers for Disease Control, 2001).

Cross-Cultural Variations

Although advancing age increases the risk of contracting both a physical disability and chronic illness, a person's race should also be considered. Within the 55- to 64- year-old age group, the proportion with a severe disability in 1999 was 20 percent among whites not of Hispanic American origin, 35 percent among African Americans, and 28 percent among people of Hispanic American origin (U.S. Bureau of the Census, 2000e).

Racial disproportion often exists for various chronic illnesses. For instance, the death rate from cervical cancer is more than twice as high for African American women as it is for white women. Deaths due to breast cancer are decreasing among white women but not among African American women. Also, the death rate from prostate cancer is more than twice as high for African American men as it is for white men. And, the prevalence of diabetes is 1.7 times higher among non-Hispanic African Americans, 1.9 times higher among Hispanic Americans, and 2.8 times higher among Native Americans than among non-Hispanic white Americans of similar age (Centers for Disease Control, 2001).

Why do such racial imbalances exist? African Americans in particular have higher rates of disabilities and chronic health problems for a number of reasons, including lower socioeconomic status, lower levels of educational attainment, and various lifestyle factors. The poor suffer the greatest economic costs because they are least likely to have good insurance or pension plans. Also, information about the importance of regular medical checkups and early diagnosis and treatment of disease are not as likely to reach poorly educated individuals. Even when such information arrives, the poor often have limited access to quality medical care. They lack health-care coverage—by private insurance, Medicare, or Medicaid.

Specific lifestyle traits have also been linked to the prevalence of certain chronic illnesses. Smoking has been connected to lung cancer and heart disease; obesity is associated with circulatory disease, diabetes, and hypertension (high blood pressure); and hypertension, in turn, is tied to strokes and heart disease. African Americans fare worse than whites on all of these factors. A higher percentage of African American men than white men smoke, are more likely to be obese (especially at older ages), and to suffer from hypertension. African Americans are also less likely than whites to visit a doctor (National Chronic Care Consortium, 2001; Centers for Disease Control, 2001; U.S. Bureau of the Census, 2000e).

Challenges Posed by Disability and Chronic Illness

Whether being born with a lifelong disability such as cerebral palsy or being afflicted in midlife with cardiovascular disease, adjusting to a long-term health impairment is difficult for the person as well as the family. We must remind ourselves of the interplay that exists between the two. Although the afflicted individual shoulders the burden of the illness, family members are also influenced by the changes in the health of a loved one. The resulting interaction can be found at all stages of the family life cycle.

Although disabilities and chronic illnesses are considered separate medical conditions, they do share certain characteristics. For example, both are usually permanent conditions that pose an assortment of limitations. Both can dramatically alter a person's life. Also, a physical disability can create a chronic illness and vice versa. Given such shared characteristics, research such as that generated by Paul Powell (2001) and William Jackson (2001) can be used to better understand the two health impairment categories and the challenges they pose. The following discussion explores some of the more important challenges facing the person and the family.

Acceptance of Health-Impaired Status. Those experiencing a loss of health usually find themselves questioning their circumstances. Many initially react to the news with shock and denial. As mentioned at the outset, we often take our health for granted, making it inconceivable for us to acknowledge that a disability or prolonged illness can happen. Anger and resentment are other common reactions. Anger and resentment are often difficult for the family to handle, largely because the person often displaces these emotions at random. Sorting through all of these reactions and emotions is a difficult but necessary chore. In so doing, most experts agree that acceptance of one's health-impaired status can be achieved. Those who have accepted their condition have had the opportunity to express their feelings: their envy of the healthy and resentment toward those who do not have to face impairment. They have accepted their disability or illness as part of themselves, a reality to be lived with, not escaped. They recognize that their best chance for future happiness lies in their understanding of their condition, and their disciplined commitment to its control.

Alteration of Personal Lifestyle. In addition to the diagnosed physical condition, a prolonged illness can impact one's emotional well-being, interpersonal relationships, and financial status. Many feel a loss of control as well as anxiety and uncertainty regarding what lies ahead. For example, day-to-day routines and tasks may have to be altered or modified. One's vocational involvement may also face change, which in turn may create financial pressures. In some instances, sexual functioning is impaired. It is often falsely assumed that sexual activity is the domain of those who are in perfect physical health; sexual intimacy is not viewed as vital to the adjustment of the health impaired or the maintenance of their every-day functioning. All people need validation that sexuality is a part of who they are; moreover, it's both the physical and psychological aspects of love that promotes psychological well-being.

Changes in Family Dynamics. Regardless of when the chronic illness or physical disability occurs, it has a significant impact on the family unit. For example, parents usually express a variety of reactions when they learn that their child is health impaired: shock, denial, sadness, fear, and anger. Many parents also believe that the child's disability was their fault. Some reason that the disability is punishment for a sin or wrongdoing. The extra care and special accommodations often required by health-impaired family members often alter how parents and siblings interact with the person, as well as with one another. The difficulty of living normally while relating to and caring for a disabled person often unleashes anxiety, confusion, and despair. Even the most competent and balanced family units can feel overwhelmed. Yet, parents and siblings usually adjust to the reality of the disability in diverse and unique ways. Indeed, many families discover that living with a health-impaired person promotes family cohesion, adaptability, and solidarity.

Necessity of Personal Reevaluation. A physical disability or chronic illness is not always a negative life experience. The restrictions imposed by the impairment causes most to reevaluate their lives, in the process assessing their limitations and taking stock of their resources. Those who inwardly energize themselves in positive ways often discover previously unknown reservoirs of resiliency, courage, and strength. Most discover that flexibility needs to be part of future plans and goals. Personal self-esteem may no longer be derived from the same occupation or activities performed while healthy. Therefore, flexible life planning might include identifying alternative pursuits and assessing available resources to engage in these pursuits. Such reevaluation enables disabled and chronically ill persons to redirect their efforts toward achieving new and meaningful goals and aspirations.

Restructuring of Priorities. People diagnosed with disabilities and chronic illnesses usually cannot expect to regain their health in the near future. Because the family lifestyle is usually disrupted in many different ways, priorities have to be restructured.

Family members soon realize that they can't do everything the way they once did. Furthermore, the type and quality of work performed by the afflicted person needs to be restructured. When a person is struggling with health problems, domestic tasks and leisure activities often need to be significantly reduced or even abandoned. For example, a household chore may take longer to accomplish, or may even have to be postponed. Whereas no outside assistance was needed before the impairment, a spouse, relative, or a home-health caregiver may now be needed on a regular basis. Pain, fatigue, or a decreased range of motion may also dictate the modification or alteration of physical activities. For many, such forced changes trigger ongoing anger, despair, and depression; one's limitations must be endured constantly and are a constant reminder of their circumstances.

Adjusting to Health Impairment: Coping Strategies

According to JoAnn LeMaistre (1999), coping with a prolonged illness requires the flexible and creative use of both internal and external resources. Effective coping often means that health-impaired persons need to become able-hearted at a time when they can no longer be able-bodied. Developing this kind of positive attitude greatly hinges on three factors: the severity of the disability or illness, the availability of a social support system, and the pre-illness personality strength and resiliency of the person. Keeping these three factors in mind, the following are suggestions and advice for healthy adjustment.

- *Be patient with yourself.* There is no predictable timetable that indicates how long or short the road to acceptance will be. The afflicted person and each member of the family may react to the situation differently. Since each particular case is unique, the overall dynamics of prolonged illness knows wide variations.
- *Approach problems actively.* An active approach to problems consists of defining the problem and determining the outcomes you want. It includes attempting to ensure that any expended energy constitutes a step toward the solution. Once the problem has been defined, one must generate as much creativity as possible to determine how a solution can be achieved. Creativity is not impaired by disability or chronic illness.

- *Do not be afraid or ashamed to express your emotions.* Reacting to disability or chronic illness includes a wide range of affective states, including anger, sadness, remorse, depression, and anxiety. Releasing these emotions, rather than suppressing them, is both normal and healthy. Be prepared for a wide range of emotions as you seek control and reorganize your life, especially during the early stages of health impairment.
- *Realize that emotional reactions to disability and chronic illness vary widely.* There will likely be days when the sorrow of loss will be more evident than others. The same holds true for anger. Energy is a significant problem for those who are health impaired and some of the most wasteful expenditures of energy are for anger and resentment. These emotions are not bad in themselves, but they tend to wear down precious internal resources.
- *Share your feelings with others.* Talk about your disability or illness with family members and other relatives, friends, or skilled helpers. Many afflicted persons tend to pull away from the mainstream and do not seek the company of others, let alone ask for help. A support group may be an excellent source of guidance, security, assistance, and trust. Working with others through your feelings also helps to combat the loneliness that is prevalent following the early stages of a prolonged illness.
- *Take steps to maintain your overall well-being.* Experiencing a disability or chronic illness has the potential of creating considerable inner turmoil and disruption. Safeguard your health by getting adequate rest, nutrition, and whatever exercise possible. Your susceptibility to illness may also be greater than it was before the diagnosis; and many afflicted persons suffer from insomnia, loss of appetite, migraine headaches, and excessive anxiety. Should any of these conditions persist, do not hesitate to see a physician.
- *Live in the present.* Don't look too far backward or too far ahead. In particular, dwelling on the past and the way things were before a disability or illness may produce feelings of depression or regret. Distant future fantasies should also be avoided since there is no way

to predict the future. Instead, live in the present with acceptance, patience, and appreciation for yourself and others. This enables you to continue life's journey in a creative way, in spite of the pain of your losses.

- *Cherish the good times.* This suggestion embodies paying attention to the positives that occur in your life and emphasizing their importance. Living with negative emotions can turn anything into proof that there are only painful events in the surroundings. Disability and chronic illness have the potential to darken a person's outlook on life. The challenge here is to focus on the positives in life and to cherish their importance.

Gay and Lesbian Families

Homosexual relationships are characterized by the sexual attraction and emotional attachment to persons of the same gender. The union of same-sex couples and the possibility of creating a family are controversial areas. Considerable disagreement exists on moral, philosophical, and religious grounds, and this disagreement has created a wide variety of issues to ponder: For example, should a couple of the same sex be legally married? If so, are they entitled to the same rights and protections as heterosexual couples? Should same-sex marriages be legally sanctioned and, if so, are the centuries of respect for traditional marriage between a man and a woman being ignored?

In considering such contemporary issues, we need to first trace our perceptions of gay and lesbian relationships as well as our treatment of same-sex couples. In the United States prior to 1973, homosexuality was labeled by the American Psychiatric Association as a disorder. Books on the topic treated homosexuality as a pathological problem to be solved, and those with same-sex orientations were viewed with a mixture of discomfort, fear, and disgust. Because homosexuality was seen as a sickness, the gay individual was usually regarded as perverted, unhappy, and desperately lonely.

In 1973, the American Psychiatric Association removed homosexuality from its classification of mental disorders. This classification change was largely the result of efforts by leaders in the gay liberation movement and their supporters, some of whom were prominent psychiatrists and clinical psychologists. Coupled with society's liberalization of sexual attitudes, the general public's perceptions of homosexuality began to slowly change. Gays banded together to assert their human rights and demanded the respect and equality that they had been denied. Many openly declared their gay sexual orientation and phrases such as "gay pride" were heard more and more. Meanwhile, researchers stepped up the pace of their scientific inquiries into the complexities of sexual orientation. As a result of this interest, homosexuality began to be better understood.

Contrary to what was once thought, homosexuality is not a form of abnormal behavior or mental illness. Indeed, most gays are well adjusted and emotionally stable. Although some may exhibit anxiety or depression, so too do some heterosexuals. When maladaptive behavior does occur in lesbians and gays, some clinicians propose that it is often attributable to the social stigma attached to homosexuality instead of to something pathological in the nature of homosexuality itself. Additionally, gays are not confused about their gender identity, the psychological awareness of being either male or female. Lesbian women are not different from heterosexual women in their sureness of being female, nor are gay men different from heterosexual men on this dimension.

Prejudice and Discrimination against Gays and Lesbians

Gays and lesbians are an oppressed group and prejudice and discrimination are aimed at them in many ways. Sometimes prejudice and discrimination is blatant and deliberate, while on other occasions it may be unintentional and unconscious. In the final analysis, though, it is harmful not only to those who are victims of it, but also to those who hold it.

Society defines gays and lesbians as deviant and punishes them in a variety of ways. The visible sanctions are primarily financial and legal. However, more pervasive and more damaging are personal attacks, constant harassment, and a wide range of negative situations, such as mimicking, jokes, and the raiding of gay bars and meeting places. Furthermore, living without a support network is a difficult and alienating experience. Combined, all of these factors do little to foster equality.

Discriminatory treatment against gays is still evident today. Despite Vermont's landmark 1999 civil union legislation, marriages between gays are still legally prohibited. Many adoption agencies are reluctant to place children with gays. The educational system has frequently denied gays teaching positions due to a fear that children will be corrupted and recruited to the so-called homosexual way of life or be abused by them in some way. The media also tends to depict gays in an unfair and unrealistic light.

Many gays and lesbians also face harassment and physical abuse simply because of their sexual orientation. Such antigay violence has risen dramatically in recent years. Many assailants tend to be white males in their teens and early twenties who are acting out their prejudices against gays. The purpose of the assaults is not theft, although this sometimes does happen. Instead, some choose to attack gays simply because they do not like their lifestyles. Violence, intimidation, and humiliation are how they make their beliefs known.

Many gays, lesbians, and other concerned persons actively seek to reduce hostility and the many types of prejudice and discrimination leveled toward gays. By the 1950s, gays and lesbians began organizing their own political groups. In 1951 the Mattachine Society was founded in Los Angeles, followed in 1955 by the Daughters of Bilitis in San Francisco (the Mattachine Society was named after a secret fraternal order of unmarried men who dressed as women and performed in thirteenth-century France. The Daughters of Bilitis were named after the lesbian poet Bilitis, who lived with Sappho on the island of Lesbos in ancient Greece).

During the 1960s the *gay liberation movement* emerged as a political force promoting the full civil rights of homosexuals and an end to discriminatory practices. The gay liberation movement embraced many subgroups, the best known being the Gay Liberation Front and the Gay Activists Alliance. In 1973, the National Gay and Lesbian Task Force (NGLTF) was founded in New York City and is now located in Washington, D.C. The purpose of the NGLTF is to re-educate society, including its gay members, to esteem gays at their full human worth and to accord them places in society that will allow them to attain and to contribute according to their full human and social potential. The organization was instrumental in getting the American Psychiatric Association to recognize that homosexuals have helped to launch legislation related to consensual sex and civil rights. At this writing, the NGLTF is the largest organization representing the gay liberation movement.

In addition, a number of organizations have been formed to combat antigay violence and to assist victims. Among these are the Violence Project of the National Gay and Lesbian Task Force, the Committee on Lesbian and Gay Victims Concerns of the National Organization for Victims' Assistance, and the Lesbian Caucus of the National Coalition Against Sexual Assault. In addition to assisting victims, such organizations seek to implement crime prevention programs, launch community education programs to dispel myths and fears about homosexuality, develop training sessions to sensitize police officers, and promote media education efforts for more accurate reporting.

Gay and Lesbian Relationships

The dynamics of gay and lesbian relationships are more similar to than different from heterosexual unions. Partners are sought so that a rewarding union may be formed, and the maintenance of a relationship hinges on mutual support, caring, love, and understanding. And, both straight and gay relationships tend to flourish when partners possess maturity and authenticity, a stable sense of self, and a willingness to share intimacy on a regular basis. For all, intimate relationships thrive on trust and commitment and offer such important social and psychological vitamins as security, affection, and comfort.

Gay and lesbian partners differ from heterosexual partners in that gays tend to maintain a more egalitarian relationship. For example, gay and lesbian couples have been found to be free from the stereotypical form of role playing or mirroring of heterosexual roles that is sometimes associated with gay couples. There is usually one personality that is more prominent or outgoing, but this "dominance" does not necessarily indicate that one partner plays the masculine, sometimes called "butch," role while the other assumes the submissive, or "femme," role. Indeed, there is probably more of an equality between partners in gay and lesbian relationships than in heterosexual relationships because homosexuals are not forced into the types of roles to which many heterosexuals feel bound.

Researchers have found that most gays want to have steady relationships, although this is somewhat more important to women than men. Heterosexuals, though, tend to value sexual exclusivity more strongly in a steady relationship. Both gay and heterosexual couples desire certain elements in a close relationship: affection, companionship, and personal development. As far as qualities sought in partners, gays and heterosexuals all value such traits as honesty, affection, and warmth. Such findings shatter the myth that sex is the sole basis for gay and lesbian relationships.

All of this means that gay and heterosexual couples are more alike than dissimilar. Thus, if we want to describe what goes on in a relationship between two gays—what makes for the success of that relationship and what may create problems—we do not have to use a different language. We can use the same terms as we would in describing a relationship between two heterosexuals.

Family Dynamics

Family law in the United States affects gay and lesbian relationships in many ways. For example, gay and lesbian couples cannot legally marry. Moreover, no state statute expressly affirms the rights of homosexual couples to marry. All courts faced with the gay/lesbian marriage issue have relied on the premise that a lawful marriage, by definition, can be entered into only by two persons of the opposite sex.

Vermont has the closest thing in the United States to gay marriage. In 1999, the Vermont Senate and House voted to enact into law a bill recognizing a *civil union* between gay and lesbian couples. A civil union represents a legal institution parallel to marriage that provides the same rights, benefits, and protections to same-sex couples (e.g., adoption, medical care, taxes, inheritance). In 2000, the civil union bill was signed by Vermont Governor Howard Dean.

In order to create a civil union, a couple obtains a license from a town clerk, has the license certified by a justice of the peace or clergy member who oversees the union ceremony, and then files the license back with the town clerk. Vermont has no residency requirement. However, if a couple chooses to dissolve their civil union, they must live in Vermont for at least a year. The couple must file for a dissolution proceeding in family court that follows the same procedures and applies the same laws as a married couple filing for a divorce.

The Vermont Supreme Court distinguished itself as the first state to give new legal status to same-sex couples. Vermont is in sharp contrast to the antigay marriage laws of more than thirty-two states and the federal government. Even civil union legislation has met with resistance. For example in 2000 California voted against same-sex civil unions, in the process denying gay and lesbian couples state benefits available only to married couples. However, in 2000 several states defeated bills that would have banned state benefits for same-sex civil unions, including New Hampshire, New Mexico, and Mississippi.

Vermont was not the first state to attempt same-sex legislation. In 1993, two men in Hawaii applied for a marriage license and were denied. The Hawaiian state Supreme Court ruled that the ban on gay and lesbian marriages was unconstitutional because it involved sexual discrimination, unless the state could show a "compelling interest" for retaining it. The case was sent back to a lower court for further consideration. In 1998, the Hawaii legislature rendered the courts' ruling null and void and passed the antigay marriage amendment.

In 2001, the Netherlands adopted legislation recognizing same-sex marriages with full and equal rights. Gays have experienced general acceptance for years in the Netherlands, but gay rights groups struggled for fifteen years for laws removing discrimination. The new Dutch legislation eliminates all reference to gender ("man" and "woman") in the laws governing matrimony. Gay same-sex marriage partners now have the legal right to use the term "spouse." Like heterosexuals, after living together for three years, gay and lesbian couples also may apply for court approval to adopt children. Legal ambiguities concerning inheritance, pension rights, taxes, and alimony no longer exist.

But in the United States, those gay and lesbian couples living outside of Vermont who wish to marry face numerous obstacles. For example, without the legal rights that are granted by a marriage license, no matter how many years a couple has been together, partners do not have the right to make medical or financial decisions for each other if one becomes incapacitated. A person may not even be allowed access to an intensive care unit in which his or her partner is being treated for a life-threatening or terminal illness. Partners cannot automatically inherit each other's property, and if they break up they are not protected by divorce laws. In an effort to combat such discrimination, many gay and lesbian couples draft legal documents designed to approximate or duplicate many of the rights of a marriage license.

The rights of gay and lesbian parents are also legally limited. Many gay and lesbian parents who have children have brought them from a prior marriage or heterosexual relationship, and the issues emerging from such situations are enormously complicated. Child custody cases invariably focus on the sexual orientation of the parent.

Adoption is also extremely difficult for openly gay and lesbian couples. Although society's tolerance for alternative lifestyles is growing, most courts continue to believe that the best interests of a child are rooted in the traditional heterosexual family. The courts do not deny parents their right to choose lifestyles, but courts do seek to restrict youngsters' exposure to alternative lifestyles. Some factors that the courts consider in determining custody and visitation rights are what peer pressures and social stigma would affect the child and how the lack of a gender role model may affect the child during the formative years.

Gay and lesbian couples often face additional problems even if they successfully adopt. Just as in any custody case, a couple's custody of an adopted child can be challenged at any time. If couples keep their relationship a secret during the adoption process, it could mean having to spend much of their lives in fear of being discovered and losing the child. In another scenario, because only one partner can legally adopt the child, if a couple splits up they could find themselves in untested legal waters and a precedent-setting custody battle.

Although parenting among gays is not widespread, growing numbers are choosing to have children. Children may be adopted by the couple, or there may already be youngsters from previous heterosexual relationships. Some lesbians utilize artificial insemination as a means to have children.

It is incorrectly assumed that gay and lesbian parents create widespread adjustment problems for children, including those related to gender identity and gender-role development. For instance, many feel that exposure to gay and lesbian parents will cause children to become gay or lesbian. Indeed, some people believe that homosexual parents try to persuade their children to be gay. Research indicates, however, that the incidence of homosexuality among children of gays is not higher than the general population. In fact, most grown children of gay and lesbian parents are heterosexual. In addition, there is evidence to suggest that most homosexuals are brought up in exclusively heterosexual households.

There is also no support for the notion that gay and lesbian parents serve as poor role models because they themselves were raised in unhappy, unstable homes. Most gay and lesbian parents were brought up in intact heterosexual families and homosexual parents highly value secure and trusting relationships with their children. The aspirations of gay parents do not differ from those of heterosexual parents. Indeed, when the two groups are compared, parenting behaviors, goals, and interests are usually the same.

In addition to legal complexities, gay and lesbian parents often face problems similar to those of single heterosexual parents. For lesbians, who as women still earn significantly less than men, economic survival can be a major struggle. Youngsters who are made the targets of ridicule by peers and others may become uncomfortable with their parents' sexual orientation. For this reason, many gay and lesbian parents inform their children as early as possible about their own sexual orientation. Most children can understand and come to accept their parents' homosexuality, and although they may have to defend their parents occasionally, they can usually expect their peers to become accustomed to their parents' lifestyles.

Caring for Aging Family Members

Never before in the history of humanity have so many people lived for so long. When the United States was founded, life expectancy at birth was only about 35 years. It reached 47 years in 1900, jumped to 68 years in 1950, and steadily rose to 76.5 years in 2000. In 2000, life expectancy was higher for women (79 years) than for men (72.5 years).

Each day in the United States about 5,000 people reach the age of 65, and those over the age of 80 represent the fastest-growing population segment in the nation. There are seven times as many elderly people in society today than there were at the turn of the last century. As the "baby boom" generation approaches the elderly ranks, the numbers will continue to swell. (The post–World War II baby boom was a high fertility period, from 1946 to 1964.) By the year 2030, as many as 1 in 5 Americans will be elderly. For a statistical portrait of the elderly population explosion, see Chapter 6, Figures 6–23, 6–24, and 6–25.

The United States is not alone in its elderly population explosion. The aging of populations is a universal phenomenon, although the rate of increase is considerably greater in today's developing nations. As in the United States, women will outlive men in every other nation. By the year 2025, the number of persons eighty and older is projected to increase by 415 percent in the developing world and 132 percent in developed nations. By the year 2030, the elderly will constitute from one-fifth to nearly one-fourth of the population of many European nations. In Chapter 6, Table 6–5 compares the aged population increase in the United States with that of other nations.

This increase of the aged population has numerous implications for individuals and families throughout the world. Contrary to popular notion, most elderly citizens are neither feeble nor sickly; indeed, most are enjoying healthy and rewarding lives. However, advancing age eventually means that many elderly persons will be in need of assistance—from financial support to various forms of medical intervention. In order to keep pace with the graying of America, the government must continue to protect the health and well-being of this important population segment. This means supporting and developing programs for the elderly that are timely and responsive, as well as comprehensive and closely monitored.

The daily living considerations of America's elderly need our close scrutiny. Although most elderly people are capable of executing daily routines and activities, the need for assistance in personal care and home management activities shows corresponding increases in the upper age ranges. Moreover, incidences of chronic illness and disability steadily increase with age, further necessitating the need for a more active caregiving role for adult children and service providers.

However, this does not mean that the elderly needing care and attention are nursing home candidates or residents. This is a myth that needs to be debunked. Only about 5 percent of the entire elderly population sixty-five or older can be found within institutional settings. However, significant age variations exist within this 5 percent total. The percentages are 1.1 for persons from 65 to 74, 4.2 for persons from 75 to 84, and 19.8 for persons eighty-five and older (U.S. Bureau of the Census, 2000d).

Patterns of Family Caregiving

Most of today's elderly reside in family settings, although living arrangements differ considerably between men and women as they age. Between the ages of 55 and 64, about 77 percent of men and 64 percent of women live with a spouse. Among persons 65 to 84 years old, most men (76 percent) are married and living with their spouse, compared with less than half (46 percent) of women the same age. For individuals 85 and over, the proportion who are married and living with their spouse is significantly lower: 49 percent of men and only 12 percent of women (U.S. Bureau of the Census, 2000d). For a statistical analysis of this information, see Chapter 6, Figure 6–26.

It is not uncommon for elderly persons to share a residency with their grandchildren or their adult children, especially when independent living in a separate location is no longer feasible. Approximately 4.7 million of the nation's elderly live with their grandchildren. Four-fifths (79 percent) of these elderly persons maintain the household in which the grandchildren live. The remainder live in households maintained by their adult children. The elderly are more likely to live with an unmarried child than with a married one, and they are more likely to live with a daughter than with a son. The proportion of elderly living with their offspring is also higher for the widowed, divorced, and separated than for married persons (U.S. Bureau of the Census, 2000a, 2000e).

When the elderly need care and assistance, it is more likely to originate from adult offspring, since most elderly persons have children. Most adult children want to provide care and support to aging family members, and not because they are obliged to do so. Adult children wanting to offer caregiving assistance cite various reasons for pitching in, but one desire looms dominant: to return the kind of support and security that was once received. Most feel it is the right and proper thing for a child to do, an unwritten expectation that is an integral part of the family life cycle (Shulman and Berman, 2001).

However, modern family life has changed the scope of caregiving. Today, for example, adult children caring for their parents have their own family and work obligations that often conflict with caregiving demands and responsibilities. In the future, the increase in childlessness and lower fertility rates will result in fewer adult children to care for increasingly large numbers of aging adults. The increased divorce rate and the population's geographic mobility will make it difficult for families to provide assistance to the elderly. Also, middle- and upper-class families tend to be more geographically scattered because of career demands and obligations.

In addition to the changing character of family life, the demands of caregiving have changed. Modern-day caregiving tends to be more difficult care for a longer time period. Also, life expectancy has increased for the disabled and chronically ill. Compared to earlier time periods, caregivers often provide care that is more physically and psychologically demanding. As medical technology continues to save lives, it is likely that the duration of disability and chronic illness, and consequently the need for help, will increase even more (Hobbs and Damon, 1996).

Most caregivers are women who are married with families of their own. Although there is some evidence that men become more involved in caregiving in their later years, this familial responsibility for the most part rests heavily on a woman's shoulders. Thus, there appears to be some truth to the maxim that "a son's a son 'til he gets a wife, and a daughter's a daughter all her life." In those homes fostering egalitarianism (equal gender roles), it is likely that more shared caregiving will occur, and that in the rest of society we may even see more sons begin to help caregiving daughters and daughters in-law (Rubin, 2000).

When traditional gender roles exist, women must learn to juggle caregiving chores, career obligations, and their own family responsibilities. As we'll see shortly, this is a heavy workload often triggering tension and stress. Thus, the increase in the labor force by women may place an additional burden on already strained family resources. Whether caregiving assistance to aged parents will change as more daughters enter the workplace (or more fathers provide assistance) amidst multiple family demands has stirred lively debate among family-life researchers. The questions to be asked in years to come are not as simple as, *Who* is going to care for Mom and Dad? Truly, modern caregivers might have to reckon with some particularly thorny issues: *How* are we going to care for Mom and Dad, and *when* are we going to care for them?

Finally, the increase in life expectancy has created a new wrinkle in family caregiving. With people living longer, it is not uncommon for older adult children to help their aging parents. In years to come, we will see more of the old helping the old, such as a sixty-five-year-old caregiver tending to the needs of ninety-year-old parents. Indeed, tomorrow we'll likely see the existence of more four and five generation families. Increases in the length of life may also result in more and more children knowing and living with their grandparents and great-grandparents (Hobbs and Damon, 1996).

Cross-Cultural Variations in Caregiving

By 2030, it is projected that people sixty-five years of age and older will represent 20 percent of the population. Minority populations are projected to represent 25 percent of the aged population, up from 16 percent recorded in 1998. Between 1998 and 2030, the white population sixty-five and older is projected to increase by 79 percent compared with 226 percent for minorities, including Hispanic Americans (341 percent), African Americans (130 percent), Native Americans (150 percent), and Asian Americans (323 percent) (U.S. Bureau of the Census, 2000d; Administration on Aging, 2000).

Most minority elderly are not isolated from family members and are the recipients of considerable intergenerational care and assistance. Traditionally, minority families have had to assume the role of caregiver. Minority families often rely on their own internal resources to provide for the social, economic, and physical needs of the aged. When outside support services are needed, family members supplement this assistance. In this fashion, rather than serving as an alternative support system, family caregivers complement more formal assistance.

Similar to majority family trends, minority family caregiving is a female-dominated activity. Although some males do help out, such assistance is clearly the exception. Family caregivers often live within visiting distance, interact by choice, and are connected to one another by means of mutual aid and social activities. When caregiving situations arise, it is not uncommon for minority family members to combine their economic resources, thus serving an important adaptive function. Given the extended family framework of many minorities, the elderly may receive care from large numbers of relatives. Thus, a network of helping hands distribute the challenges posed by caregiving and become important modifiers of stress.

The elderly are a key component of minority families and represent a strong social force. The elderly are respected for the wisdom they possess, and they are neither ignored nor rejected by younger family members. Among Asian Americans, respect and reverence for the elderly are taught at early ages. Moreover, Asian Americans consider it an honor to provide supportive care and assistance to the aged. Among Native Americans such as the Navajos, enduring and reciprocal kin relationships are part of tribal lore. The elderly are appreciated as important individuals who still have much to contribute to the good of the family.

Most minority families are characterized by cohesion and intergenerational connections. Regular contact with family members is practiced and also stressed to younger generations. Among Korean Americans, for example, regular contact with aged relatives and shared family activities are commonplace. Although most elderly Korean Americans want to live independently, most rely on their children for assistance when it is needed. Mexican, Puerto Rican, and Cuban families living in the United States reflect similar patterns of contact and interaction. Among African American families, a norm of reciprocity or mutual assistance serves to weave generations together.

African American elderly typically have extensive interaction with other family members, provide extensive affective (emotional) support, and report a high degree of satisfaction with their later years. Hispanic American families also emphasize affective support as well as the provision of instrumental support, such as the goods and services associated with caregiving. Strong intergenerational relations among African Americans and Hispanic Americans are particularly important in later life because they serve to buffer the negative effects of aging.

In some instances, socioeconomic status rather than race or ethnicity is a better predictor of the structure and nature of family caregiving. Aging parents from low socioeconomic backgrounds have a greater likelihood than those from high socioeconomic levels to have more contact with their children and to receive higher levels of caregiving. This is because working-class people are more likely to live near their relatives, while middle- and upper-middle-class persons have a greater tendency to move to another town or part of the country because of career demands and other obligations.

The Costs of Caregiving

Today, the typical caregiver is middle aged and often caught in the "squeeze" of the "sandwich" generation. That is, many adults now become acutely aware of the conflicting pressures of caring for aging parents at the same time as they are trying to satisfy the demands of work and caring for their own children. The rigors of caregiving while maintaining one's own household and balancing a career is physically and psychologically exhausting. The loss of personal freedom, the lack of time for social and recreational activities, and other restrictions are often part of the sacrifices. Simply put, caregiving presents multiple, time-consuming responsibilities that alter the caregiver's life course (Applegate and Thorne, 2000).

Unrelenting friction and turbulence between adult child and dependent parent has been known to produce a dark side to caregiving patterns: abuse of the elderly. Abusers of the aged are not maladaptive personality types such as those portrayed in the media. Rather, the abuser is more likely to be a parent's middle-aged caregiver, often the daughter. In most instances, abusers are typically normal persons who are tending to multiple responsibilities and encountering escalating stress levels. In addition to caregiving tasks and chores, it is not uncommon for caregivers to experience family conflict or deterioration of their own physical and mental health. Negative behaviors, then, tend to reflect the emotional strain of caregiver burdens (Ilardo and Rothman, 2001; Marcell and Shankle, 2000).

For middle-aged female caregivers, such stress may accompany their traditional nurturing role. Women most likely start caring for an elderly parent at the time when their own children are beginning to leave home. Being placed back into a nurturing role, just when it is expected that this responsibility is finished, may prove overwhelming. The caregiver's age, the quality of the relationship between the caregiver and the elderly person, as well as the amount of assistance provided by other family members are important factors to consider when examining the caregiver's burden (Rubin, 2000).

In recognition of the responsibilities and demands placed on caregivers, a wide range of supportive assistance has emerged. For example, in 1993 the Family and Medical Leave Act ensured that employers address the needs of their employees with regard to eldercare. The federally sponsored Administration on Aging works closely with the national network of aging organizations to plan, coordinate, and provide home and community-based services to meet the needs of elderly persons and their caregivers. At the local level, organizations such as Area Agencies on Aging provide caregivers with access to service providers, adult-care centers, and volunteers. Support groups such Children of Aging Parents have also sprung up in the recent past to help adult children better handle the pressures of caregiving.

Finally, whether sharing a residence or tending to the needs of the elderly on a visitation basis, caregivers must reckon with the financial burden. The material support of an aging parent is an expensive venture, be it the amount of time given or actual dollars expended. Medical costs at hospitals and nursing homes have increased dramatically, resulting in depleted Medicare and Medicaid funds.

The income of older people often brings little or no financial relief. In 1999, about 3.4 million elderly persons were below the poverty level. Older women had a higher poverty rate than older men. One out of every eleven (8.9 percent) elderly whites was poor in 1999, compared to 26.4 percent of elderly African Americans, and 21.2 percent of elderly Hispanic Americans. Older citizens living alone or with nonrelatives were much more likely to be poor (20.4 percent) than were elderly persons living with families (6.4 percent). The highest poverty rates, taking all of these variables into account, were reported by elderly African American women who lived alone (Administration on Aging, 2000).

Adult children need to seriously address the issue of family caregiving and, obviously, planning in advance is the key. When an aged parent is stricken with an illness or faces acute financial hardship, it is often too late to do the most effective planning. The time to work out financial and legal considerations possibly lurking ahead is *before* they occur, when parents are optimally healthy and content with their lives. Nothing has to be decided definitively after the first conversation since most strategies and decisions need to evolve. Family discussions and advance planning need not be restricted to finances, either. Frank, open discussions are needed about all aspects of family life such as lifestyle considerations, funeral arrangements, and issues related to inheritance. When this is done in productive and healthy ways, an assortment of parents' plans and wishes usually unfolds. Better yet, difficult situations in later years can be eased, since a well-informed adult child is in a better position to ensure that parents' best interests are protected (Robertson, 2000; Greenberg, 2000).

Families of Divorce

"Do you promise to love, honor, and cherish . . . until death do you part?" How often we've heard these traditional wedding vows exchanged, but in the wake of widespread divorce rates, how realistic are they? Consider that question as we explore the magnitude and scope of divorce in this section. Why are divorce rates so high? What is it like to go through a divorce? Let's explore these and other issues and discover what it is that transforms romance at the altar into marital unhappiness, disappointment, and eventual separation.

Divorce is the legal dissolution of marriage. Divorce is widespread in the United States today; indeed, America has the rather dubious distinction of having a higher divorce rate than any other Western nation. Divorce rates hit an all-time peak in 1946 and then steadily declined until the late 1950s. Since then, however, the proportion of first marriages ending in divorce has sharply risen. Approximately one million divorces were granted in 1974, marking the first time in American history that more marriages ended in divorce than through death. Between 1970 and 1980, the number of divorces in this country increased almost 70 percent. In 1999, approximately one million divorces were granted (U.S. Department of Health and Human Services, 1999; National Center for Health Statistics, 2000).

One method of computing the frequency of divorce is to examine the *crude divorce rate*. The crude divorce rate indicates the number of divorces per 1,000 people in a given year. In the United States in 1999, there were about 4.2 divorces per 1,000 population. This is considered to be a high rate of divorce. Compare this to Poland, for example, where the divorce rate is 1.3, while in El Salvador it is only 0.3. The U.S. crude divorce rate of 4.2 in 1999 was almost double the rate recorded in 1965 (U.S. Department of Health and Human Services, 1999; National Center for Health Statistics, 2000).

It is often reported that almost 50 percent of all marriages end in divorce. This is a very misleading statement, and such a statistical analysis must be placed into a proper perspective. This percentage was arrived at by comparing the divorces granted in one year with the marriages performed in that same year. This is quite different from the crude divorce rate and tends to be somewhat misleading because divorces granted in any one year are the result of marriages performed in many earlier years. Also, divorce does not affect all social groups equally. The poor and the poorly educated, members of the working class, and those who marry young have higher divorce rates than better-educated and middle-class professionals (U.S. Bureau of the Census, 2000a; U.S. Department of Health and Human Services, 1999; National Center for Health Statistics, 2000).

Divorce Legalities

Obtaining a divorce today is simpler in scope than it was years ago. However, divorce proceedings still encompass a number of legal complexities, something we will investigate. Before doing so, though, let's first explore the concepts of annulment, legal separation, and divorce mediation.

Annulment is the invalidation of a marriage on the basis of some reason that existed at the beginning of that marriage. (Annulment is less common than divorce.) Some of the acceptable reasons for a legal annulment are insanity, fraud, or being underage.

A *legal separation* often occurs before the proceedings and allows couples to live apart. More specifically, it entails a contract between the two that focuses on the issues that have to be resolved before a divorce is granted, such as property division or child custody. Typically, the contract is submitted to a judge, who has the power to modify it if the terms are not clear or they favor one partner over another.

Divorce mediation is a conflict resolution process in which the disputants meet with a third-party mediator whose role is that of a facilitator and an impartial guide to negotiation. The mediator serves as an adviser who suggests options and can describe the range of decisions that courts are likely to make about a given issue.

Divorce mediation respects and supports the participants' ability to make decisions that affect their lives. In mediation, the separating partners control the results, taking responsibility for the final outcome instead of handing decisions over to the courts. Mediation provides a clearinghouse for cooperative solutions in which everyone can have his or her needs considered. This is especially important where children are involved and joint custody is anticipated.

Divorce mediation differs from the traditional adversary process, be it the public judiciary (judgment in court) or private arbitration (judgment made by an arbitrator in a closed session), in several important ways. Most important, mediation is generally informal and less structured than either of the alternative procedures. Because it is private, it encourages an openness that is impossible in a public setting. The disputants retain control of the outcome rather than turning the decision-making power over to a judge or an arbitrator.

Divorce mediation offers several distinct advantages to couples. It is often cheaper than a traditional divorce. Also, proponents maintain that disputes are settled faster when there is a mediation process rather than an adversarial process. Third, participants are more likely to perceive a mediated settlement as fairer than a court resolution to the divorce.

There are different styles of divorce mediation, although each strives for the same goal: an agreeable settlement without the cost of a court suit. In its simplest form, mediation can be performed by a single lawyer and a single mediator. However, other arrangements exist, such as with a lawyer-therapist interdisciplinary team. Court-sponsored public mediation programs are also available.

Divorce Law

There are many legal sides to the dissolution of a marriage, and divorce laws have changed over the years. For centuries, divorce law centered around the concept of fault. By this, there was the requirement that one party had done something wrong while the other party was without fault. Thus, traditional divorce law represented an adversarial process. It should be noted, too, that once fault was determined, financial terms of the divorce were directed to this party.

At one time, the notion of "fault" included only adultery and physical cruelty. Later, though, "fault" included such grounds as mental cruelty or desertion. Because divorce was an action in equity, it could only be granted if the party seeking the divorce was innocent of any wrongdoing. If both parties happened to be at fault, the divorce was typically not allowed. Also, proof that parties colluded to obtain a divorce would bar a divorce.

In addition, traditional divorce law perpetuated the gender-typed division of roles and responsibilities apparent in traditional marriages. That is, in a traditional marriage a woman presumably agreed to devote herself to being a wife, mother, and homemaker in return for her husband's promise of lifelong support. If the marriage did not endure, and if the wife was virtuous, she would be granted alimony. Alimony represents the husband's continued economic support, a perpetuation of the husband's continued financial obligation. Traditional divorce laws also perpetuated the gender-typed division of roles as far as the children were concerned: The wife was typically responsible for their care while the husband was responsible for their economic support.

In 1969, California passed legislation making it the first state to recognize the breakdown of a marriage as a ground for divorce. This legislation, the Family Law Act, heralds the concept of *no-fault divorce*. The concept of no-fault divorce changes several basic elements of traditional divorce legislation. It eliminates the fault-based grounds for divorce and removes the adversary process. Neither party is accused of creating the marital breakdown, a factor that makes divorce proceedings simpler. No-fault divorce also helps to reduce the bitterness associated with property settlements, alimony, and the like. Financial settlements no longer originate on the concept of fault or gender-based role assignments. No-fault divorce redefines the traditional responsibilities of husbands and wives by implementing a new norm of gender equality. It attempts to institutionalize gender-neutral obligations between partners, including that related to economic support, division of property, and child support. Since its inception in 1969, nearly every state has some variation of no-fault divorce proceedings.

Whether no-fault divorce achieves all of the foregoing, however, remains to be seen. Some researchers have found that divorcing mothers are faring more poorly under the no-fault concept of divorce than they did under the former adversary system. Others have discovered that no-fault divorce reduces the bargaining power of spouses who did not want to divorce, which ultimately leads to significant declines in the financial settlements received by women. Furthermore, some maintain that the concept of no-fault divorce has led to a casual commitment to marriage among many segments of the population (Maher, 2000).

Divorce Transitions

Divorce involves a number of transitions and mentally taxing decisions for both couples and families. Family studies researcher Constance Ahrons (2000) maintains that divorce is an event that consists of five stages or transitions. These five stages represent a process during which family members acquire new roles and the family itself takes on a new definition.

Individual Cognition Stage. During this stage, there is an awareness that something is wrong in the marital relationship. Individual reactions vary during the early phases of this stage: blaming one's partner, anger, depression, or even denial of the problem. Any resolution chosen at this stage depends on the couple's history of coping strategies. Some couples may decide to stay in the marriage until the children are grown. Others may decide to spend time and energy on interests outside the family while attempting to maintain the facade of an intact marriage. This process of emotional divorce, the withdrawal of emotional investment in the marital relationship, is self-protective and may have some positive benefits for the individual. However, this withdrawal will have implications for the entire family system. How long this stage lasts hinges on the coping behaviors used and other factors related to the family's vulnerability to stress.

Family Metacognition Stage. Here, the entire family begins to realize that the marriage is deteriorating. Metacognition means that the family system begins to change in recognition of the problem. The problem is typically discussed by the family and the dialogue often sums up each member's anxieties. It is also a time for potential solutions and consequences of the problem to be discussed. A key element of this stage is the family's adaptive ability. If the family has not demonstrated adequate and rational problem solving in past crisis situations, it is not apt to do so at this time.

Separation Stage. At this time, one parent moves out of the home and away from the family. The family at this time is in a state of flux and family members often express more doubt in regard to family roles and boundaries. The family typically faces stress at this time, even if it has successfully coped with earlier stages. Also during this transition, the family typically shares its marital separation with extended family, friends, and the community as they begin the tasks of the economic and legal divorce. Ahrons believes these mediating factors can help and/or hinder the transitional process.

Family Reorganization Stage. During earlier stages, the lack of clear boundaries caused much of the confusion and stress. Now, the clarification of the boundaries themselves creates distress.

One of the most stressful chores confronting divorcing parents is that of redefining their co-parental relationship, the relationship that permits them to continue their child-rearing obligations and responsibilities after divorce. Ahrons takes this a step further, though, by saying adults must separate their spousal roles from their parental roles, terminating the former while redefining the latter. This complex process of ceasing to be husband and wife while still continuing to be mother and father creates the foundation for divorced family reorganization. Although divorce creates structural changes in the family, the relationship between former spouses is still the key to redefinition of relationships in the divorced family.

Family Redefinition Stage. The redefinition of relationships in the divorced family depends on the relationship between the parents. Although a continued and cooperative relationship between divorced parents reduces the crisis potential associated with divorce, its relationship dynamics remain largely unexplored. The growing debate over custody rights reveals our lack of knowledge about the time-honored concept "best interests of the child" and brings the custom of sole custody into serious question. We'll discuss later how the trend toward shared custody and co-parenting represents an alternative, and thus plays a role in the family redefinition stage.

Ahrons's research enables us to see the individual and family factors involved in divorce. However, none of her identified processes or transitions exist in a vacuum, nor are they independent or mutually exclusive of one another. Also, since reactions to divorce are highly individualized, variations of the identified stages are more than likely. They should not be taken as precise and rigid blueprints that everyone follows. Nonetheless, her theory is useful in helping us to understand the changes that people face when negotiating this painful process. Her theory also succeeds in capturing how divorce represents a complex and multifaceted experience.

Children and Divorce

Each year, nearly one million children will see their parents' marriage collapse. Should current rates hold, one of every three white children and two of three African American children born within marriage will experience a parental marital dissolution by age sixteen. Most children of divorced parents live with their mother, and the majority will experience living in a fatherless home for at least five years. Moreover, the divorce experience is not necessarily over when the mother remarries. About one-third of white and one-half of African American children whose mothers remarry will experience a second parental marital dissolution before they reach adulthood (U.S. Bureau of the Census, 2000b; U.S. Department of Health and Human Services, 1999; National Center for Health Statistics, 2000).

Divorce has the potential of creating numerous problems for children. Some children feel personally responsible for the divorce. Many are persuaded to take sides by their parents. Others may bear the brunt of displaced parental aggression. Coping with the divorce may also spill over to other aspects of the child's life and create additional problems, such as in schoolwork. And children may exhibit a wide range of emotional reactions, such as anger, sadness, irritability, distractibility, and rejection (James, Friedman, and Matthews, 2001; Benedek and Brown, 2001).

One of the most extensive and comprehensive investigations focusing on the effects of divorce on children was undertaken by Judith Wallerstein and a team of researchers (2000). Wallerstein, who launched her research in 1971, identified and tracked the lives of sixty families in which the parents had separated and filed for divorce in California. Over the course of time, Wallerstein discovered that the children of divorce—now in their twenties, thirties, and forties—still suffer from the fallout of their parents' split. Many of the adult children reported fears of betrayal, feelings of powerlessness, unrealistic ideas about love and partnership, and shying away from intimacy altogether.

It should be pointed out, though, that many children of divorce show remarkable resilience in the face of domestic turmoil. Resiliency as a response to divorce tends to be enhanced by open and honest family communication, not placing the blame on the child, and not trapping the child in the middle of a divorce crossfire. Resilient children also tend to have access to a meaningful support system, such as the presence and reassurance of other family members, friends, and teachers (Hetherington, 2000; Ahrons, 2000; Teyber, 2001).

What else can parents do to help children in the face of an impending divorce? According to Matthew McKay and colleagues (2001), no matter how hard it is to face children and talk about divorce, it must be done and it cannot be done in the form of a simple announcement. The dialogue between parent and child is the beginning of a process where youngsters can express feelings, get reassurance, and gradually integrate this important change into their lives. McKay and colleagues offer the following helpful suggestions:

Tell children clearly and directly what divorce means. Parents should explain to children in an understandable way what problems and issues have led to the divorce decision. They should also be prepared to repeat this information several times before the younger children really acknowledge what has happened.

Encourage children to ask questions. Parents need to help children openly express their thoughts and feelings about the divorce, not just at the beginning but throughout the long process of adjustment. Children should also be told that the communication channels are always open.

Do not assess blame. State that each parent has been hurt in his or her own way and that each has felt pain. If a parent is angry, he or she should acknowledge it, but negative feelings should not be directed toward children.

Emphasize that the children in no way caused the divorce, nor are they responsible for marital problems. Parents need to explain that they are divorcing each other, not the children. It is equally important to let children know that nothing they can do can bring about a reconciliation. Young children often harbor fantasies of mending a broken marriage.

If possible, describe any changes the children can expect in their day-to-day experiences. Children tend to fear the unknown, and this fear magnifies when the future is unknown or uncharted. Parents need to carefully explain pending lifestyle changes with a particular emphasis placed on the maintenance of domestic stability and security.

Do not force children to take sides. Assure children that they will always remain free to love both parents. No pressure will be brought to reject one parent in order to continue getting nurtured by the other. Parents need to emphasize how they will continue to love and care for the children.

Custodial Arrangements

Finally, custodial arrangements greatly influence a child's adjustment to divorce. Unfortunately, conclusive answers about the best arrangements remain elusive. Judicial decisions over time regarding child custody reflect the uncertainty that has plagued this issue. For example, until the middle of the nineteenth century, children automatically went to their fathers. But, as economic conditions changed, the laws were modified to award custody to mothers as the natural nurturers of children during their "tender years." Now, judges make custodial decisions on the basis of the child's best interests. Mothers still obtain custody in about nine out of ten cases; but fathers are seeking custody more often than they used to. Grandparents can also go to court to obtain the right to visit with their grandchildren (Hetherington, 2000; Lee, 1999).

An alternative that brings flexibility to the courts is *joint custody*. Joint custody embodies mutual sharing of parental rights and responsibilities after the divorce. Many believe that joint custody requires children to make the fewest adjustments. Joint custody may also reduce the loss that a noncustodial parent often experiences under traditional sole custody (Swindoll, 2000; Booth, 2000).

Joint custody actually has two meanings. One is that both parents retain the rights they always have had as parents: for instance, the right to participate in decisions about schooling or health/medical considerations. The other meaning of joint custody is that every week, month, or year parents will alternate in providing the child's shelter. This is called joint residential custody.

It needs to be pointed out, though, that joint custody may not be best for all families. For instance, children and adolescents often want a single home as a base and find alternating homes confusing. Moving from home to home can also disrupt a child's school education. Beyond this, joint custody does not ensure that each parent is capable of handling the responsibilities of child rearing. Experts point out that children might be best served if their parents have joint custody in the legal sense, but the children are not required to alternate residences. At the same time, children should have easy access to the parent with whom they do not live (Benedek and Brown, 2001; Beyer and Winchester, 2001; Teyber, 2001).

Remarried Families

The noted eighteenth-century writer Samuel Johnson once described remarriage as "the triumph of hope over experience." How realistic is this rather gloomy and cynical appraisal of remarriage? Are remarriages programmed for failure or are they instead characterized by heightened levels of satisfaction and happiness? For that matter, is love better the second time around, as many lyricists would lead us to believe? Answers to such questions are difficult and complex.

The United States has the highest remarriage rate in the world. Statistics tell us that over 40 percent of marriages are remarriages for one or both partners. Each year, about 1. 5 million people will remarry. This means that in the United States today, divorce tends to be a transitional rather than a terminal event. However, it is important to point out that the pathways to remarriage are varied. For example, partners can be divorced or widowed with no children, divorced or widowed with custody of children, divorced or widowed without custody of children, or divorced or widowed with custody of some children but not others (U.S. Bureau of the Census, 2000a; U.S. Department of Health and Human Services, 1999; National Center for Health Statistics, 2000).

Those who choose to remarry do so within relatively short periods of time. The average interval between divorce and remarriage is approximately three years. Widowed men and women who do remarry tend to take longer to remarry than do divorced individuals, even when age is considered. A divorced person at any given age has a greater chance of marrying a second time than a never-married person has of marrying a first time. Also, divorce rates among the remarried are high, about 25 percent higher than for first marriages (Swindoll, 2000; National Center for Health Statistics, 2000).

Additionally, remarriage rates for women of all ages has diminished over the last twenty years. White women are more likely than African American women to remarry, and for the most part, they remarry more quickly. Younger women are far more likely to remarry quickly following a divorce, especially when their first marriages were relatively brief. Rapid remarriage is also more likely among females who were married when they were young and who had less than a college education. Also, men and women in remarriages tend to differ in age by a greater margin than do men and women in first marriages. In both first marriages and remarriages, the man is the same age or older than the woman in approximately four in five marriages. However, the magnitude of the difference is significantly greater in remarriages than in first marriages (U.S. Bureau of the Census, 2000a;

U.S. Department of Health and Human Services, 1999; National Center for Health Statistics, 2000).

Rates of remarriage among African Americans are only one-quarter those of white non-Hispanics, and remarriage rates have been declining disproportionately among African Americans over the last two decades. The low rate of African American remarriages reinforces a pattern that has already been established due to lower rates of first marriages and higher rates of divorces and illegitimacy. The pattern is one in which a much smaller proportion of African Americans than whites spend their lives in conventional two-parent families. African Americans also spend many more years in female-headed households, both in childhood and as grown women (National Center for Health Statistics, 2000).

A large number of remarriages involve children. Today, there are over 11 million remarried families in the United States, including 4.3 stepfamilies. About one out of five married-couple families with children are remarried families, and about 8 percent of all married-couple families are stepfamilies. Approximately 10 million children under the age of eighteen are in remarried families, about 9 million are in stepfamilies, and almost 7 million are stepchildren. The reason for the differences in the numbers is that some children are born to remarried parents while others are brought into the remarriage. For all youngsters in the United States under the age of eighteen, nearly one in six lives in a remarried family, and about one out of ten is a stepchild (Kelley and Burg, 2000; Dunn, 1999; Lauer and Lauer, 1999).

Of the nearly 6 million stepchildren living in a two-parent home, one of every seven are under the age of eighteen. Because some children who are not now stepchildren will become stepchildren before eighteen and some children who were formerly stepchildren have seen their parent and stepparent divorce, it is reasonable to expect that one-third of the children now under eighteen have already experienced or will experience being a stepchild in a two-parent family (U.S. Bureau of the Census, 2000a; U.S. Department of Health and Human Services, 1999; National Center for Health Statistics, 2000).

We need to acknowledge that those who remarry are likely to differ from those in a first marriage in a number of ways. For example, they may be older and, consequently, in a different phase of their life cycle than first-marrieds. Remarried couples may have different ideas about the meaning of love. Partners may be unclear as to what their roles and expectations are within the family. They also have experiences in marriage, and know the pain of divorce (Pino, 2001; Booth, 2000; Lauer and Lauer, 1999).

Karen Bruns (2000) observes that the blending of families is not an easy process. Adjusting to the new relationships takes time. Merging families bring together many differences. For example, an adolescent may now be followed around by a five-year-old stepsister. Holiday celebrations will change as the newly created stepfamily integrates customs and begins new ones. Parents must learn to develop realistic expectations concerning the children's periods of adjustment. Everyone needs to realize that it will be necessary to adjust to the loss of the former family structure and to accept the new situation.

In addition, Robert and Jeanette Lauer (1999) point out that there are a number of issues unique to remarriage that influence overall patterns of adjustment: complex kin relations and ambiguous roles, unresolved emotional issues related to the first marriage, financial issues, legal issues, and the adjustment of children. Let's examine each more closely.

Complex kin relations and ambiguous roles. Acquiring an entire new set of kin relationships, including step relations, coupled with ambiguity about many of the roles, often creates uncertainty and confusion. This is particularly true for boundary ambiguity; that is, family members uncertainty regarding their perceptions about who is in or who is out of the family and who is performing what roles and tasks within the family. Furthermore, many in a remarriage have to contend with a partner's continuing relationship with an ex-spouse. Because there are no social norms for such relationships, it is difficult to determine what is appropriate or expected.

Unresolved emotional issues related to the first marriage. Beyond problematic relationships, there may be unresolved emotional issues from the first marriage and the divorce that continue to affect the person and the remarriage. For instance, a wife may react to something her husband says or does because it reminds her of a problem in her first marriage. Some couples also have difficulty in developing trust in the remarriage. Trust is crucial to the well-being of any intimate relationship, but the failure of a first marriage often represents a crisis of lost trust. Having found their trust in the first spouse betrayed, individuals often have to work hard to learn to trust a second spouse.

Financial issues. Financial issues are likely to represent a source of stress in remarriages. Financial problems can be complex and painful because of obligations to ex-spouses and children. In addition, there are often questions about the inheritance rights of children and stepchildren. The issue of how family finances are to be managed may also warrant special consideration. For example, should both partners put their total income (including any alimony and child support) into a common pot and allocate it among family members according to need instead of according to who deposited what? Or, should there be two separate accounts?

Legal issues. Legal issues also become numerous and complex in remarriages. While the biological children and the ex-spouse may all have legal rights, what about the stepchildren? There are no laws that are specific to stepparent-stepchild relationships. Consequently, some couples may choose to draft a premarital agreement that takes into account what each has brought into the relationship. Such a document usually protects each spouse as well as any existing children each has and any future children they may have together.

Adjustment of children. When a parent having physical custody of a child remarries, a *blended* or *reconstituted* family is formed. Special adjustment challenges often accompany such families. For example, children have loyalties to parents. A youngster may feel that exhibiting affection toward a stepparent is betraying the biological parent. Or, the child who has lived in a single-parent household may have difficulty sharing that parent (Bruns, 2000).

It should be realized that remarriage with children is part of a unique process of family redefinition. According to Emily and John Visher (1996), such relationships begin with a loss: a spouse or parent has died or there has been a divorce. A once-existing love relationship has disappeared. Children and parents have been separated either totally or partially, depending on the custody and visitation arrangements. In some situations, brothers and sisters have been separated. There may have been a severing of relationships with grandparents, or alienation from friends and a familiar community. Thus, the parent's remarriage sometimes looms as a significant crisis—both as a risk and as an opportunity. In the remarriage of one or both parents, children often find an additional parental figure who may effectively complement what can't be secured from one or both biological parents. This whole process can be one of growth for children and adults (or it can be a disaster) or anything in between (Benedek and Brown, 2001; Brey and Kelly, 1999; Ganong and Coleman, 1999).

Many adults enter a remarriage expecting the impossible of themselves and the rest of the family. For example, stepmothers try to be super-moms so they overcome the "wicked stepmother" image (remember the evil portrayals of stepmothers in *Cinderella, Hansel and Gretel,* and *Snow White?* Notice the absence of myth regarding the stepfather). Whereas once stepmothers remained relatively silent regarding adjustment difficulties, today many are sharing their feelings. Many report preoccupation with their new position in the family, feelings of rejection or ineffectiveness, guilt, hostility, exhaustion, and loss of self-esteem. Clearly the majority of them experience distress that is normal within the context of their adjustment reaction (Teyber, 2001; Booth, 2000; Dunn, 1999; Kelley and Burg, 2000).

Also, stepfathers often rush in and try to take command immediately, while stepchildren may balk and drag their heels in resentment. Many grandparents feel somewhat isolated and uncertain of their roles, while ex-spouses may compete for the love and loyalty of their children. The issue of "turf," or who owns which possessions in the redesigned family network, is also difficult for many. Add to this mosaic of emotions and unrealistic expectations the ways in which stepfamilies are different from biological families, and it is clear why remarried families experience their particular tensions (Pino, 2001; Swindoll, 2000).

In general, research reveals that stepchildren are usually a well-adjusted lot. Compared to children from natural families, most are just as happy and emotionally stable. They tend to have no more behavior problems than do children from intact homes, and they usually have similar levels of self-esteem. However, some research indicates that stepchildren exhibit more internalizing behavior (e.g., anxiety, depression) than children from nuclear families. Yet, stepchildren do as well as other children in such areas as academic achievement and problem-solving resourcefulness (Beyer and Winchester, 2001; James, Friedman, and Matthews, 2001; Lee, 1999).

What can parents do to promote stability and equilibrium in blended families? Obviously, all parties must work at building domestic solidarity and harmony. This is usually difficult given the complexities of assimilating new family members and defining new family roles and relationships. According to Jeannette

Lofas (1998), the natural family alone contains enough of its own stresses and conflicts. When one or two stepparents are added, along with a set of ready-made brothers and sisters, added pressures begin to mount. To help deal with these special demands, Lofas offers the following suggestions:

Recognize that the stepfamily is a unique family system. The stepfamily has unique structure and operating mechanisms. Special dynamics surface as new relationships are forged, such as the execution of roles, rules, and responsibilities. The functioning of a stepfamily cannot and should not be compared to the functioning of a natural family.

Don't expect instant love. Adjusting to any kind of new relationship takes time and patience. Children, especially, are often guarded and tentative regarding new relationships. Initially, trust may be fleeting and needs time to establish itself. Stepparents are often alarmed when emotions expressed toward them fluctuate between love and hate, security and insecurity. For these reasons, it is important to go slow and not to come on too strong.

Expectations should be realistic and flexible. Stepparents need to abandon rigid expectations for themselves and their children. It is vital for the survival of the stepfamily to be able to see and delineate expectations for each member of the family. This is especially true in such areas as money, discipline, relations with prior spouses, and territory (i.e., physical, emotional). Being flexible and open-minded goes a long way toward promoting domestic stability.

Seek to minimize changes in family schedules. As we've seen throughout this book, children need predictability and structure in their lives. The creation of a stepfamily brings change and the potential for confusion and upheaval. To counter this, children need some activities to remain the same. Parents should avoid making unnecessary changes. By adhering to an established schedule, all family members benefit from continuity and equilibrium.

Establish clear roles and rules. It is important to stay away from unclear expectations, since ambiguity lends itself to confusion and distortion of domestic assignments. Furthermore, unclear expectations often create rejection and resentment. For a system to run smoothly, members need to know what their jobs are, as well as those assigned to others. Clear job descriptions need to be established between the parent, stepparent, and children.

Expect ambivalence and conflict of loyalties. Mixed emotional reactions are normal when two families merge. Anger and resentment are not uncommon reactions among those children torn between an absent natural parent and a stepparent. Conflicts of loyalties often create emotional confusion and must be recognized right from the beginning. Stepparents should not take this as a form of personal rejection.

Establish effective disciplinary strategies. Parents need to identify what is considered acceptable as well as unacceptable behavior. Consequences for misbehavior must be clearly identified. Initially, this may prove to be difficult since parents are likely bringing together differing strategies and techniques. Parents need to strive for consistency and seek to support one another when rules need to be enforced.

Seek supportive assistance. Becoming an effective stepparent is hard work and takes time. Creating a healthy and strong stepfamily requires patience and dedication. Parents may benefit from turning to informal or formal support mechanisms for guidance or resources. Such assistance can include professional literature on the topic, local support groups, or national stepfamily organizations or foundations.

Abusive Family Relationships

Home sweet home. For countless Americans, the family unit represents a safe haven and the source of love, care, security, and comfort. Yet for a growing number of people, the household has been transformed into a battleground filled with violent assaults, sexual abuse, neglect, and even death for those living under the same roof. For the abused, there's no place worse than home.

Consider the following, with regard to not only the extent of the problem but also to how violent the family has become: a person runs a greater chance of being killed by his/her spouse than by any other individual encountered throughout life. Also, the family looms as the most violent and assaulting group or institution in the country, with the exception of the police or the military at war. Why has the family become so prone to physical violence? What do we know about the abused and the abuser? What kinds of intervention are available for survivors of domestic violence? This section addresses itself to these important family issues.

Spousal Abuse

Spousal abuse, referring to maltreatment between husbands and wives, is quite prevalent in the United States today. Like other forms of domestic violence, husband-wife abuse may be one of our best-kept secrets because it happens behind closed doors. We also need to emphasize that abuse against any family member does not restrict itself to physical measures. On the contrary, pain and suffering can be inflicted on others in a number of different ways. Beyond physical abuse is verbal, emotional, and sexual abuse as well as neglect and abandonment, to name but a few major forms.

Domestic violence is not confined to any one socioeconomic, ethnic, religious, racial, or age group. Domestic violence is not confined to mentally disturbed or sick people. Batterers are not psychopathic personalities, nor are they violent in all of their relationships. Additionally, abusers are at times loving, sensitive people. And surprisingly, the abused frequently love their batterers in spite of the pain they inflict.

Men who batter their wives often harbor low levels of self-esteem and frequent depression. In addition, a wife batterer typically has a lower occupational status than that of his neighbors. Interestingly, his occupational and educational status is frequently lower than that of his wife. Abusive males also are likely to be jealous and insecure, and many lack direction in life. Many male batterers feel powerless and inadequate. They turn to violence as a way of trying to demonstrate power and adequacy (Lloyd-Still, 2000).

It is difficult to fit battered women into any particular age classification since wife abuse can occur at any age. It has been found, however, that pregnant women seem particularly susceptible to physical violence. Some research also indicates that battered women are more likely to be unassertive and to have low levels of self-esteem. Finally, abuse typically begins early in the marriage and tends to increase as time goes on.

Abused women often remain in, rather than leave, the home that promotes violence. Why ? The wife may be ashamed. Because wife beating is so well secluded in our society, the victim often feels isolated and alone; she may feel that she is the only abused wife in the community (Rouse, 2000). A second reason is fear. A battered wife may fear retaliation from the abuser. Third, many experience a sense of helplessness because they feel little will come of their efforts to improve their situation. Finally, some battered women stay at the site of violence for practical reasons—many have children, few job skills, no place to go, and no means of financial support. They are literally trapped by the economics of their situation (LaViolette and Barnett, 2000; Glassman, 2000).

Marital Rape

Marital rape is a type of sexual assault in which a woman is forced by her husband to have sexual intercourse or other forms of sexual activity against her will. Many states do not recognize marital rape as a violation of the law, but a growing number of people believe it should be a crime subject to prosecution. At present, in over half of our states, a husband can force his wife to have intercourse and this act is not legally considered a rape. In several states, marital rape is not even a crime when the husband and wife are separated.

There are several reasons why marital rape isn't a crime in so many states. For one, implicit in the civil marriage contract is the belief that a married man has the right to have sex with his wife whenever he so desires. Within marriage, women who do not comply can be forced to do so. A man may perceive that sexual intercourse and other sexual acts within the marriage are a woman's duty and that she has no right to refuse participation. Such acts may therefore not even be viewed by the wife as rape. What activities constitute marital rape, how to assess the degree of force or coercion, and how to categorize long-term live-in relationships are factors that have prevented marital rape from achieving uniform legal status.

Explanations regarding why men rape their wives are speculative. Indeed, there may be as many reasons why husbands rape their wives as there are men who do it. However, researchers offer certain motivations for consideration, many of which are intertwined. For example, it is believed that some men do not see their wives as people with a right to say no to sex. They hold the traditional idea that a wife belongs to her husband, and that sex can occur whenever they want, regardless of a woman's desires. Such men do not see women as their equals or as people who have as much choice over their sex life as they do. Whether their wife's desire equals their own does not seem to matter (Sattler, 2000; Dalton and Schneider, 2000).

As far as other motivations are concerned, some men make their wives into symbols of things they hate and want to get back at. Other men are threatened by their wives—their intelligence, perhaps, or their independence—and the husbands want to regain some superiority by dominating them. Still others believe that their wives deny them sex all the time and that they therefore have a right to take it by force. Finally, some men think that getting sex all the time is the only proof of their manhood, regardless of how they get it (Braun-Haley and Haley, 2001; Beattie and Shaughnessey, 2000).

Researchers agree that marital rape is a vicious and brutal form of abuse. Victims of marital rape endure intimate violation and experience trauma, just as much as survivors of other types of sexual assault do—yet their suffering remains the most silenced, because the crime against them in many states is not legally regarded as a crime at all. Many investigators contend that as long as marital rape remains legal, it can only be concluded that society condones it—which must in turn be interpreted as a threat to all women. They propose that while criminalizing marital rape is by no means a solution, it must be regarded—if only in a symbolic sense—as an important first step to making this a safer society for women (Eisikovits and Edleson, 2000; Profitt, 2001; Campbell, 2000; Dalton and Schneider, 2000).

Child Abuse

Child abuse, like spousal abuse, is widespread in the United States. It has been estimated that over one million children and teenagers are victims of maltreatment each year. Broken bones, lacerations, concussions, limb dislocations, and abrasions are commonplace. However, family abuse is not restricted to just physical measures. Pain and suffering are inflicted on children and adolescents in a number of different ways—through neglect and abandonment, as well as verbal, emotional, and sexual abuse, to name but a few major forms (MacDonald, 2001; Hobbs and Wynne, 2001; Bartholet, 2000).

Child abuse tends to be widespread among children six years of age and younger for several reasons. The child at this time is especially susceptible to parental frustration as adults must adjust to the rather tedious chores of early child care. Early economic hardships also cause tensions, and frustration on the parent's part may develop because of the child's inability to interact with the adult in a socially meaningful manner.

Other factors help explain why parents maltreat their offspring. Pressures from work, the home, financial difficulties, and low levels of self-esteem are frequently cited as reasons behind violence. And, research indicates that many abusive parents were abused themselves or witnessed violence between parents when they were youngsters. Some parents abuse their children in much the same way that they were abused as children. Moreover, research exists showing that husbands tend to abuse their wives in many of the same ways the husbands were abused when they were young (Grapes, 2001; Tubbs, 2000).

Many child abusers are lonely, frequently depressed, and have never learned how to contain their aggression. Physical illness, untimely childbearing, and a parent's poor ability to empathize with youngsters can substantially increase the likelihood of child maltreatment. This is particularly true when social stress, social isolation, and family dysfunction exist. Evidence also exists that certain child and adolescent characteristics such as a difficult temperament or a health problem heightens the risk for maltreatment.

Many parents also abuse their children in an effort to enforce discipline. Some have an overpowering need to impress other adults with a well-behaved youngster. Still other abusers identify with the youngster and consider every fault and mistake of their youngster to be their own. Also, there are those who perceive themselves as failures in life and feel they are attaining superiority and command by exerting such forceful dominance.

A particularly bothersome feature of family abuse is the consequence of battering in later life. Many maltreated children and teenagers run a risk for aggressiveness, self-destructive behaviors, school failure, running away from home, delinquency, and other maladaptive behaviors (Everett and Gallop, 2000). Research often shows that early harsh discipline is associated with later aggressive behavior in both children and teenagers. Maltreated children and adolescents also tend to have more discipline referrals and school suspensions. Emotional abuse in the form of name-calling, bullying, or rejection has the potential of undermining a child and teenager's sense of well-being, self-image, and self-esteem. Finally, many abused children are insecure, mistrusting, and have low overall levels of self-confidence and self-reliance (Schwartz-Kenney, McCauley, and Epstein, 2000).

Child Sexual Abuse

The sexual maltreatment of children can occur both inside and outside of the family. *Incest* is sexual contact between close blood relatives. *Child sexual abuse*, on the other hand, is sexual contact between an adult and a child who are in no way related. Both usually refer to interactions between a child and adult when the youngster is being used for the sexual stimulation of that adult or another person.

Virtually every society prohibits intrafamilial sexual relationships. This prohibition is often called the *incest taboo*. In the United States, incest is a crime, and although laws vary in different states regarding the type of sexual relationship forbidden, close blood relatives always include father, mother, grandfather, grandmother, brother, sister, aunt, uncle, niece, nephew, and sometimes first cousins. Many states include stepparent-stepchildren, stepsibling, and in-law relationships, although these individuals are not blood related.

It is difficult to assess the prevalence of incest because it happens behind closed doors and most victims live with secrecy and isolation. However, it is estimated that as many as 20 million Americans may be incest victims, meaning about one in ten are affected. The average age of a child encountering incest is eleven, with many experiencing incestuous activity somewhere between the ages of 5 and 8. Contrary to the belief that incest is a problem only among the poor, incestuous families are found in every socioeconomic and educational group (Ainscough and Toon, 2000).

Experts maintain that father-daughter and stepfather-daughter incest represent most of the reported incest cases. Mother-son and mother-daughter incest constitute most of the remaining reports. Sibling incest is also believed to be widespread, but it is rarely reported. The most prevalent sibling incest pattern appears to be the abuse of younger sisters and brothers by an older male sibling.

When the incestuous activity begins, victims often believe that they are holding the family together. They fear that the offending parent will go to jail if the incest is discovered. Some children acquiesce because they are desperate for any type of affection. And in many situations, children believe that there is no one to help them, even if they wanted help. Offenders often try to convince themselves that there is nothing wrong with what they are doing. But most use either subtle coercion or direct threats to keep the children silent.

In many father-daughter incestuous relationships, the mother is aware of the circumstances. A number of mothers choose to remain uninvolved, perhaps because they were victims of incest, or they are so frightened by and insecure with their husbands that they are immobilized. Given the mother's passive stance, the youngster often searches for an available and safe person with whom to communicate. However, in so doing the child runs the risk of not being believed or even rejected (Herman and Hirschman, 2000).

Like incest, the sexual abuse of a young child by an adult is a punishable crime in the United States. However, the incidence of child sexual abuse is not much easier to assess than the incidence of incest. Most researchers agree that the problem is occurring at a significant rate, and they acknowledge that male children are abused less frequently than females. However, reported cases barely scratch the surface. Many reports of child sexual abuse are never even passed on to protective agencies. Furthermore, many sexual abuse cases are investigated, but they do not stand up to the rigors of the court. And, there are unknown numbers of youngsters who remain silent, never tell, or never seek therapeutic assistance (Cairns, 2000).

The effects of all forms of child sexual abuse are multiple and diverse. For example, the survivor's suffering may be expressed in physical ailments such as chronic pelvic pain or the psychological disturbances of depression or acute anxiety. Many survivors are left with strong feelings of guilt, betrayal, and powerlessness. Because of the trauma of sexual abuse, later sexual behavior may be affected, such as with sexual preoccupation or compulsive masturbation and sex play. Many female survivors of sexual abuse are hostile and angry, distrustful of men or intimate relationships in general, and have a history of failed relationships or marriages. Finally, many child sexual abuse victims often feel isolated and turn to self-destructive behaviors, such as drug abuse or delinquency (Draucker, 2000).

Therapeutic Intervention

Therapy aimed at survivors of violent relationships is designed to break the cycle of abuse and to deal with whatever effects have occurred. Therapeutic interventions as well as prevention efforts designed to stop abuse face a formidable challenge. Although numerous and commendable attempts have been made, experts are quick to point out that continued research and more innovative approaches are needed. Most contend that while dealing with the aftermath of violence and abuse is critical, the causes of relationship violence and abuse must be the focal point of future efforts. Many believe that we have placed too much emphasis on remedial attention and not enough on stopping the problem before it occurs. In other words, we need to implement more proactive strategies rather than reactive measures (Ketterman, 2001; Kearney, 2001).

A number of therapeutic approaches are available. Individual approaches or family therapy are among the most popular approaches. Therapeutic strategies typically focus on the resolution of conflicts in nonviolent ways and on establishing more effective communication techniques among family members. Although progress has been reported with such approaches, obstacles can develop in therapy. Individuals may continually deny the use of violence or the existence of personal problems. Hostility is typically present, and frequently there is little guilt expressed over violent and abusive behavior.

Self-help groups such as Parents Anonymous as well as other community organizations have also proven to be effective modes of intervention. The basic underlying theme of these programs is group support. Abused parties usually meet in small groups under the guidance of trained counselors and offer understanding and empathy to one another. Such therapeutic self-help systems not only help abused parties, but they also place the family in a more meaningful social context. Therapists point out that the family should not be treated as an independent social unit, but as embedded in a broader social network of informal and formal community-based support systems.

Unfortunately, many individuals and families fail to seek psychotherapy or assistance from self-help groups. For example, many battered women remain in the home that promotes violence rather than seek help. Some are ashamed of their situation and feel that they are the only abused person in the community. Many refuse to get help because they fear retaliation from the abuser. Many also experience a sense of helplessness because they feel little will come of their efforts to improve their situation (Berry, 2000).

The provision of support and services for all abused parties needs to be continually stressed (Deaton and Hertica, 2001). Emergency shelters for abused family members are considered critical in our overall intervention efforts. Transportation, food, and emergency money are frequently provided by these temporary facilities. Some shelters even help survivors of violence and abuse to find new jobs and homes. Most agree that these are indispensable services when a family member is seeking refuge from violence. Telephone hotlines available 24 hours a day are also valuable therapeutic tools. Toll-free telephone numbers to national organizations are especially valuable. (The National Resource Center on Domestic Violence is 800–537–2238.) Trained counselors assist the abused with obtaining legal assistance in such matters as formal complaints, child custody, and general legal rights. And, self-defense training sessions for women are also valuable (Canfield, 2000; Davies, Lyon, and Monti-Catania, 2000).

Surprisingly, there are many people in society who refuse to acknowledge the severity of violence and abuse in relationships. Psychologists, sociologists, and other professionals feel that educating the public about the magnitude of this social problem may be one of our highest priorities in combating this problem. Training workshops for those that deal with abuse, such as police officers, social workers, lawyers, and counselors are needed. Family life education in schools also needs to be strengthened, with a particular emphasis placed on the realities of domestic abuse and intervention strategies.

Legislation combining tough new penalties with programs to prosecute batterers and help victims of violence is also important. The Crime Bill of 1994 strengthened efforts by the Department of Health and Human Services to prevent violence and crime. Under the Violence Against Women Act (VAWA), passed as part of the Crime Bill, women and children are protected against violence through rigorous law enforcement strategies. Additionally, efforts are being made to alleviate possible abusive conditions and to promote a better understanding of domestic violence issues.

In years to come, experts agree that the shroud of secrecy that surrounds all forms of violence and abuse has to be removed. To effectively implement all of these strategies, more federal, state, and local funding is needed. Financial aid is needed to establish more shelter homes, to provide more efficient types of legal assistance, and to support those researchers exploring the causes and cures of violence and abuse in relationships.

Summary

This chapter presented some of the most important issues and controversies characterizing family life in America today. The chapter began by examining family planning issues and reasons behind America's declining fertility rates. We spent time exploring variations in traditional fertility patterns, including delayed parenthood, voluntary childlessness, and adoption. Attention was also given to reproductive technologies, including the many controversies they have created.

We saw how parenthood poses numerous adaptations, including adjusting to new roles and deciding on appropriate child-rearing strategies. Contemporary parents typically juggle an assortment of work and household demands. Although the dual-earner family brings the potential for happiness and reward, this chapter discussed the potential for family turbulence. Many dual-earner families also report considerable difficulty locating suitable child care, particularly in terms of quality, affordability, and accessibility. We emphasized how improvements in child-care availability for youngsters of all ages are needed.

Another aspect of families we examined is the widespread nature of single-parent households. Unfortunately, a number of misconceptions and myths surround single-parenthood, usually conveying a picture of doom and gloom. A deliberate effort was made to shatter some of the more common stereotypes about single-parent families and to replace these stereotypes with the strengths that do exist. We took the same positive stance with those families facing physical disability and chronic illness. Rather than emphasizing the drawbacks and shortcomings of these challenges, we instead chose to highlight positive coping strategies and successful family lifestyles.

We then explored the dynamics of gay and lesbian families, a topic too often ignored or given limited attention in other reference handbooks. Contrary to what was once thought, homosexuality is not a form of abnormal behavior or mental illness. Today, many gays and lesbians are choosing to raise children in a family unit. Research tends to show that the aspirations of gay and lesbian parents do not differ from those of heterosexual parents, and there is no support for the idea that they serve as poor role models.

Also in this chapter we discussed the current elderly population explosion going on in the United States, as in other developed countries. With the aged population increasing, the amount of family care given by adult children is also increasing. We observed that caregiving in these modem times often embraces more difficult care and, thanks to medical sophistication, occupies longer durations of time. Although caregiving brings its share of rewards, it also has the potential of triggering emotional strain and the depletion of physical and psychological resources.

Since divorce is widespread in the United States, we discussed the need for considerable family adjustment to this situation. Each year, divorce will impact the lives of approximately one million children. Because divorce has the potential of creating numerous problems for younger generations, supportive assistance and understanding are critical. We also noted that remarriage is an extremely popular lifestyle in the United States today. There are numerous adjustments required among remarrieds; indeed, the blending of families often heralds complex relationships and ambiguous roles, particularly for children. Generally speaking, though, children from blended families exhibit healthy adjustment and have no more behavior problems that do youngsters from intact homes.

We concluded this chapter with a look at abusive family relationships—the characteristics of the abused as well as the abuser, including the features of home life that influence the risk of battering and the ingredients that produce violent behaviors. The chapter ended with a look at preventative measures and intervention strategies for dealing with abusive family relationships. In years to come, most experts agree that proactive, rather than reactive, strategies are needed to curb family violence.

References

Administration on Aging. 2000. "Older and Younger People with Disabilities: Improving Chronic Care Throughout the Life Span." http://www. aoa.dhhs.gov/factsheets/disabilities.htm. Accessed on 17 February 2001.

Ahrons, Constance. 2000. *Divorced Families*. New York: HarperCollins.

Ainscough, Carolyn, and Kay Toon. 2000. *Surviving Childhood Sexual Abuse.* LaVergne, TN: Fisher Books.

Applegate, Barbara, and Jean Thorne. 2000. *Parent Care: A Survival Guide for Adult Children of Aging Parents.* New York: A.G.E. Consultants Press.

Bachu, Amara, and Martin O'Connell. 1999. *Fertility of American Women.* Washington, DC: U.S. Government Printing Office.

Balswick, Jack, and Judith Balswick. 1999. *The Two-Paycheck Marriage.* New York: McGraw-Hill.

Barnett, Rosalind, and Caryl Rivers. 1998. *She Works/He Works: How Two-Income Families Are Happy, Healthy, and Thriving.* Cambridge, MA: Harvard University Press.

Bartholet, Elizabeth 2000. *Nobody's Children.* Westminster, MD: Beacon Press.

Beattie, L. Elisabeth, and Mary Angela Shaughnessey. 2000. *Sisters in Pain: Battered Women Speak Out.* Lexington: University Press of Kentucky.

Becker, Gaylene. 2000. *The Elusive Embryo: How Women and Men Apporach New Reproductive Technologies.* Los Angeles: University of California Press.

Beecham, Jahnna, and Malcolm Hillgartner. 2001. *I'm Counting to Ten: Hope and Humor for Frazzled Parents.* South Royalton, VT: Sorin Books.

Benedek, Elissa P., and Catherine F. Brown. 2001. *How to Help Your Child Overcome Divorce: A Support Guide for Families.* New York: Newmarket Press.

Bentley, Gillian R., and C. G. Nicholas Mascie-Taylor. 2001. *Infertility in the Modern World: Present and Future Prospects.* Port Chester, NY: Cambridge University Press.

Berne, Eric. 1964. *Games People Play.* New York: Grove.

Berne, Suzanne. 2001. *A Perfect Arrangement: A Novel.* Chapel Hill, NC: Algonquin.

Berry, Dawn Bradley. 2000. *The Domestic Violence Sourcebook.* Lincolnwood, IL: Lowell House Publishers.

Beyer, Roberta, and Kent Winchester. 2001. *Speaking of Divorce: How to Talk with Your Kids and Help Them Cope.* Minneapolis, MN: Spirit Publishing.

Booth, James. 2000. *Divorce and Remarriage.* Gordonsville, VA: Universe Publications.

Braun-Haley, Ellie, and Shawn Haley. 2001. *War on the Homefront.* Herndon, VA: Berghohn Books.

Brey, James and John Kelley. 1999. *Stepfamilies.* Shelter Island, NY: Broadway Books.

Brubaker, Timothy. 2000. *Family Relations.* Thousand Oaks, CA: Sage.

Bruns, K. 2000. "Ten Steps toward Successful Stepparenting." http://www.ag.ohio-state.edu/ohioline/5231.htm. Accessed 6 November 2000.

Burns, Linda, and Sharon N. Covington, eds. 2000. *Infertility Counseling: A Comprehensive Handbook for Clinicians.* Foreword by Roger Kempers. Pearl River, NJ: Parthenon Publishing.

Cairns, Kate. 2000. *Surviving Pedophilia.* Herndon, PA: Stylus Publishing.

Campbell, Jacqueline C., ed. 2000. *Empowering Survivors of Abuse: Health Care for Battered Women and Their Children.* Thousand Oaks, CA: Sage.

Canfield, Muriel. 2000. *Broken and Battered.* West Monroe, LA: Howard Publishing.

Centers for Disease Control. 2001. "About Chronic Disease." http://www.cdc.gov/nccdphp/about.htm. Accessed 17 February 2001.

Dalton, Clare, and Elizabeth Schneider. 2000. *Battered Women and the Law.* New York: Foundation Press.

Darnell, Shellee. 2000. "How to Be the Best Single Parent You Can Be." http://www.divorcewizards.com/top10singleparenting.htm. Accessed 17 June 2001.

Davies, Jill M., Eleanor Lyon, and Diane Monti-Catania. 2000. *Safety Planning with Battered Women: Complex Lives, Difficult Choices.* Thousand Oaks, CA: Sage.

Deaton, Wendy S., and Michael Hertica, eds. 2001. *Therapist's Guide to Growing Free: A Manual for Survivors of Domestic Violence.* Binghamton, NY: Haworth.

Draucker, Claire B. 2000. *Counseling Survivors of Childhood Sexual Abuse.* Thousand Oaks, CA: Sage.

Dreikurs, Rudolph. 1964. *Children: The Challenge.* New York: Hawthorne.

Duncan, Stephen. 2000. "The Unique Strengths of Single Parent Families." *http://www.Singleparentcentral.com/sparticlesstrengths2.htm.*

Dunn, Dick. 1999. *Preparing to Marry Again.* Alpharetta, GA: Discipleship Resources.

Eisikovits, Zui, and Jeffrey Edelson, eds. 2000. *Future Interventions with Battered Women and Their Families.* Thousand Oaks, CA: Sage.

Everett, Barbara, and Ruth Gallop. 2000. *The Link Between Childhood Trauma and Mental Illness.* Thousand Oaks, CA: Sage.

Ganong, Lawrence H., and Marilyn Coleman. 1999. *Changing Families, Changing Responsibilities.* New York: Lawrence Erlbaum.

Gesell, Arnold. 1940. *The First Five Years of Life.* New York: Harper.

Gill, Gurjeet K. 1998. *Third Job Employed Couples' Management of Household Work Contradictions.* Brookfield, VT: Ashgate Publishing.

Ginott, Haim. 1965. *Between Parent and Child.* New York: Avon.

Glassman, Ronald. 2000. *Witness to the Pain.* Gordonsville, VA: Universe Publications.

Gordon, Thomas. 1978. *P.E.T. in Action.* New York: Bantam.

Grapes, Brian J., ed. 2001. *Child Abuse.* San Diego, CA: Greenhaven Press.

Greenberg, Vivian. 2000. *Children of a Certain Age: Adults and Their Aging Parents.* Missoula, MT: University Press.

Haupt, Arthur, and Thomas T. Kane. 1998 *International Population Handbook.* 4th ed. Washington, DC: Population Reference Bureau.

Herman, Judith L., and Lisa Hirschman. 2000. *Father-Daughter Incest.* Cambridge, MA: Harvard University Press.

Hertz, Rosanna, and Nancy Marshall. 2001. *Working Families: The Transformation of the American Home.* Los Angeles: University of California Press.

Hetherington, E. Mavis, ed. 2000. *Coping with Divorce.* Mahwah, NJ: Lawrence Erlbaum.

Hobbs, Christopher, and Jane Wynne. 2001. *Physical Signs of Child Abuse.* Philadelphia: W. B. Saunders.

Hobbs, Frank B., and Bonnie L. Damon. 1996. *65+ in the United States.* Washington, DC: U.S. Government Printing Office.

Hochschild, Arlie R. 2000. *The Time Bind: When Work Becomes Home and Home Becomes Work.* Gordonsville, VA: Henry Holt.

Ilardo, Joseph A., and Carole R. Rothman. 2001. *Are Your Parents Driving You Crazy? How to Resolve the Most Common Dilemmas with Aging Parents.* Acton, MA: Vanderwyk and Burnham.

Jackson, William. 2001. "Coping with Chronic Illness." Charter Hospital of Mobile, Alabama. http://www.sunflower.org/chronic.htm. Accessed 17 February 2001.

James, John W., Russell Friedman, and Leslie Landon Matthews. 2001. *When Children Grieve: For Adults to Help Children Deal with Death, Divorce, Moving, Pet Loss and Other Losses.* New York: HarperCollins Publishers.

Jeffers, Susan. 2001. *I'm Okay, But You're a Brat: Freeing Yourself from the Guilt of Parenthood.* Gordonsville, VA: Renaissance Books.

Jequier, Anne M. 2000. *Male Infertility: A Guide for the Clinician.* Williston, VT: Blackwell.

Kearney, R. Timothy. 2001. *Caring for Sexually Abused Children.* Downers Grove, IL: InterVarsity Press.

Kelley, Susan. C., and Dale Burg. 2000. *The Second Time Around: Everything You Need to Know to Make Your Remarriage Happy.* New York: William Morrow.

Ketterman, Grace. 2001. *Real Solutions for Abuse-Proofing Your Child.* Ann Arbor, MI: Sevant Publications.

Lauer, Robert H. and Jeannette C. Lauer. 1999. *Marriage and Family: The Quest for Intimacy.* 4th ed. New York: McGraw-Hill.

LaViolette, Alyce D., and Ola W. Barnett. 2000. *It Could Happen to Anyone: Why Battered Women Stay.* Thousand Oaks, CA: Sage.

Lee, Michael. 1999. *Marriage, Divorce and Remarriage.* Gordonsville, VA: Universe Publications.

LeMaistre, JoAnn. 1999. *After the Diagnosis.* Dillon, CO: Alpine Guild.

Lloyd-Still, John. 2000. *Family Violence.* San Diego, CA: Greenhaven Press.

Lofas, Jeannette. 1998. *Family Rules: Helping Stepfamilies and Single Parents Build Happy Homes.* New York: Kensington Publications.

MacDonald, Geraldine. 2001. *Effective Interventions for Child Abuse and Neglect.* New York: Wiley.

Maher, Bridget. 2000. "Divorce Reform: Forming Ties That Bind." *Family Research Council.* http://www.frc.org/get/is99h1.cfm. Accessed 7 November 2000.

Marcell, Jacqueline, and Rodman Shankle. 2000. *Elder Rage.* Chicago, IL: Imprint Publishers.

McFalls, Joseph. 1998. *Population: A Lively Introduction.* Washington, DC: Population Reference Bureau.

McKay, Matthew, et al. 2001. *The Divorce Book.* Edited by Kirk and Susan Johnson. Oakland, CA: New Harbinger.

National Center for Health Statistics. 2000. *Health, United States: 2000.* Hyattsville, MD: National Center for Health Statistics.

National Chronic Care Consortium. 2001. "Chronic Illness Care." http://www.nccconline.org/.

Nee, Tekla S. 2000. *The Mommy Zone: Tales from the Trenches of Parenthood.* New York: Xlibris.

Pino, Christopher J. 2001. *Divorce, Remarriage, and Blended Families: Divorce Counseling and Research Perspectives.* Gordonsville, VA: Universe Publications.

Pollard, Kelvin, and William O'Hare. 1999. *America's Racial and Ethnic Minorities*. Washington, DC: Population Reference Bureau.

Population Reference Bureau. 1997. *Population Handbook*. 4th ed. Washington, DC: Population Reference Bureau.

———. 2000. *America's Diversity and Growth: Signposts for the 21 Century*. Washington, DC: Population Reference Bureau.

Powell, Paul. 2001. "A Guide to Chronic Illness." http://www.webaccess.net/~evolvhiv/chronic.html. Accessed 17 February 2001.

Profitt, Norma J. 2001. *Women Survivors, Psychological Trauma, and the Politics of Resistance*. Binghamton, NY: Haworth.

Robertson, Betty B. 2000. *TLC for Aging Parents: A Practical Guide*. Kansas City, MO: Beacon Hill Press.

Rosenthal, Masood S., and M. Sara Khatamee. 2001. *The Fertility Sourcebook*. Lincolnwood, IL: Lowell House.

Rouse, Linda P. 2000. *You Are Not Alone: A Guide for Battered Women*. Holmes Beach, FL: Learning Publishers.

Rubin, Lillian B. 2000. *Tangled Lives: Daughters, Mothers, and the Crucible of Aging*. Westminster, MD: Beacon Press.

Sattler, Cheryl L. 2000. *Teaching to Transcend: Educating Women against Violence*. New York: State University of New York Press.

Schwartz-Kenney, Beth M., Michelle A. McCauley, and Michelle A. Epstein, eds. 2000. *Child Abuse: A Global View*. Westport, CT: Greenwood Press.

Shulman, Bernard H., and Raeann Berman. 2001. *How to Survive Your Aging Parents: So You and They Can Enjoy Life*. Chicago, IL: Surrey Books.

Skinner, B. F. 1953. *Science and Human Behavior*. New York: Macmillan.

Spraggins, R. E. 2000. *Women in the United States: A Profile*. Washington, DC: U.S. Government Printing Office.

Stephen, Elizabeth H. 1999. "Assisted Reproductive Technologies: Is the Price Too High?" *Population Today* 275: 1–7.

Sugarman, Stephen D. 1998. "Single Parent Families." In *All Our Families: New Policies for a New Century*. Edited by M. Mason. New York: Oxford University Press.

Swindoll, Charles R. 2000. *Divorce and Remarriage*. San Francisco: Insight Press.

Teyber, Edward. 2001. *Helping Children Cope with Divorce*. San Francisco: Jossey-Bass.

Treiser, Susan, and Robin K. Levinson. 2001. *Infertility*. East Rutherford, NY: Kensington Publishers.

Tubbs, Janet. 2000. *Child Abuse.* New York: Arcadia Press.

U.S. Bureau of Labor Statistics. 1999. *Handbook of Labor Statistics.* Washington, DC: U.S. Government Printing Office.

————. 2000. *Handbook of Labor Statistics.* Washington, DC: U.S. Government Printing Office.

U.S. Bureau of the Census. 2000a. *Statistical Abstract of the United States.* 120th Edition. Washington, DC: U.S. Government Printing Office.

————. 2000b. *Marital Status and Living Arrangements.* February 11. Washington, DC: U.S. Government Printing Office.

————. 2000c. *Current Population Reports.* March 15. Washington, DC: U.S. Government Printing Office.

————. 2000d. *The Older Population in the United States: Population Characteristics.* September 15. Washington, DC: U.S. Government Printing Office.

————. 2000e. *Census Bureau Facts for Features: Americans with Disabilities.* January 15. Washington, DC: U.S. Government Printing Office.

U.S. Department of Commerce. 2001. *United States Department of Commerce News.* Washington, DC: U.S. Government Printing Office.

U.S. Department of Health and Human Services. 1999. *United States Health Facts.* Hyattsville, MD: National Center for Health Statistics.

Visher, Emily, and John S. Visher. 1996. *Therapy with Stepfamilies.* New York: Brunner/Mazel.

Wallerstein, Judith S., Julia Lewis, and Sandra Blakeslee. 2000. *The Unexpected Legacy of Divorce: A Twenty-Five Year Landmark Study.* Westport, CT: Hyperion.

Westman, Jack. 2001. *Parenthood in America.* Green Bay: University of Wisconsin Press.

Williams, Christopher D. 2001. *The Fastest Way to Get Pregnant Naturally.* Westport, CT: Hyperion.

World Health Organization. 1999. *Her Way to Work: The Road to Quality Jobs for Women.* Washington, DC: International Labour Organization.

————. 2000a. *ABC of Women Workers. Rights and Gender Equality.* Washington, DC: International Labour Organization.

————. 2000b. *World Labor Report.* Washington, DC: International Labour Organization.

4

Chronology

1900 **Family Life at the Turn of the Century**

Marriages per 1,000 of Total Population: 10.1
Median Age at First Marriage: Men, 25.9; Women, 21.6
Divorces per 1,000 of Total Population: 1.3
Fertility Rate of Women: 3.5
Percentage of Married Women in Labor Force: 4.6

1902 Psychosocial theorist Erik Erikson born in Frankfurt, Germany.

1903 Noted child-care expert Benjamin Spock born in New Haven, Connecticut.

Women's Trade Union League of New York is founded, an organization dedicated to the rights of working women and to women's suffrage.

1908 Sex researcher Edward Carpenter publishes ground-breaking text *The Intermediate Sex,* an examination of homosexuality.

1910 **A Decade of Family Change**

Marriages per 1,000 of Total Population: 11.2
Median Age at First Marriage: Men, 25.1; Women, 21.6
Divorces per 1,000 of Total Population: 1.2
Fertility Rate of Women: 3.4
Percentage of Married Women in Labor Force: 5.6

1916   Margaret Sanger establishes the first birth control clinic in New York City. The concept of "planned" parenthood opens a new chapter in the reproductive lives of women and men.

1920   **A Decade of Family Change**

Marriages per 1,000 of Total Population: 11.9
Median Age at First Marriage: Men, 24.6; Women, 21.2
Divorces per 1,000 of Total Population: 1.7
Fertility Rate of Women: 3.3
Percentage of Married Women in Labor Force: 9.3

The Nineteenth Amendment is ratified and extends suffrage to women. No United States citizen can be denied the right to vote based on his or her sex.

The Department of Labor establishes The Women's Bureau, an organization designed to promote equal rights and protective legislation for women.

1923   The Equal Rights Amendment, the most comprehensive legal statement promoting sexual equality, is introduced into Congress. It has never been ratified.

Arnold Gesell establishes the Clinic of Child Development at Yale University. Gesell provides parents and educators alike with detailed information on childhood growth, including developmental milestones and specific behavioral sequences.

1926   Publication of Jean Piaget's first book in the United States, *Language and Thought of the Child.*

Estimated cost of raising a child from birth to age 18 is $16,337.

1928   John Watson publishes *Psychological Care of the Infant and Child,* one of the nation's earliest child-rearing publications.

1930 **A Decade of Family Change**

Marriages per 1,000 of Total Population: 9.1
Median Age at First Marriage: Men, 24.3; Women, 21.3
Divorces per 1,000 of Total Population: 1.6
Fertility Rate of Women: 2.3
Percentage of Married Women in Labor Force: 11.4

American Institute of Family Relations is founded in Los Angeles, one of the nation's first centers for marriage therapy.

1938 National Council on Family Relations, an organization designed for family professionals to plan and act together on concerns relevant to families, is founded.

1940 **A Decade of Family Change**

Marriages per 1,000 of Total Population: 9.2
Median Age at First Marriage: Men, 24.3; Women, 21.5
Divorces per 1,000 of Total Population: 2.1
Fertility Rate of Women: 2.2
Percentage of Married Women in Labor Force: 15.2

1942 Establishment of the American Association for Marriage and Family Therapy, which is geared to the professional development of marriage and family therapists throughout the United States, Canada, and abroad.

1945 Benjamin Spock's *Baby and Child Care*, an enormously popular book on child rearing, is published.

1948 Alfred Kinsey and a team of researchers publish *Sexual Behavior in the Human Male*.

1950 **A Decade of Family Change**

Marriages per 1,000 of Total Population: 11.1
Median Age at First Marriage: Men, 22.8; Women, 20.3
Divorces per 1,000 of Total Population: 2.6
Fertility Rate of Women: 3.1

1950   Percentage of Married Women in Labor Force: 24.6
(cont.)

1951   Average family income is $3,700. Fewer than 12 million families have incomes over $5,000.

1953   Alfred Kinsey and a team of researchers publish *Sexual Behavior in the Human Female.*

1954   Family therapist Murray Bowen becomes the first director of the Family Division at the National Institute of Mental Health (NIMH).

1957   Parents Without Partners, a support organization devoted to the welfare and interests of single parents and their families, is founded.

1958   Therapists Don Jackson and Jay Haley are recognized as influential figures in shaping the family therapy movement. Working in Palo Alto, California, the two explore family therapy against the backdrop of communications analysis.

1960   **A Decade of Family Change**

Marriages per 1,000 of Total Population: 8.5
Median Age at First Marriage: Men, 22.8; Women, 20.3
Divorces per 1,000 of Total Population: 2.2
Fertility Rate of Women: 3.6
Percentage of Married Women in Labor Force: 31.9

A middle-income, two-parent family with a child born this year can expect to spend about $25,230 for food, shelter, and other necessities to raise that youngster over the next seventeen years.

One-half million unmarried couples live together.

1961   The first family therapy research journal, *Family Process,* is founded by Don Johnson, Jay Haley, and Nathan Ackerman.

1963   Congress passes the Equal Pay Act, making it illegal for employers to pay a woman less than a man for the same job.

Family therapist Jay Haley publishes *Strategies of Psychotherapy*.

1964   Family therapist and noted researcher Virginia Satir publishes *Conjoint Family Therapy*.

1966   The National Organization for Women is formed to promote equality in such areas as family life, the workplace, and the educational sphere.

William Masters and Virginia Johnson co-author the book *Human Sexual Response*. In it, the researchers detail four physiological phases that accompany sexual arousal.

1967   Congress passes the Age Discrimination in Employment Act, which prohibits employers, employment agencies, and labor organizations from discriminating against employees who are over 40 years old.

1969   California enacts the Family Law Act, thus becoming the first state to legislate a "no-fault" divorce concept. The no-fault concept recognizes the breakdown of a marriage as a ground for divorce and helps reduce the adversarial process often associated with traditional divorce proceedings. In the years that follow, nearly every state will adopt some form or variation of the no-fault divorce concept.

1970 A Decade of Family Change

Marriages per 1,000 of Total Population: 10.6
Median Age at First Marriage: Men, 23.2; Women, 20.8
Divorces per 1,000 of Total Population: 3.5
Fertility Rate of Women: 2.4
Percentage of Married Women in Labor Force: 40.5

1971   National Organization for Nonparents, an organization promoting voluntary childlessness, is established.

1972   The Equal Rights Amendment (ERA) is passed by both the Senate and the House of Representatives and sent to the states for their action. However, over a ten-year period, only 35 of the required 38 states (three-fourths of all states must ratify a constitutional amendment) ratified the ERA.

1973   *Roe v. Wade* Supreme Court ruling declares that the decision to abort is one exclusively between the mother and her doctors during the first three months of pregnancy.

Children's Defense Fund, an organization designed to investigate, plan, and execute reforms for children in both public and private institutions, is launched. A particular emphasis is placed on poor, minority, and disabled children.

The American Psychiatric Association removes homosexuality from its official diagnostic manual of mental illness.

1974   The birth of the National Clearinghouse on Child Abuse and Neglect. The organization provides information and technical assistance on child abuse, neglect, and related child welfare issues.

More than 15 percent of all children under age six—2.8 million youngsters—live in single-parent households.

The National Gay Task Force is founded in New York City.

Family therapist Salvador Minuchin publishes *Families and Family Therapy,* a classic text identifying family structural components, such as subsystems and boundaries.

1976   The federal tax code is changed so that working parents may claim a tax credit: up to 20 percent of the first $2,000 spent on the care of one child (a maximum of $400), up to 50 percent of the first $4,000 for the care of two or more children (a maximum of $800).

Benjamin Spock's *Baby and Child Care* enters its fourth printing and has now sold over 29 million copies.

California's Supreme Court ruling in *Marvin v. Marvin* introduces the concept of "palimony," a type of alimony given to a partner after a cohabitation relationship terminates.

1978   The Pregnancy Discrimination Act bans employment discrimination against pregnant women.

Louise Brown, the world's first "test-tube" (in-vitro fertilization) baby is born in Oldham, England.

Establishment of the Center for Parent Education, a national organization addressing the needs of families and children.

Over one million unwed adolescent females become pregnant.

1979   Officially designated as "The Year of the Child" by the United Nations.

One infant out of every six is born out of wedlock.

1980   A Decade of Family Change

Marriages per 1,000 of Total Population: 10.6
Median Age at First Marriage: Men, 24.7; Women, 22.1
Divorces per 1,000 of Total Population: 5.2
Fertility Rate of Women: 1.9
Percentage of Married Women in Labor Force: 49.9

First baby delivered by a surrogate mother in Louisville, Kentucky. The couple, childless because the wife was unable to conceive, paid the surrogate mother to have the baby using the husband's stored sperm.

First United States infant born at an in-vitro fertilization clinic at Eastern Virginia Medical School.

1980   Family studies researcher Ellen Galinsky publishes the
(cont.) book *Between Generations: The Six Stages of Parenthood.* In it,
Galinsky provides a sequential narrative of how parents'
self-images are shaped by interactions with their children.

1982   Congress establishes the House Select Committee on
Children, Youth, and Families.

1984   Approximately 7 million children 13 and younger are designated as "latchkey" children. They are without adult
care before and after school while their parents work.

The number of divorces declines for the first time in two
decades.

1985   Forty percent of single-parent families headed by white
women and sixty percent headed by African American
women live in poverty.

Almost 2 million unmarried couples cohabit, an increase
of over 300 percent from the previous decade.

One infant in five is born to an unmarried woman.

1987   Over 3.8 million babies are born, the most since 1964.

1989   Families and Work Institute is founded, a nonprofit organization promoting mutually supportive connections
among workplaces, families, and communities.

The number of children in child-care centers doubles
since 1977.

1990 **A Decade of Family Change**

Marriages per 1,000 of Total Population: 9.8
Median Age at First Marriage: Men, 26.1; Women, 23.9
Divorces per 1,000 of Population: 4.7
Fertility Rate of Women: 2.2
Percentage of Married Women in Labor Force: 58.4

The National Center for Fathering, an organization dedicated to developing practical resources to prepare men for fatherhood and the challenges associated with this parental role, is founded.

1992   Family Institute of New Jersey is founded by Monica McGoldrick.

1993   Family and Medical Leave Act makes it illegal to fire employees who must take time off to care for babies or ill family members. The law mandates up to twelve weeks of leave per year for various family medical emergencies and for the birth or adoption of a child. It also stipulates that employers must continue to provide health-care benefits and that returning workers must be given their old job or an equivalent position.

Hawaii's Supreme Court rules that the ban placed on gay marriages is unconstitutional because it involves sexual discrimination. The case, *Baehr v. Miike*, was sent back to a lower court for further consideration. The debate continued over a constitutional amendment to ban same-sex marriages and render the courts' ruling null and void. In 1998, legislators would pass an anti-gay marriage amendment.

Of the 3.6 million families with an adult welfare recipient, 90 percent are single-parent families, most of whom are headed by women.

1994   Violence Against Women Act combines tough law enforcement strategies with safeguards for victims of domestic violence and sexual assault. It increases penalties for sex offenders and domestic abusers, provides additional funding to assist state and local law enforcement agencies, and enhances restitution for victims of domestic violence.

National Fatherhood Initiative, a broad-based organization designed to heighten the visibility of fatherhood and make effective fathering a national priority, is launched.

1995   About 25 percent of babies are born out of wedlock.

1996   Jay Haley publishes *Learning and Teaching Family Therapy.*

1998   Alliance for Children and Families, an international association representing more than 350 private, nonprofit child and family oriented organizations is founded.

The popular image of the "traditional family"—a married couple with children and in which only the husband works—declines to 6.8 million, representing only 24 percent of all households.

The U.S. Department of Health and Human Services reports an estimated 903,000 cases of child maltreatment. Of the reported cases 53.5 percent suffered neglect, 22.7 percent were physically abused, 11.5 percent were sexually abused, and the remaining percentages suffered psychological abuse and medical neglect. Over one-quarter of the reported cases suffered more than one type of maltreatment. Over 1,000 children died of abuse and neglect.

About 28 percent of all children under age 18 live with only one parent.

1999   A middle-income, two-parent family with a child born this year can expect to spend about $160,140 for food, shelter, and other necessities to raise that youngster over the next 17 years.

The state of Vermont votes to enact into law a bill recognizing civil unions between gay or lesbian couples. Civil union, a legal institution parallel to marriage, grants the same rights and benefits to same-sex couples as married couples.

2000   **A Decade of Family Change**

Marriages per 1,000 of Total Population: 8.3
Median Age at First Marriage: Men, 26.7; Women, 25.1
Divorces per 1,000 of Total Population: 4.2
Fertility Rate of Women: 2.1
Percentage of Married Women in Labor Force: 62.1

5

Biographical Sketches

Gordon Allport (1897–1967)

Gordon Allport was born in Montezuma, Indiana. He received his Ph.D. from Harvard University in 1922. Although originally interested in philosophy and economics, he developed a strong interest in psychology, especially the study of personality. Following his graduation, Allport traveled abroad for two years and studied in a number of European cities, including Berlin, Hamburg, and Cambridge. During this time, Allport had the opportunity to meet and share ideas with a number of notable psychologists, including Sigmund Freud.

After serving as an assistant professor of psychology at Dartmouth College, Allport returned to Harvard University in 1930. In 1937 he was appointed chairman of the psychology department and earned the distinction of being appointed the first Richard Cabot Professor of Social Ethics. Remaining at Harvard until his death in 1967, Allport was also instrumental in developing the Department of Social Relations at the university.

Allport's contributions to the field of psychology are both numerous and diverse. His most significant involvement was in the areas of personality and social psychology, including an extensive investigation of adult maturity, values, and communication. His analysis of maturity, in particular, helps us to better understand how family relationships are forged and maintained throughout life. He described how mature adults bring recognized skills and competencies to their relationships, including heightened levels of self-insight and understanding. Mature adults have learned to accept themselves as well as their partners,

including shortcomings and weaknesses. In addition, their interactions are characterized by such important dimensions as empathy, confidence in self-expression, and a realistic appraisal of
needs and purposes. From Allport's perspective, all of this contributes to the likelihood that a relationship will be guided by a
common purpose and by shared goals and values.

Allport was president of the American Psychological Association in 1937 and served as editor of the Journal of Abnormal
and Social Psychology from 1937 to 1949. During his professional
career, he received numerous honors and awards, including the
American Psychological Association Distinguished Scientific
Contribution Award in 1959.

Urie Bronfenbrenner (1917–)

Urie Bronfenbrenner is one of the leading figures in the field of
ecological psychology, a major theory of lifespan development
(the growth of humans from birth to death). He was born in
Moscow. Bronfenbrenner spent many years of his professional
life developing this conceptual framework, which is best seen as
a progressive, mutual accommodation between an active, growing human and the changing properties of the settings in which
the person lives. The manner in which family relationships converge within these settings, as well as within the larger contexts
where the settings are embedded, is detailed in Bronfenbrenner's
numerous articles and books.

Bronfenbrenner is also internationally known for his cross-
cultural research in such locations as the Soviet Union, China,
Israel, Nova Scotia, and Western Europe. His research in the
Soviet Union during the 1960s earned critical acclaim among
developmental researchers and child-care experts. His research
focused on child rearing in the family and in collective settings,
and how Soviet children compared with youngsters from the
United States. While in the Soviet Union, Bronfenbrenner also
served as exchange scientist at the Institute of Psychology in
Moscow.

In the United States, Bronfenbrenner is well known as a
developmental and social psychologist who translates the results
of social research into public policy. He is one of the founding
fathers of Project Head Start (a federally funded early childhood
education program established in 1965) and has served as a frequent advisor to the federal government on matters affecting

national policy on children. Bronfenbrenner served for many years as professor of psychology and of child development and family studies in the College of Human Ecology at Cornell University.

Robert N. Butler (1927–)

Robert N. Butler is an internationally known gerontologist, author, and consultant. He was born in New York and received a medical degree from Columbia University's College of Physicians and Surgeons in 1953. He has been Brookdale Professor and chairman of the Gerald and May Ellen Ritter Department of Geriatrics and Adult Development of Mount Sinai Medical Center in New York City since 1982. As chairman of the first Department of Geriatrics in an American medical school, Butler is a leader in improving the quality of life for older people, including within the family context.

Before he came to Mount Sinai, Butler worked at the National Institutes of Health, where he created the National Institute on Aging in 1976 and served as its first director. Under his leadership, the need for federal funding for research in gerontology gained recognition. He was particularly outspoken about the few service-related research activities available to enhance the health and social service delivery to the elderly in terms of efficiency, cost, and quality. Butler felt that future research on aging had to be unusually inventive, taking advantage of a broad range of collaboration while seeking to telescope research's natural development.

A prolific writer, Butler won the Pulitzer Prize in 1976 for his book *Why Survive? Being Old in America,* a penetrating social analysis of the elderly in the United States. He is a member of the Institute of Medicine of the National Academy of Sciences and is a founding fellow of the American Geriatrics Society. Butler has also served as a consultant to the United States Senate Special Committee on Aging, the National Institute of Mental Health, the Commonwealth Fund, and numerous other organizations.

Milton H. Erickson (1901–1980)

Milton H. Erickson was born in Aurum, Nevada. He is considered one of the founders of "strategic family therapy," a short-term approach to counseling that emphasizes problem-focused intervention. Erickson was known for his development of pragmatic and flexible therapeutic approaches, as well as helping his clients devise alternative problem-solving strategies. Erickson was also considered one of the nation's leading practitioners of medical hypnosis.

Erickson completed his undergraduate degree in psychology at the University of Wisconsin and received his medical degree at Colorado General Hospital. Among his appointments, Erickson served as chief psychiatrist at Worcester State Hospital (MA), director of psychiatric research at Wayne County General Hospital and Infirmary (MI), and professor of psychiatry at Wayne State University and Michigan State University.

Throughout his professional life, Erickson maintained a private practice and spent time researching, consulting, and conducting seminars on strategic family therapy. He was the founding president of the American Society for Clinical Hypnosis as well as the founder and editor of that organization's professional journal. Erickson was also a fellow of both the American Psychiatric Association and the American Psychological Association.

Erik H. Erikson (1902–1994)

Erik H. Erikson was born in Frankfurt, Germany, and was one of the world's foremost psychoanalytic scholars. After finishing high school Erikson declared a "moratorium" on his education and visited various parts of Europe to study art. During one of his journeys, he was given an opportunity to study child analysis at the Vienna Psychoanalytic Institute. It was at this institute, under the guidance of Anna Freud, among others, that Erikson launched a brilliant career in the field of developmental psychology.

When Hitler rose to power, Erikson left his native Europe and served as a research associate in psychiatry, first in the Harvard Medical School and then at Yale University from 1936 to 1939. Following his stay at Yale, he accepted research and teaching posts at the University of California from 1939 to 1951. From 1951 through 1960, Erikson was senior consultant at the Austen-Riggs Center and a visiting professor at the University of Pittsburgh School of Medicine. He then became professor of human development and lecturer on psychiatry at Harvard University, from which he retired in 1970 as professor emeritus.

Erikson focused considerable energy on exploring the individual's personality development throughout the life cycle. Following Freud, who placed emphasis on psychosexual stages of development, Erikson stressed *psychosocial development* throughout life. At each stage of development, he theorized, from birth to old age, is a psychosocial crisis that must be resolved. Harmonious personality development is characterized by the successful resolution of these psychosocial crises.

Sigmund Freud (1856–1939)

Sigmund Freud was an Austrian physician who forged a revolutionary theory of personality in which sexual motivation played a dominant role. Born in what is now Czechoslovakia, Freud received a medical degree from the University of Vienna in 1881. While practicing medicine in clinics, he became interested in neurophysiology, especially the functions of the brain. He spent considerable time seeking to understand abnormal brain functions and mental disorders, a pursuit that would eventually bring him to the fields of psychiatry and psychology.

Gradually, through treating neurotic patients with such techniques as hypnosis and free association (asking the patient to say spontaneously whatever came into his head), Freud became convinced that sexual conflict was the cause of most neuroses. Freud traced such conflict to the forces of sexual and aggressive urges and the clashes of these forces with the codes of conduct required by society.

Eventually Freud developed *psychoanalytic theory*, which proposes, among other things, that our past plays an important role in determining our present behavior. Fundamental to Freud's theory are the notions that behavior is unconsciously motivated and that neuroses often have their origins in early childhood experiences that have subsequently become repressed. Freud also suggested that sexual urges are responsible for most human motivation. He held that because sexual thoughts and needs are often repressed they are likely to provide unconscious motivation.

Although many of Freud's views are controversial, many researchers in the field of lifespan development have been influenced by his theories, such as psychosexual development. According to this theory, the development and maturation of sexual and other body parts has great impact on early life experiences. Critics of psychoanalytic theory claim that many of Freud's concepts cannot be scientifically measured and are based on poor methodology. Some argue that his theories were bound to nineteenth-century Vienna and, furthermore, that he downplayed female sexuality.

Nevertheless, Freud's theories have lost none of their luster over the years. Proponents point out how Freud's ideas have extended into many disciplines including history, literature, philosophy, and the arts. However we view Freud's specific theories, we cannot deny the power of his intellect and the strength of his motivation to discover new dimensions of human behavior.

Erich Fromm (1900–1980)

Erich Fromm was a noted psychoanalytic scholar who explored the nature of productive and nonproductive facets of behavior within interpersonal relationships, including expressions of love. Fromm trained at the Berlin Psychoanalytic Institute and received his Ph.D. in psychology from the University of Heidelberg in 1922. He held teaching positions at Columbia University, Yale University, New York University, and Michigan State University.

Fromm maintained that men and women sometimes tend to alienate themselves and demonstrate hostile and aggressive forms of behavior. Fromm concentrated his energies on studying such negative behavior, particularly ways to overcome it. His works are directed toward the regulation of humanity, including the need for people to unite with others and to feel part of a group, such as within a family, church, or nation. Fromm saw control as a necessary way of life, including the setting of limits through boundaries, rules, and regulations.

In his writings, Fromm often stressed the importance of relating to others in a loving, caring fashion. In so doing, he felt that individuals nurtured their own integrity and self-worth. He stressed the importance of altruistic love, which embodies the unselfish concern for the well-being of another person. Fromm felt that loving should be an act of giving rather than receiving, and he believed it should embrace such elements as respect, concern, and understanding.

Ellen Galinsky (1942–)

Ellen Galinsky is a professor of the Bank Street College of Education in New York and a specialist in human development and family relations. Galinsky was born in Pittsburgh, Pennsylvania, and received a graduate degree from the Bank Street College of

Education in 1970. She is recognized for exploring the developmental dynamics of parenthood, particularly how it unfolds through a series of predictable stages.

In all, Galinsky maintains that the experience of parenthood consists of six stages. She feels that these stages bring a progressive transformation of parental self-image. Parents mentally picture the way they think things should be, especially in terms of their own personal behavior and that of their children. If such images are successfully achieved, satisfaction and happiness are experienced. If they are not attained, parents typically feel anger, resentment, and even depression. Consequently, parents' self-images—not to mention parental development—are shaped by interactions with their children. Put another way, a child's development leads the parent from one stage to the next. The following is a summary of Galinsky's stages of parenthood.

Parental-Image Stage. This first stage occurs when the baby is born. During this time, parents seek to treat their children as they would have liked their parents to treat them. Images of parenthood are constructed around a desire for perfection, even though most adults are fully aware that child-rearing perfection is nearly impossible.

Nurturing Stage. The nurturing stage is the second phase of parental development and lasts approximately through the second year of the child's life. Forming bonds of attachment to the baby is the major chore at this point, in addition to learning how much and when to give to oneself, one's spouse, job, and friends.

Authority Stage. The authority stage, between two and four years, is a phase where adults critically question their effectiveness as parental figures. For the child, this is a time of newly discovered social independence, testing of new powers, and saying "no." Witnessing such developments may cause parents to discover flaws in their images of parental perfection. Parental growth at this time may well be measured by rejecting the images that are simply unrealistic.

Integrative Stage. The integrative stage, encompassing the preschool years through middle childhood, is the fourth phase proposed by Galinsky. Further childhood gains in autonomy and initiative, as well as expanding social horizons, force parents to re-examine and then test their own implicit theories about the way things should be ideally and how they are in fact. Discrepancies between these two polarities are difficult for adults groping for effective parenting skills to accept.

Independent Teenage Years. During this stage, adolescents struggle for greater levels of freedom, responsibility, and, in some cases, emancipation from the home. In perhaps one of parenthood's most impactful stages, adults must learn to redefine authority due to the teenager's growing independence, while lending support to the growing pains characteristic of adolescence.

Departure Stage. The departure stage, approximately after age 18, occurs when adolescents leave the home. For the parents, this final stage becomes a period of assessment and evaluation of their overall past performances. Taking stock of the entire experience of parenthood reveals positive as well as negative features: the loose or crumbling pieces and the cracks, in addition to the cohesiveness, of their whole lives. Such an overview at this time in the family cycle, coupled with the assessments inherent in each of the previous stages, provides adults with a thought provoking analysis and narrative of their performance as parents.

Arnold L. Gesell (1880–1961)

Arnold L. Gesell was a leading child development researcher and was influential in shaping child-rearing strategies in the early part of the twentieth century. Born in Alma, Wisconsin, Gesell obtained a Ph.D. degree from Clark University in 1906 and an M.D. degree from Yale University in 1915.

Among Gesell's more notable contributions to the field of child psychology was the establishment of the Clinic of Child Development at Yale during the 1930s. At the clinic, Gesell stressed the notion that growth and development take place in orderly stages and sequences. He expended considerable energy in exploring this principle, leading him to devise numerous norms of infant development and to undertake detailed investigations of specific behavior sequences such as walking and prehension.

Gesell also translated this developmental-maturational theme into applied child-rearing formulations for parents. Because of this, Gesell was largely viewed as an authoritative figure in the child-rearing movement during the 1930s and 1940s and his numerous books and publications were sought by parents as well as professionals. His popularity was likely due to his ability to translate the theoretical into the practical world of everyday parenting and child development.

Roger Gould (1935–)

Roger Gould is a psychoanalyst and a professor of psychiatry at the University of California at Los Angeles who created a theory of adult personality development. Gould was born in Milwaukee and received a medical degree from Northwestern University in 1959. His theory suggests that adulthood is not a plateau but rather a time for the continuous unfolding of the self. Gould's primary emphasis is on the importance of striving toward adult levels of consciousness and discarding irrational childhood notions about oneself and the world in general.

According to Gould, irrational childhood ideas have a tendency to restrict maturity and responsibility. These false assumptions frequently embody the concept of parental dependency. Ideally, as life experience builds, adults must abandon these unwarranted expectations, rigid rules, and inflexible roles, which hinder individual autonomy and independence. If this is accomplished, in time adults will come to be true owners of their selves with a more mature level of consciousness.

Gould maintains that young adulthood, in particular, is a critical period of development, since it is at this point that individuals realize how they can begin to take control of their lives. In particular, four irrational childhood assumptions need to be questioned: Children will always live with their parents; parents will always be there to help when things go wrong or not exactly as expected; parents can always offer a simplified version (and solution) to complicated inner realities; and no evil or death exists in the world.

Gould proposes that by the time young adulthood is reached, individuals know intellectually that these assumptions are factually incorrect, but emotionally they retain hidden control of adult life until significant events unveil them as emotional and intellectual fantasies. The gradual shedding of these false assumptions, a process that lasts throughout adulthood, signifies an individual's shift from childhood consciousness to more mature levels of adult reasoning.

Jay Haley (1931–)

Jay Haley is a well-known family therapist, teacher, and author. Haley holds degrees from the University of California at Los

Angeles, the University of California at Berkeley, and Stanford University. He is one of the founders of family therapy, having earned that distinction with Don Jackson and other notable therapists at the Mental Research Institute in Palo Alto, California, in 1958. Haley promoted "strategic therapy," which places an emphasis on short-term, focused efforts to solve specific problems.

In addition to his work at the Mental Research Institute, Haley served as director of family therapy research at the Philadelphia Child Guidance Clinic and was a consultant to the Family Committee Group for the Advancement of Psychiatry. He also served as editor of the research journal *Family Process*. Haley has also taught at the University of Maryland, Howard University, and the University of Pennsylvania.

Haley regularly conducts workshops and seminars on family therapy. He has also authored numerous books, including *Strategies of Psychotherapy, Problem-Solving Therapy, Uncommon Therapy, Leaving Home*, and *Ordeal Therapy*. His latest book, *Learning and Teaching Therapy*, was published in 1996.

Harry F. Harlow (1905–1981)

Harry F. Harlow was a psychologist who conducted laboratory research on various aspects of infant attachment and the need for contact and comfort. Harlow was born in Fairfield, Iowa, and received his Ph.D. from Stanford University in 1930. He taught at the University of Wisconsin for many years and was president of the American Psychological Association in 1958. He also was editor of the *Journal of Comparative and Physiological Psychology* and a member of the National Academy of Science.

Harlow's long-term research focused on the contact-comfort behaviors of rhesus monkeys and the manner in which they sought attachment and security. In Harlow's now classic studies, two surrogate mothers were built and placed in a cage; one was constructed of wire meshing and the other of the same material covered with a terry cloth wrapping. Each "mother" was equipped with a nursing bottle (the nipple of which protruded through the chest) and a light bulb behind the body, which provided heat for the infant.

The infant monkeys were then divided into two groups; Group A could receive milk from only the nursing bottle placed in the wire mother, whereas Group B could receive milk from only the nursing bottle of the cloth-covered mother. The monkeys in Group A fed from the wire mother, but they gradually spent less time with her. Eventually, these monkeys took nourishment and then spent the intervening time with the more comforting cloth mother. Several infants even clung to the cloth mother while reaching over to feed from the wire mother. On the other hand, the infants in Group B spent considerable time clinging to the soft covering of their cloth mother and almost never ventured over to the other wire figure.

The cloth mother also played a central role in reducing the infant's fear and anxiety. This was apparent when a strange object (a mechanical teddy bear) was introduced into the cage with the infant, the cloth mother, and the wire mother. The infant invariably ran to the cloth mother and clung to her for security. After its fear was reduced by this form of contact and comfort, the infant would venture short distances from the mother and eventually attempt to explore the new object.

Harlow also studied the later behavior of those monkeys not benefiting from a real mother. It was learned that the mother's absence had severely hampered the monkeys' normal development, particularly in the formation of attachment bonds as well as in other aspects of social behavior. Whereas the monkeys reared with cloth mothers showed no overt problems in infancy, some were retarded later in life when compared with monkeys brought up by real mothers. More specifically, the experimental monkeys became socially maladjusted, ignoring others, and frequently passing time by biting and hugging themselves. Later, some of the females in the study group proved to be poor mothers, neglecting and abusing their young. However, when placed in the company of normal monkeys, the socially isolated monkeys began to recover from the effects of their experimental environment. This was largely because the normal monkeys encouraged social interaction and play behavior and discouraged solitary behavior.

All of Harlow's research provided much insight into the contact-comfort motive as well as attachment behaviors. His research showed that satisfaction of the hunger drive does not by itself promote and nurture the infant's attachment to the mother, a belief held for years by many. Rather, the attachment to the mother is encouraged by the need to establish contact with something that can offer comfort, softness, and warmth. Moreover, this need often manifests itself in the young child's selection of a cuddly or huggable doll or stuffed animal, called a *transitional object* by child psychologists. The use of a transitional object is considered a normal phase of child development, particularly when youngsters encounter novel, irritating, or threatening situations. Transitional objects are typically outgrown as immature and dependent behavior is replaced with more independence and a more secure sense of self.

Robert J. Havighurst (1900–1991)

Robert J. Havighurst made many contributions to the field of lifespan development, most notably the concept of *developmental tasks*. He was born in Wisconsin and received a Ph.D. from Ohio State University in 1924. Havighurst, who served as a professor of human development at the University of Chicago, stressed the importance of mastering developmental tasks appropriate to a given life stage. In his research, he used Erik Erikson's concepts of the interaction between the individual and society and noted that most societies appear to have a timetable for the accomplishment of various tasks.

According to Havighurst, a developmental task is unique to each major stage of the lifespan (e. g., infancy, adolescence), and may originate from physical maturation; from the pressure of the surrounding society on the person; and from the desires, aspirations, and values of the emerging personality. For example, children must learn to walk and talk, to distinguish right from wrong, and so forth. Adults, too, have developmental tasks appropriate to various stages of their personal and social growth. Embarking on a vocation and assuming civic responsibility are examples of adult developmental tasks. Achievement of developmental tasks is not only a building block to success, but it also helps future tasks lead toward happiness. Failure to satisfactorily complete these tasks can lead to unhappiness, difficulty with accomplishing future tasks, and disapproval by society.

Magnus Hirschfeld (1868–1935)

Magnus Hirschfeld, who founded the Institute of Sexual Science in Berlin, was a German physician best remembered for his progressive and outspoken views on human sexuality. Following his graduation from medical school in 1894, Hirschfeld devoted much of his attention to studying problems in sexual functioning and was particularly drawn to the study of sexual deviations and their etiology.

Homosexuality was of particular interest to Hirschfeld, and he wrote several books on the topic. In a departure from the thinking of the day, Hirschfeld maintained that homosexuality was biologically determined and not a disease or a crime. He felt strongly that homosexuals should be protected by law and not prosecuted. Furthermore, Hirschfeld argued that therapy should be aimed at helping clients accept themselves as members of what he called "the third sex" and at assisting them to be useful citizens.

During the 1920s, Hirschfeld was instrumental in organizing the World League for Sexual Reform. This organization brought professionals in the field of human sexuality together and promoted such causes as sexual equality, sex education, and the prevention of sexually transmitted diseases. Hirschfeld's many professional contributions and innovative ideas helped to construct a foundation for the infant field of human sexuality research.

Don Jackson (1920–1968)

Don Jackson was one of the early contributors to the field of family therapy. He graduated from Stanford University's School of Medicine in 1943 and launched a career that spanned teaching, therapy, and research. Many leaders in the field of family therapy acknowledge Jackson as a major contributor to our understanding of family dynamics and therapeutic intervention. More specifically, Jackson was instrumental in developing "interactional family therapy," which emphasizes that the key to understanding family members is to focus on their present-day behaviors, not past influences.

Before his untimely death in 1968 at the age of 48, Jackson published more than 125 articles and book chapters and seven books. Two of the titles he coauthored, *Mirages of Marriage* and *Human Communication,* are regarded as classic family therapy textbooks. Additionally, he cofounded the journal *Family Process* with colleagues Jay Haley and Nathan Ackerman. He also helped to launch the national publishing firm Science and Behavior Books.

In 1958, Jackson helped to establish the Mental Research Institute in Palo Alto, California, and worked with such notable therapists as Jay Haley and Virginia Satir. Among his many honors and awards, Jackson won the Frieda Fromm-Reichmann Award for contributions to understanding schizophrenia, the Edward R. Strecker Award for contributions to in-patient treatment of hospitalized patients, and a special citation from the American Psychiatric Association.

Alfred C. Kinsey (1894–1956)

Alfred C. Kinsey ranks as one of the most influential human sexuality researchers in the United States. He was born in Hoboken, New Jersey, and received his Ph.D. in biology from Harvard in 1920. He became an instructor in biology at Indiana University shortly thereafter, and earned academic recognition for his work in the field of taxonomy (the science of identifying, naming, and classifying organisms). He remained on the faculty at Indiana University until his death in 1956.

Kinsey launched his detailed investigation of human sexual behavior in 1938. Over a span of ten years, Kinsey and his staff had interviewed over 11,000 individuals (about 5,300 males and 5,900 females) using a sex history questionnaire that contained 521 items. The subjects represented a cross-section of geographical location, education, occupation, socioeconomic level, age, and religion in the United States. However, only white male and white female respondents were included in the published findings. This was because Kinsey deemed the population sample of black respondents insufficient in size for making analyses comparable to those made for whites.

In 1948, the research team of Kinsey and Indiana University associates Wardell Pomeroy and Clyde Martin published *Sexual Behavior in the Human Male*. In 1953, Kinsey was joined by Pomeroy, Martin, and Paul Gebhard and they published *Sexual Behavior in the Human Female*. These four researchers were chiefly responsible for the thousands of interviews conducted, with Kinsey himself handling over 7,000. This is a staggering total considering that the average interview required between an hour and a half to two hours of time.

Never before had a strictly scientific investigation like this aroused so much interest, not only among fellow researchers but among the general public as well. When the findings were released, prevailing conceptions of many facets of human sexuality were radically altered. Indeed, most readers of the Kinsey studies were astonished to discover how widespread certain sexual activities were in the United States. For example, most men and almost one-half of the women reported that they had engaged in premarital sex. Many couples also engaged in sexual practices considered objectionable by society at the time, such as oral sex. About 50 percent of married men and approximately 25 percent of married women also reported having had at least one extramarital affair.

Kinsey's research marked a major breakthrough in social science research. Although critics pointed to several research flaws (e. g., using a disproportionate number of uneducated males and too many college-educated females; interviewing only those subjects who were willing to disclose their sex lives), Kinsey's research had many positive dimensions. In addition to its magnitude and scope, an outstanding feature of Kinsey's research was the unprecedented sophistication and expertise in employing the interview technique. Kinsey's staff provided scholarly objectivity and sophisticated interviewing throughout the project. Thanks to Alfred Kinsey and his dedicated team of associates, human sexuality research began to emerge as a legitimate and respectable branch of social science inquiry.

Daniel Levinson (1920–)

Daniel Levinson is an important contributor to the study of adult personality development. He earned a Ph.D. at the University of California at Berkeley in social psychology and had a distinguished teaching and research career at Yale University from 1966 to 1992. Levinson maintains that adult personality development unfolds in a series of predictable stages. In his research, Levinson describes what he calls a *life structure*, which is the underlying pattern of a person's behavior at a given time in life. There are three aspects to a person's life structure: sociocultural world (e. g., ethnicity, occupation, class, status, religion); self-aspects (complex patterns of wishes, anxieties, conflicts, moral values, talents and skills, fantasies, and modes of feeling, thought, and action); and participation in the world (how a person uses and is used by the world).

Utilizing the concept of a life structure, Levinson suggests that adulthood is divided into *eras* of approximately twenty-five years each, and each era consists of unique developmental periods for personality dynamics. Between each era (for example, the *early adult transition,* the *age 30 transition,* and the *midlife transition)* a major transition occurs. Levinson calls the initial time when individuals enter a new era and they are making psychological adjustments the *novice phase.* A reassessment of the developing life structure occurs during the middle of each era, labeled by Levinson as the *transition phase.* Finally, one enters the *culminating phase* of the era where the life structure is reassessed and fine-tuned.

According to Levinson, the nature of adult personality dynamics can be best understood within this developmental framework. For example, the early adult transition enables us to see the developmental bridge that exists between preadulthood and early adulthood. We can study how becoming less dependent on one's family of origin requires launching a new life structure and making choices, defining goals, and establishing an occupation. During the midlife transition, Levinson's conceptual model is useful in studying how individuals assess earlier established life goals and how they modify unsatisfactory aspects of their life structure. Finally, the late adult transition enables researchers to explore personality dynamics as middle adulthood's heavy responsibilities are reduced and individuals face living in a changed relationship with society and themselves.

William H. Masters (1915–) and Virginia E. Johnson (1925–)

William H. Masters and Virginia E. Johnson are perhaps the most famous team of investigators in the history of human sexuality research. Masters received his M.D. from the Rochester School of Medicine in 1943. At Washington University in St. Louis, Masters began exploring the physiology of sex, as well as the treatment of sexual dysfunction. Spurred on by the generally favorable response to Alfred Kinsey's human sexuality research, Masters decided to launch a more detailed investigation on sexual functioning and enlisted the services of research associate Virginia Johnson, who had studied psychology and sociology at Missouri University. Masters and Johnson, who later married and then divorced, began a laboratory physiological study of human sexual response in 1957. The two founded and served as codirectors of the Masters and Johnson Institute in St. Louis.

Unlike Kinsey, Masters and Johnson directly and systematically observed (and filmed) sexual intercourse and self-stimulation, or masturbation. Whereas Kinsey's research represented a statistical analysis of sexual behavior, Masters and Johnson broke new ground by using sophisticated instrumentation to measure the physiology of sexual response. They recruited a total of 694 female and male volunteers for laboratory study (all were paid for their services), including 276 married couples. The unmarried subjects participated primarily in noncoital research activities, such as studies of ejaculatory processes in males or studies of the ways in which different contraceptive devices affected female sexual response. Although most subjects were between the ages of 18 and 40, Masters and Johnson included a group of subjects over the age of 50 in order to study the effects of aging on sexual response. A careful screening procedure was designed to weed out exhibitionists and people with emotional disturbances.

Following a tour of Masters and Johnson's laboratory facilities and inspection of the equipment to be used in the studies, each subject was invited to a private practice session. The purpose of this was to accustom people to engaging in sexual activity in a laboratory environment. When actual experimental sessions began, subjects performed acts of masturbation or sexual intercourse while being filmed or wearing devices that recorded physiological response to sexual stimulation. For example, a subject might wear electrode terminals connected to an electrocardiograph that would produce a record of her heart's activity during sexual intercourse. Or a subject might have a band placed around his penis to record size and speed of erection in response to manual stimulation.

In over 10,000 sessions, Masters and Johnson recorded subjects' responses to sexual stimulation and discovered striking similarities between the responses of men and women. From this research, Masters and Johnson developed a sexual model of response called the *sexual response cycle*. The model consists of four stages of physiological response during which two basic physiological reactions occur: an increased concentration of blood in bodily tissues in the genitals and female breasts and increased energy in the nerves and muscles throughout the body.

The Masters and Johnson research model was not without its critics, For example, many viewed the laboratory setting as dehumanizing and mechanizing sex. Many critics felt that the emphasis placed on the physiology of sex downplayed its interpersonal and emotional aspects. Some objected to the research design on ethical grounds, claiming the project was an invasion of privacy. Finally, critics wondered if Masters and Johnson had selected a representative sample of the population. In fact, most of the subjects were well educated and more affluent than the average person. Moreover, their willingness to perform sexually under laboratory conditions suggested that they were not typical. Overall, though, the research of Masters and Johnson had enormous impact on the field of human sexuality. For the first time, scientific evidence on the physiology of the orgasmic response was systematically gathered. Because of these researchers' efforts, laboratory studies of sexual arousal achieved a new level of respectability among scientific researchers.

George Herbert Mead (1863–1931)

George Herbert Mead was an early social psychologist and sociologist. Among his many contributions to both disciplines, Mead explored how one's personality is shaped and molded by society. He emphasized the importance of role-taking and role-playing, and how the learning of social expectations contributes to a person's developing sense of self. Role-taking and role-playing are social processes evident throughout life, from the play stage of childhood to the roles demanded throughout adulthood.

According to Mead, one's sense of self is greatly influenced by *significant others*, people of importance such as parents, siblings, and peers. Over the course of the lifespan, a person will internalize the values and attitudes of significant others and apply them to society as a whole, which Mead termed the *generalized other*. Although significant others represent real persons, the generalized other consists of societal values and attitudes.

Mead also expounded upon an individual's *social self*, which he believed was composed of two related elements: the "me" and "I." The me represents the individual's objective involvement in social roles and role-playing. The I represents the individual's subjective side, and mirrors individual attributes. Compared to the predictable nature of the me, the I is spontaneous, nonconforming, and creative. Mead argued that society needs both components of the social self in order to operate smoothly. If everyone behaved exclusively at the I level, there would be social chaos and disorganization. And, if the me level dominated, there would be no creativity, innovation, or social change. Finally, Mead argued that the social self undergoes change and modification throughout the lifespan, particularly as one's social statuses and relationships change.

Margaret Mead (1901–1978)

Margaret Mead was a noted anthropologist who explored and carefully detailed cross-cultural differences in a wide range of topics, including family dynamics, gender, temperament, and rites of passage. In her most famous fieldwork, Mead set out for Samoa in 1925 to test the notion that puberty creates social and psychological stress for all adolescents. In her classic book *Coming of Age in Samoa: A Psychological Study of Primitive Youth for Western Civilization,* Mead concluded that puberty need not be a period of stress and turbulence. On the contrary, Mead observed that adolescence in Samoa was a smooth and tranquil period. For most, it was a time for happiness, self-indulgence, and a relatively carefree—and conflict-free—lifestyle. Such observations prompted Mead to discount the notion that a difficult adolescence was a universal experience, that it was always a period of conflict and turmoil. Rather, she maintained that the experience of adolescence varies according to cultural influences. Because of the role of culture, it is incorrect to assume that all adolescents share the same experiences.

In later research, Mead also analyzed three primitive societies (Arapesh, Mundugumor, and Tchambuli) on the island of New Guinea to see whether temperamental differences are universal. Her fieldwork disclosed that among the Arapesh, both men and women behaved in what our culture would call feminine fashions. In the Mundugumor tribe, both women and men possessed such masculine traits as assertiveness and competitiveness. And among the Tchambuli, women were independent, dominant, and managerial, whereas men were emotional, submissive, and dependent. Mead's research demonstrated that while individuals are born with a biological sexual identity, it is society and culture that truly impact peoples' lives and leave an indelible imprint on the course of development.

Carl R. Rogers (1902–1987)

Carl R. Rogers was an internationally known therapist and an important contributor to humanistic theory, a major school of thought in psychology. Born in Oak Park, Illinois, Rogers is also recognized as the founding figure of *client-centered* or *person-centered therapy*. Rogers received his Ph.D. from Teacher's College and over the years taught at a number of universities, including Ohio State University, the University of Wisconsin, and the University of Chicago. He received many honors over his professional career, including the Distinguished Scientific Contribution Award, bestowed on him in 1956 by the American Psychological Association.

Rogers believed that people can become fully functioning human beings only when they are given the freedom and emotional support that enables them to grow psychologically. He maintained that each of us has a *real self*, which consists of our self-perceptions, and an *ideal self*, which represents the self we would like to become. When these two selves are congruent, we are probably living without conflict and likely in the process of developing into fully functioning people. Thus, healthy growth and development is seen as embracing congruency and movement toward such important personality dimensions as flexibility, autonomy, and self-acceptance.

However, when these two selves are incongruent, we likely suffer from such conditions as lack of self-esteem, rigidity, feelings of inferiority, guilt, and other negative emotions, all of which serve to stifle positive self-development. The essence of his person-centered therapy is to overcome such negative states. This is an "insight" therapy (so-called because it stresses self-knowledge and growth) that emphasizes providing a supportive climate for clients, who play a major role in determining the pace and direction of therapeutic intervention.

Margaret Sanger (1883–1966)

Margaret Sanger initiated and led the movement to find safe and effective methods of birth control. She became interested in women's health issues through her experiences in nursing. Sanger worked with many poor women in New York for whom pregnancy was a "chronic condition" and who often induced their own abortions, frequently dying in the process.

Frustrated in her efforts to help these women within the medical context, Sanger left nursing and founded the National Birth Control League in 1914. Although the league's magazine

Woman Rebel did not violate the Comstock Act of 1873, which made it illegal to send contraceptive information through the mail, Sanger barely escaped imprisonment by fleeing to Europe, where she visited the world's first birth control clinics.

In 1916, Sanger opened a birth control clinic in Brooklyn where women could obtain diaphragms and birth control information, including the publication *Birth Control Review*. She was jailed for thirty days and the clinic was closed. But ultimately she won the right to keep the clinic open, and within two years doctors were legally allowed to dispense contraceptive information.

Sanger began the American Birth Control League in 1921, and she promoted the concepts of women's health and reproductive rights both at home and abroad. Sanger also promoted birth control research, fighting for a reliable birth control method that could be controlled by women, but it was not until 1960 that birth control pills became available in the United States.

Virginia Satir (1916–1988)

Virginia Satir is recognized as one of the pioneers of family therapy. She believed that the family unit is an integral force in the growth and development of its members. Because individuals are constantly changing and evolving, the family must create optimal levels of functioning. She was particularly interested in improving patterns of family communication and problem-solving strategies.

Satir attended graduate school at the University of Chicago. Early in her career she worked with families at the Dallas Child Guidance Center and later at the Illinois State Psychiatric Institute. In 1959, Satir was invited to join Don Jackson and a team of therapists to launch the Mental Research Institute in Palo Alto, California. The Mental Research Institute would become the first formal program in family therapy in the United States.

Satir's first book, *Conjoint Family Therapy*, was published in 1964 and is considered a classic in the field. She has written many other books, including *Peoplemaking* in 1972 and *The New Peoplemaking* in 1988. Satir is also the author of many articles, and she has conducted workshops and training seminars on the topic of family therapy. She remained involved in the family therapy movement for almost fifty years. She died in 1988 from pancreatic cancer.

Benjamin Spock (1903–1998)

Benjamin Spock was a world-renowned pediatrician who achieved everlasting fame as the author of *Baby and Child Care*, a book that revolutionized child raising. The book, first published in 1945, sold over 45 million copies and was translated into 39 languages. It remains the best-selling book ever written by an American author.

No one has had a greater impact on child care than Spock. Trained as a pediatrician, Spock taught at Cornell University's Medical College in New York City between 1933 and 1943. At age 39 he wrote *Baby and Child Care*, blending his training in pediatrics with psychology to provide parents with practical and sensible child-care advice. Throughout his book, Spock stressed the importance of treating children with affection and respect, rather than with rigid structure and physical punishment. His humanitarian method of raising children became known as the "permissive" approach to child care.

Spock's approach to parenting encouraged parents to trust and respect themselves, as well as their children. The key to successful parenting is flexibility, patience, and the ability to understand a child's various developmental needs. Although such advice was generally welcomed by parents, it was not met with open arms by all concerned. Among critics, Spock's permissiveness approach was seen as creating undisciplined and problem-prone children. Some critics accused Spock's permissiveness for creating the youth rebellions of the 1960s.

Spock also became known for his opposition to nuclear weapons and America's involvement in the Vietnam War. He often took part in nonviolent protest activities, such as demonstrations to end the war and encourage men to avoid the military draft. In 1972, he unsuccessfully ran for president as a candidate of the People's Party. He died of respiratory failure at his home in San Diego at the age of 94.

6

Facts and Statistics

This chapter provides readers with a statistical portrait of modern family life. Americans are a very curious people; as the statistical graphics, surveys, studies, and opinion polls that the media continually bombard us with suggest. The fact that so much of this research is concerned with marriage and family life is understandable if we look closely at our culture. As we have seen in previous chapters, marriage and the family have always been integral and important parts of our lives. From birth until death we are embraced by marriage and family and they present us with a wide assortment of challenges, issues, and controversies.

The goal of the statistical portraits contained in this chapter is to provide accurate, meaningful, and reliable information to the general public as well as to others who are engaged in such fields as research, education, or therapy. Statistical portraits can help us see data related to marriage and family clearly and systematically, which in turn promotes careful, critical, and systematic thinking. On a practical level, research in marriage and family can help us make informed decisions about our behavior, allow us to compare our attitudes with other people's, and enable us to better understand our partners, children, parents, and grandparents.

In addition to complementing important textual material, the statistical portraits in this chapter are used to summarize key points or provide a visual display when words alone cannot adequately describe a concept. The graphics thus serve to offer a variation of text material, in the process providing readers with ways to better understand important concepts and with visual aids to better remember them.

Most of the tables and graphs in this chapter represent displays of demographics, or population trends, as they relate to marriage and family life. The statistical portraits are largely drawn from government sources, such as United States Census Bureau or the Population Reference Bureau. The United States Census Bureau is a particularly instrumental source since it conducts a decennial census of the population, a monthly population survey, a program of population estimates and projections, and a number of periodic surveys relating to population characteristics.

Figure 6.1   Median Age at First Marriage of the Population 15 Years and Over by Sex: Selected Years, 1970 to 2000

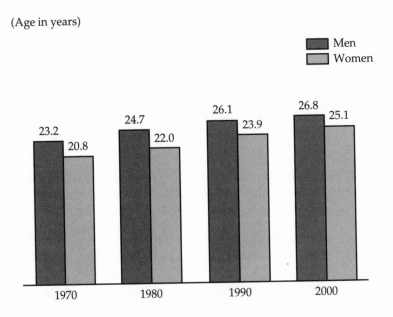

Source: U.S. Census Bureau, *Current Population Survey*, March Supplements: 1970 to 2000.

Figure 6.2 Projected Number of Persons Living Alone by Age: 1995 and 2010

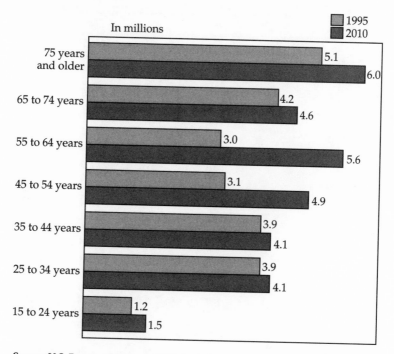

In millions

	1995
	2010

75 years and older — 5.1 / 6.0
65 to 74 years — 4.2 / 4.6
55 to 64 years — 3.0 / 5.6
45 to 54 years — 3.1 / 4.9
35 to 44 years — 3.9 / 4.1
25 to 34 years — 3.9 / 4.1
15 to 24 years — 1.2 / 1.5

Source: U.S. Bureau of Census. (1996). *Projection of the Number of Households and Families in the United States: 1995 to 2010.* Washington, DC: U.S. Government Printing Office.

TABLE 6.1
Persons Living Alone by Age and Sex: 1995, 2000, 2005, and 2010
(in thousands)

Age and sex	1995	2000	2005	2010
Total	**24,304**	**26,231**	**28,336**	**30,727**
15 to 24 years	1,181	1,239	1,370	1,472
25 to 34 years	3,911	3,706	3,743	4,079
35 to 44 years	3,850	4,288	4,278	4,118
45 to 54 years	3,098	3,850	4,500	4,926
55 to 64 years	2,964	3,488	4,479	5,556
65 to 74 years	4,201	4,019	4,031	4,584
75 years and over	5,098	5,640	5,936	5,993
Female	**14,131**	**15,035**	**16,083**	**17,327**
15 to 24 years	526	553	613	659
25 to 34 years	1,499	1,421	1,443	1,579
35 to 44 years	1,459	1,575	1,539	1,462
45 to 54 years	1,570	1,932	2,244	2,448
55 to 64 years	1,830	2,090	2,611	3,155
65 to 74 years	3,124	2,931	2,888	3,233
75 years and over	4,124	4,533	4,754	4,791
Male	**10,173**	**11,195**	**12,244**	**13,400**
15 to 24 years	656	685	757	813
25 to 34 years	2,411	2,285	2,300	2,499
35 to 44 years	2,392	2,713	2,738	2,657
45 to 54 years	1,528	1,918	2,256	2,477
55 to 64 years	1,134	1,399	1,868	2,400
65 to 74 years	1,077	1,088	1,143	1,351
75 years and over	974	1,107	1,182	1,203

Source: U.S. Bureau of the Census. (1996). *Projection of the Number of Households and Families in the United States: 1995 to 2010.* Washington, DC: U.S. Government Printing Office.

TABLE 6.2
Average Size of Household and Family: 1940 to 2010

	Series 1					
	Persons per household			Persons per family		
Year	All persons	Under 18 years	18 years and over	All persons	Under 18 years	18 years and over
CENSUS ESTIMATES						
1940	3.67	1.14	2.53	3.76	1.24	2.52
1950	3.37	1.06	2.31	3.54	1.17	2.37
1960	3.33	1.21	2.12	3.67	1.41	2.26
1970	3.14	1.09	2.05	3.58	1.32	2.26
1980	2.76	0.79	1.97	3.29	1.05	2.24
1990	2.63	0.69	1.94	3.15	0.96	2.19
						(continues)

TABLE 6.2 (continued)

	Persons per household			Persons per family		
Year	All persons	Under 18 years	18 years and over	All persons	Under 18 years	18 years and over
PROJECTIONS						
1995	2.62	0.70	1.92	3.15	0.98	2.17
2000	2.59	0.68	1.91	3.12	0.97	2.15
2005	2.57	0.66	1.91	3.09	0.94	2.15
2010	2.53	0.63	1.90	3.05	0.91	2.14

Source: U.S. Bureau of the Census. (1996). *Projection of the Number of Households and Families in the United States: 1995 to 2010*. Washington, DC: U.S. Government Printing office.

Figure 6.3 Total Fertility Rate, 1920 to 1999

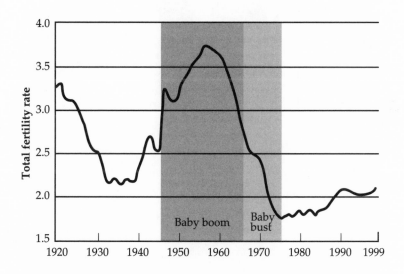

Source: Population Reference Bureau. AmeriStat. "Fertility: U.S. Fertility Trends: Boom and Bust and Leveling Off," accessed online at *http://www.ameristat.org/fertility/FertilityTrendsBoomBustLevelingOff.html* (August 1, 2001).

**Figure 6.4 Projections of Changing Family Composition:
1995, 2000, 2005, and 2010**

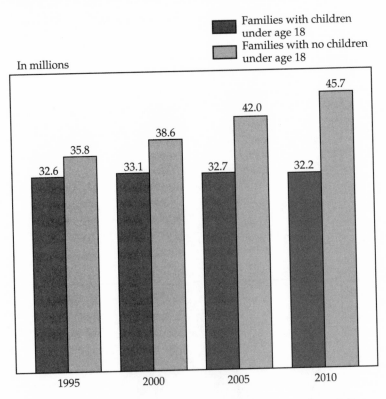

Source: U.S. Bureau of the Census. (1996). *Projection of the Number of Households
and Families in the United States: 1995 to 2010.* Washington, DC: U.S. Government
Printing Office.

Figure 6.5   Projections of Changing Household Composition: 1995 and 2010

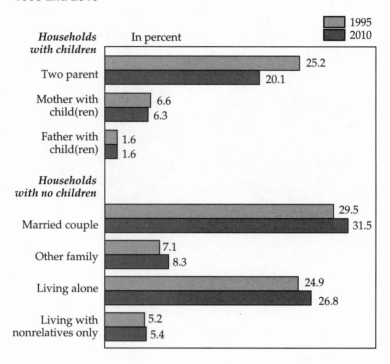

Source: U.S. Bureau of Census. (1996). *Projection of the Number of Households and Families in the United States: 1995 to 2010.* Washington, DC: U.S. Government Printing Office.

Figure 6.6   Race and Ethnic Composition for United States, 1999 and 2025

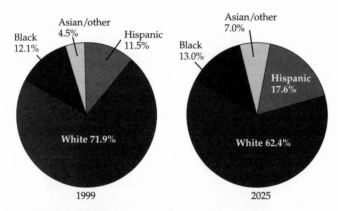

1999

2025

Note: White, Black, and Asian/other categories exclude Hispanics, who may be of any race. The Asian/other category includes American Indians, Eskimos, Aleuts, and Pacific Islanders.

Source: Population Reference Bureau. AmeriStat. "Race and Ethnicity: The Changing American Pie, 1999 and 2025," accessed online at *http://www.ameristat.org/raceethnic/pie.html* (August 1, 2001).

Figure 6.7   People in Poverty by Age, Sex, and Race: 1998
(Percent of population)

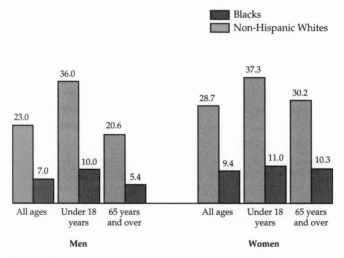

Source: U.S. Census Bureau, *Current Population Survey*, March 1999.

Figure 6.8   Family Size by Type and Race of Householder

(Percent of families*)

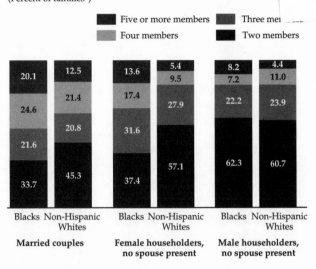

■ Five or more members   ▨ Three me~ ____
▨ Four members   ■ Two members

	Blacks	Non-Hispanic Whites	Blacks	Non-Hispanic Whites	Blacks	Non-Hispanic Whites
Five or more	20.1	12.5	13.6	5.4	8.2	4.4
Four members	24.6	21.4	17.4	9.5	7.2	11.0
Three members	21.6	20.8	31.6	27.9	22.2	23.9
Two members	33.7	45.3	37.4	57.1	62.3	60.7

Married couples   **Female householders, no spouse present**   **Male householders, no spouse present**

*The percentages may not add to 100.0 percent because of rounding.
Source: U.S. Census Bureau, *Current Population Survey,* March 1999.

Figure 6.9   Family Size by Income/Family Type and Race of Householder: 1998

(Percent of families*)

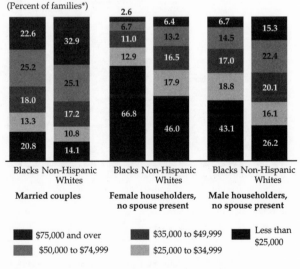

	Blacks	Non-Hispanic Whites	Blacks	Non-Hispanic Whites	Blacks	Non-Hispanic Whites
$75,000 and over	22.6	32.9	2.6	6.4	6.7	15.3
$50,000 to $74,999	25.2	25.1	6.7	13.2	14.5	22.4
$35,000 to $49,999	18.0	17.2	11.0	16.5	17.0	20.1
$25,000 to $34,999	13.3	10.8	12.9	17.9	18.8	16.1
Less than $25,000	20.8	14.1	66.8	46.0	43.1	26.2

Married couples   **Female householders, no spouse present**   **Male householders, no spouse present**

■ $75,000 and over   ▨ $35,000 to $49,999   ■ Less than $25,000
▨ $50,000 to $74,999   ▨ $25,000 to $34,999

*The percentages may not add to 100.0 percent because of rounding.
Source: U.S. Census Bureau, *Current Population Survey,* March 1999.

Figure 6.10 Percent Black and Hispanic Origin of the Total Population 65 Years and Over: 1990 to 2050

Black

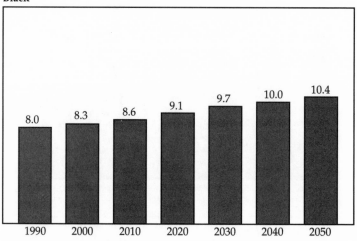

Hispanic Origin[1]

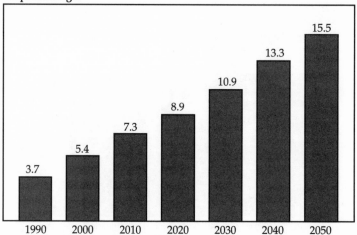

[1] Hispanic origin may be of any race.

Source: U.S. Bureau of the Census, 1990 from 1990 Census of Population and Housing, CPH-L-74, *Modified and Actual Age, Sex, Race, and Hispanic Origin Data;* and 2000 to 2050 from *Population Projections of the United States, by Age, Sex, Race, and Hispanic Origin: 1993 to 2050,* Current Population Reports, P25-1104, U.S. Government Printing Office, Washington, DC, 1993.

Figure 6.11   Black and Hispanic Origin Population 85 Years and Over: 1990 to 2050

Black

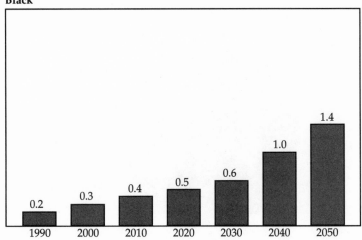

Hispanic Origin[1]

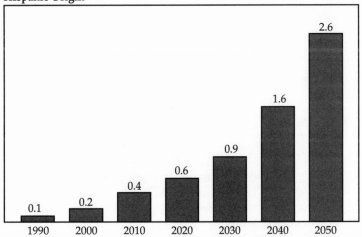

[1] Hispanic origin may be of any race.

Source: U.S. Bureau of the Census, 1990 from 1990 Census of Population and Housing, CPH-L-74, *Modified and Actual Age, Sex, Race, and Hispanic Origin Data;* and 2000 to 2050 from *Population Projections of the United States, by Age, Sex, Race, and Hispanic Origin: 1993 to 2050,* Current Population Reports, P25-1104, U.S. Government Printing Office, Washington, DC, 1993.

Figure 6.12   Hispanics, by Type of Origin: 1999

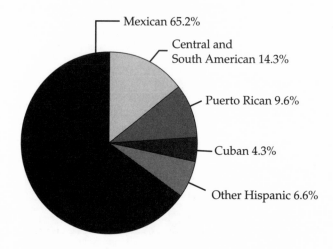

Source: U.S. Bureau of the Census, *Current Population Survey,* March 1999.

Figure 6.13   Type of Family by Hispanic Origin: March 1999
(In percentage)

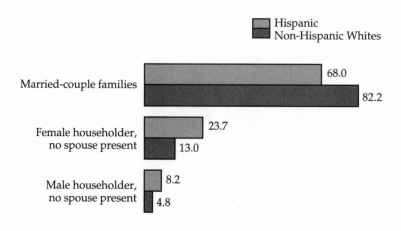

Source: U.S. Bureau of the Census, *Current Population Survey,* March 1999.

Figure 6.14   Percent of People 55 Years and Older by Race and Hispanic Origin: 1999

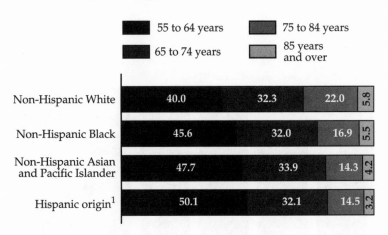

■ 55 to 64 years   ■ 75 to 84 years

■ 65 to 74 years   ▨ 85 years and over

	55 to 64	65 to 74	75 to 84	85+
Non-Hispanic White	40.0	32.3	22.0	5.8
Non-Hispanic Black	45.6	32.0	16.9	5.5
Non-Hispanic Asian and Pacific Islander	47.7	33.9	14.3	4.2
Hispanic origin[1]	50.1	32.1	14.5	3.2

[1] Hispanic origin may be of any race.

Source: U.S. Census Bureau, *Current Population Survey*, March 1999.

Figure 6.15   Childlessness Among Women 40 to 44 Years Old: Selected Years, June 1976 to June 1998

(Percent)

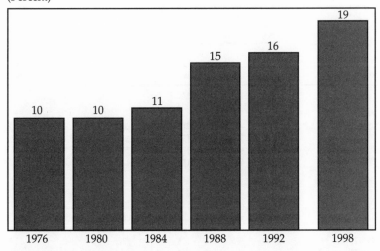

1976	1980	1984	1988	1992	1998
10	10	11	15	16	19

Source: U.S. Census Bureau, *June Current Population Surveys*, 1976 to 1998.

Figure 6.16   Labor Force Participation Among Women With Infants: Selected Years, June 1976 to June 1998

(Percent)

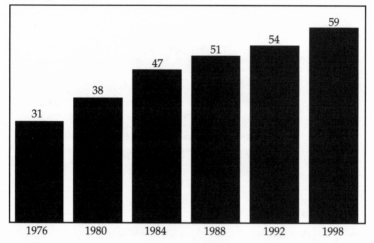

Source: U.S. Census Bureau, *June Current Population Surveys*, 1976 to 1998.

TABLE 6.3

Labor Force Participation Among Mothers 15 to 44 Years Old by Fertility Status and Selected Characteristics: June 1998 (Numbers in thousands. Limited to women with at least one child ever born)

	Mothers who had a child in the last year					Mothers who did not have a child in the last year				
		Percent in labor force					Percent in labor force			
Characteristic	Number of mothers	Total	Full-time	Part-time	Unem-ployed	Number of mothers	Total	Full-time	Part-time	Unem-ployed
Total	3,671	58.7	35.8	17.3	5.6	31,303	72.8	51.8	17.0	4.0
Age										
15 to 19 years	460	43.2	9.0	21.9	12.3	483	57.4	24.4	20.8	12.3
20 to 24 years	864	56.4	31.9	15.3	9.3	2,306	66.1	38.8	17.9	9.5
25 to 29 years	950	61.9	40.5	17.2	4.2	4,387	69.3	50.3	14.8	4.1
30 to 44 years	1,397	63.0	43.7	17.1	2.2	24,127	74.4	53.8	17.3	3.2
Births to Date and Age of Woman										
First birth	1,490	60.8	38.3	16.2	6.3	9,188	76.9	57.3	14.9	4.6
15 to 19 years	280	48.4	12.6	22.9	12.9	360	58.3	23.9	20.9	13.5
20 to 24 years	444	54.8	30.8	16.1	7.9	1,443	68.9	44.4	16.6	8.0
25 to 29 years	395	68.5	49.3	14.8	4.4	1,824	75.8	58.6	13.8	3.4
30 to 44 years	370	69.3	54.9	12.9	1.4	5,562	80.5	62.5	14.4	3.6

(continues)

TABLE 6.3 (continued)

| | Mothers who had a child in the last year | | | | | Mothers who did not have a child in the last year | | | | |
| | Percent in labor force | | | | | Percent in labor force | | | | |
Characteristic	Number of mothers	Total	Full-time	Part-time	Unem-ployed	Number of mothers	Total	Full-time	Part-time	Unem-ployed
Second or higher order birth	2,181	57.3	34.0	18.0	5.2	22,115	71.1	49.5	17.9	3.7
15 to 19 years	180	35.2	3.4	20.5	11.3	124	54.9	25.8	20.4	8.7
20 to 24 years	420	58.2	33.0	14.5	10.7	863	61.5	29.6	20.0	11.9
25 to 29 years	555	57.3	34.3	18.9	4.0	2,563	64.6	44.4	15.5	4.7
30 to 44 years	1,026	60.7	39.7	18.6	2.4	18.565	72.5	51.2	18.2	3.1
Race and Ethnicity										
White	2,947	58.4	36.3	17.5	4.6	24,647	72.1	50.4	18.6	3.1
White non-Hispanic	2,374	61.6	38.9	19.2	3.5	20,690	73.7	51.3	19.7	2.6
Black	554	63.0	33.5	17.9	11.6	5,079	77.5	58.4	10.8	8.4
Asian and Pacific Islander	138	49.9	34.7	11.0	4.2	1,250	67.6	50.3	14.4	2.9
Hispanic (of any race)	618	45.7	26.1	11.2	8.4	4,182	64.5	46.3	12.7	5.5
Marital Status										
Married, husband present	2,469	60.0	39.3	17.4	3.3	21,121	70.7	49.1	19.1	2.5
Separated[1], divorced or widowed	202	64.5	50.2	9.3	5.0	5,731	82.1	65.2	12.0	4.9
Never married	1,000	54.4	24.2	18.6	11.6	4,451	70.8	46.9	14.0	9.9
Educational Attainment										
Not a high school graduate	793	37.7	13.6	13.5	10.6	4,871	56.3	35.4	12.9	7.9
High school graduate	1,034	58.4	33.5	17.0	7.9	11,511	73.8	52.8	16.5	4.5
College, 1 or more years	1,844	67.9	46.6	19.1	2.2	14,920	77.4	56.3	18.8	2.2
no degree	690	66.4	39.8	22.1	4.4	6,329	75.8	56.4	16.7	2.6
Associate degree	288	69.7	50.4	17.3	2.0	2,664	81.5	57.5	21.1	2.9
Bachelor's degree	627	66.5	45.8	19.9	0.8	4,509	76.3	54.0	20.8	1.4
Graduate or professional degree	239	73.6	63.2	10.4	*	1,418	80.6	61.1	17.5	2.1
Family Income										
Under $10,000	413	41.8	14.4	13.8	13.6	3,179	56.7	26.0	16.8	13.8
$10,000 to $19,999	514	49.5	26.4	15.2	7.8	3,763	69.8	48.5	15.7	5.6
$20,000 to $24,999	301	58.8	35.4	12.9	10.5	2,024	71.2	52.5	14.5	4.2
$25,000 to $29,999	236	57.2	36.6	12.0	8.5	2,013	75.2	55.7	14.8	4.7
$30,000 to $34,999	230	54.8	26.0	24.7	4.1	2,006	76.2	56.7	16.1	3.4
$35,000 to $49,999	522	67.3	41.1	24.3	1.8	5,080	76.7	58.0	16.3	2.5
$50,000 to $74,999	663	69.6	46.7	21.2	1.7	5,634	80.1	58.9	20.0	1.6
$75,000 and over	484	66.9	48.3	16.2	2.4	4,526	75.1	53.0	20.9	1.2
Income not reported	308	49.9	34.7	9.8	5.5	3,078	66.9	51.9	12.7	2.4

* Represents zero or rounds to zero.
[1] Includes married, husband absent.
Source: U.S. Census Bureau, June Current Population Survey, 1998.

TABLE 6.4
Composition and Representation of Female and Male Vocations, 2000

Composition of the Female and Male Work Forces, by Occupation, 2000 (Numbers in thousands)

Category	# women	% or female work force in group	# men	% of male work force in group
Executives, managers	8,888	14.1	10,877	15.3
Professional, specialty	11,309	17.9	9,420	13.2
Technicians	2,324	3.7	2,060	2.9
Sales	7,931	12.6	8,207	11.5
Administrative support	15,112	23.9	3,908	5.5
Private household	843	1.3	40	0.1
Protective service	431	0.7	1,934	2.7
Other services	9,938	15.7	5,485	7.7
Farming, forestry, fishing	729	1.2	2,515	3.5
Precision production	1,410	2.2	12,975	18.2
Machine operators	2,576	4.1	4,775	6.7
Transportation, material moving	554	0.9	4,786	6.7
Handlers, laborers	1,056	1.7	4,254	6
Total	63,102	100	71,237	100

Representation of Women and Men in Major Occupations, 2000 %

	Women	Men	Total
Executives, managers	45	55	100
Professional, specialty	55	45	100
Technicians	53	47	100
Sales	49	51	100
Administrative support	80	20	100
Private household	95	5	100
Protective service	18	82	100
Other services	64	36	100
Farming, forestry, fishing	23	77	100
Precision production	10	90	100
Machine operators	35	65	100
Transportation, material moving	10	90	100
Handlers, laborers	20	80	100
Total work force	47	53	100

Source: Population Reference Bureau. AmeriStat. "Labor Force and Employment: What Jobs Do Women and Men Have?", accessed online at http://www.ameristat.org/labor/jobs.html (August 1, 2001).

Figure 6.17 Common Child Care Combinations Used for Preschoolers During Their Parent's Work/School Hours: Fall 1995

(Percent in specified combination)

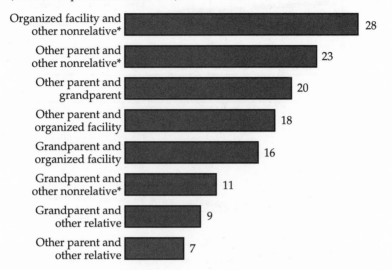

Note: Data are for preschoolers in two or more arrangements. Children may be in other arrangement types as well as these combinations.
*Includes care in the child's home or the provider's home.
Source: U.S. Census Bureau, *Survey of Income and Program Participation (SIPP),* 1993 Panel Wave 9.

**Figure 6.18   Living Arrangements of Children,
1980 to 1999**

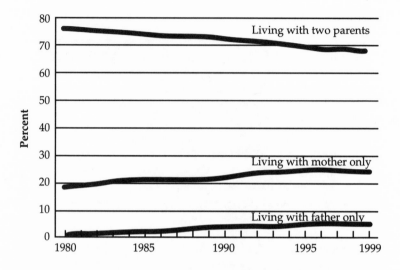

Source: Population Reference Bureau. AmeriStat. "Children: Two-parent Families
on the decline," accessed online at
http://www.ameristat.org/children/TwoParentFamiliesDecline.html (August 1, 2001).

Figure 6.19 Living Arrangements of Children by Race/Ethnicity, 1999

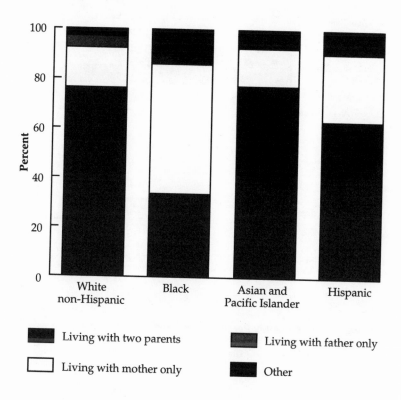

Source: Population Reference Bureau. AmeriStat. "Children: Two-parent Families on the Decline," accessed online at http://www.ameristat.org/children/TwoParentFamiliesDecline.html (August 1, 2001).

Figure 6.20 Children with Divorced and Never-Married Mothers, by Family Income: March 1995

(In millions)

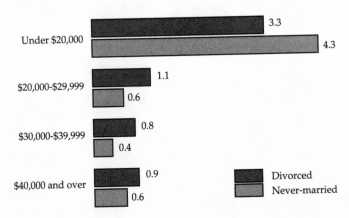

Source: U.S. Bureau of the Census. (1997). *Children with Single Parents: How Do They Fare?* Census Brief, September. Washington, DC: U. S. Government Printing Office.

Figure 6.21 Disability Prevalence by Age

Percent with specified level of disability

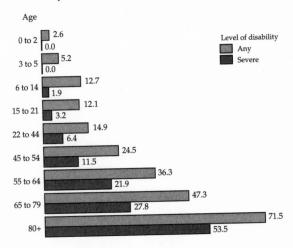

Source: U.S. Bureau of the Census. (1995). *Current Population Report*, March. Americans with Disabilities. Washington, DC: U.S. Government Printing Office.

Figure 6.22 Severe Disability Distribution by Age

Percent distribution of persons with a severe disability by age

45 to 54
years of age
13.4%

22 to 44
years of age
23.4%

55 to 64
years of age
17.4%

Less than 22
years of age
5.7%

65 to 79
years of age
26.2%

80+ years
of age
14.0%

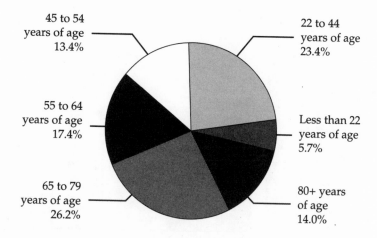

Source: U.S. Bureau of Census. (1995). *Current Population Report*, March. Americans with Disabilities. Washington, DC: U.S. Government Printing Office.

Figure 6.23 Average Annual Growth Rate of the Elderly Population: 1910–30 to 2030–50

(In percent)

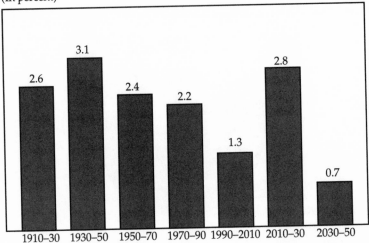

Source: U.S. Census Bureau of the Census. Data for 1910 to 1940, 1960, and 1980 shown in 1980 Census of Population, *General Population Characteristics*, PC80-1-B1, Tables 42 and 45, U.S. Government Printing Office, Washington, DC, May 1983; data for 1990 from 1990 Census of Population and Housing, CPH-L-74, *Modified and Actual Age, Sex, Race, and Hispanic Origin Data*; data for 2000 to 2050 shown in *Population Projections of the United States by Age, Sex, Race, and Hispanic Origin: 1993 to 2050*, Current Population Reports, P25-1104, U.S. Government Printing Office, Washington, DC, 1993; data for 1950 shown in *Estimates of the Population of the United States and Components of Change, by Age, Color, and Sex: 1950 to 1960*, Current Population Reports, Series P-25, No. 310, U.S. Government Printing Office, Washington DC, 1965; data for 1970 from unpublished tables consistent with *United States Population Estimated by Age, Race, Sex, and Hispanic Origin: 1988*, Series P-25, No. 1045, U.S. Government Printing Office, Washington, DC, 1990.

Figure 6.24 Sex Ratio of People 55 Years and Older by Age: 1999

(Number of men per 100 women)

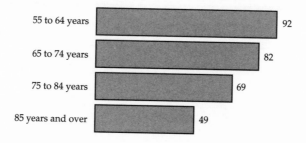

Source: U.S. Census Bureau, *Current Population Survey*, March 1999.

Figure 6.25 Population 85 Years and Over: 1900 to 2050

(In millions)

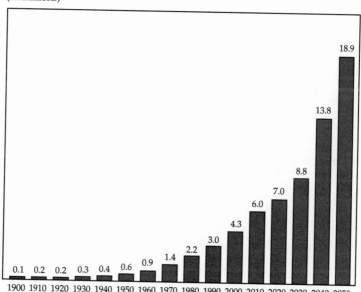

Source: U.S. Bureau of the Census, Decennial Censuses for specfied years and *Population Projections of the United States by Age, Sex, Race, and Hispanic Origin: 1993 to 2050,* Current Population Reports, P25-1104, U.S. Government Printing Office, Washington, DC, 1993. Data for 1990 from *1990 Census of Population and Housing,* CPH-L-74, *Modfied and Actual Age, Sex, Race, and Hispanic Origin Data.*

TABLE 6.5

Projected Population for Countries With More Than One Million
Persons Aged 80 Years and Over: 1994 and 2020
(in thousands, based on rank in 1994)

Country/area	Rank		Population aged 80 years and over	
	1994	2020	1994	2020
China, Mainland	1	1	9,010	28,737
United States	2	2	7,760	13,007
India	3	3	4,021	12,639
Japan	4	4	3,597	9,362
Russia	5	5	3,317	7,191
Germany	6	6	3,313	5,889
France	7	8	2,563	3,754
United Kingdom	8	9	2,342	3,400
Italy	9	7	2,221	4,142
Ukraine	10	12	1,421	2,923
Spain	11	13	1,287	2,488
Brazil	*	10	*	3,132
Indonesia	*	11	*	3,034
Mexico	*	14	*	2,296
Poland	*	15	*	1,877
Turkey	*	16	*	1,751
Canada	*	17	*	1,595
Thailand	*	18	*	1,477
Pakistan	*	19	*	1,385
Romania	*	20	*	1,264
South Korea	*	21	*	1,221
Vietnam	*	22	*	1,199
Argentina	*	23	*	1,072
Iran	*	24	*	1,039

Note: * indicates population 80 years and over in 1994 was less than one million.
Source: U.S. Bureau of teh Census, International Data Base.

Figure 6.26   Percentage of People 55 Years and Older Who Were Married with Spouse Present or Widowed by Age and Sex: 1999

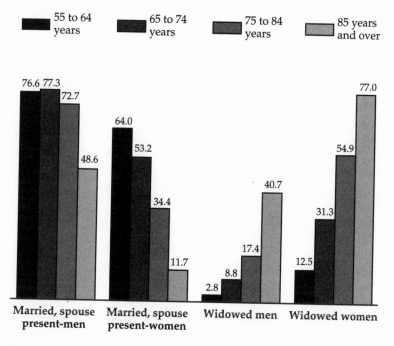

Source: U.S. Census Bureau, *Current Population Survey*, March 1999.

7

Agencies and Organizations

This chapter contains a comprehensive listing of family agencies and organizations. For the dual purpose of convenience and organization, the agencies and organizations are arranged according to their relevance to each of the chapters.

Chapter 1: History and Scope of American Families

Alliance for Children and Families
11700 West Lake Park Drive
Milwaukee, WI 53224–3099
(414) 359–1040
http://www.alliance1.org

The Alliance for Children and Families is an international association representing more than 350 private, nonprofit child- and family-serving organizations. Alliance members provide a wide variety of services ranging from residential care to domestic abuse prevention and intervention. The alliance's mission is to strengthen members' capacity to serve and advocate for children, families, and communities.

Board on Children, Youth, and Families
National Academy of Sciences
2101 Constitution Avenue, NW, HA156
Washington, DC 20418
(202) 334–1935
http://www4.nationalacademies.org/cbsse/bocyfweb.nsf

The Board on Children, Youth, and Families addresses a variety of policy-relevant issues related to the health and development of children, youth, and families by convening experts to weigh in on matters from the perspective of the behavioral, social, and health sciences. The Board's Committee on Adolescent Health and Development focuses attention on critical national issues of importance to youth and their families. The board operates under the National Research Council and the Institute of Medicine of the National Academies.

Center for the Future of Children
The David and Lucile Packard Foundation
300 Second Street, Suite 200
Los Altos, CA 94022
(650) 917–7110
http://www.futureofchildren.org

This national organization researches and distributes timely information on major issues related to children's well-being and the maintenance of healthy families. A particular emphasis is placed on providing objective analysis and evaluation, translating existing knowledge into effective programs and policies, and promoting constructive institutional change.

Children, Youth, and Family Consortium
McNamara Alumni Center, Suite 270A
200 Oak Street Southeast
Minneapolis, MN 55455
(612) 625–7849
http://www.cyfernet.org

This organization, established in 1991, seeks to bring together the varied competencies of the University of Minnesota and the vital resources of Minnesota's communities to enhance the ability of individuals and organizations to address critical health, education, and social policy concerns in ways that improve the well-being of children, youth, and families.

Facts for Families
American Academy of Child and Adolescent Psychiatry
3615 Wisconsin, NW
Washington, DC 20016–3007

(202) 966–7300
http://www.aacap.org/factsfam

Sponsored by the American Academy of Child and Adolescent Psychiatry, Facts for Families provides concise and up-to-date information on issues that affect children, teenagers, and their families. The AACAP provides this important information as a public service and the Facts for Families may be duplicated and distributed free of charge as long as the American Academy of Child and Adolescent Psychiatry is properly credited and no profit is gained from their use.

Families and Education
1000 Market Street
Portsmouth, NH 03801
(800) 258–0802
http://www.rmcres.com/famed/index.html

This organization promotes an understanding of the bridge that exists between home and school. It provides a wide range of information and ideas on how to help parents understand how schools and other educational programs work; how children learn; and how parents and families can best contribute to the learning process.

Families USA
1334 G Street, NW
Washington, DC 20005
(202) 628–3030
http://www.familiesusa.org

Families USA is a national nonprofit, nonpartisan organization dedicated to the achievement of high-quality, affordable health and long-term care for all Americans. Working at the national, state, and community levels, this organization provides a voice for health-care consumers. Among other services, it releases health policy reports describing the problems facing health-care consumers and outlining steps to solve them.

Family Life Development Center
N202 Martha Van Rensselaer Hall
Ithaca, NY 14853

(607) 255–7794
http://fldc.cornell.edu/

Located at Cornell University in New York, the Family Life Development Center seeks to improve efforts to understand and act upon risk and protective factors in the lives of children and families. As an interdisciplinary unit of Cornell's College of Human Ecology, the center accomplishes its mission through research, training, outreach, and education.

Federation of Families for Children's Mental Health
State Organizations, Chapters & Representatives
Contact List
1101 King Street, Suite 420
Alexandria, VA 22314
(703) 684–7710
http://www.ffcmh.org

This parent-run association focuses on the needs of children and youth with emotional, behavioral, or mental disorders and their families. Serving as an advocacy group, it embraces more than 120 state organizations, chapters, and representatives in all states and Ontario, Canada. It represents children, youth, and families from all cultures and backgrounds.

Chapter 2: Exploring the Diversity of Family Life

ADL: A World of Difference
823 United Nations Plaza
New York, NY 10017
(212) 885–7700
http://www.adl.org/awod/awod_institute.html

This organization first began in Boston in 1985 when the Anti-Defamation League (ADL) and WCVB-TV joined to fight prejudice and discrimination. Among its program goals are to recognize bias and the harm it inflicts on individuals and society; to explore the value of diversity and improve intergroup relations; and to combat racism, anti-Semitism, and all other forms of prejudice and bigotry.

American Institute for Managing Diversity
50 Hurt Plaza, Suite 1150
Atlanta, GA 30303
(404) 302–9226
http://aimd.org/

Founded in 1984, the American Institute for Managing Diversity (AIMD) was the first national, nonprofit organization created for the study of diversity issues. It is known as the innovator of research-based information on diversity issues. AIMD has provided individuals and organizations an opportunity to take proactive measures to make their work place and community better environments for all.

Center for Research on Women
Wellesley Centers for Women
Wellesley College
106 Central Street
Wellesley, MA 02481
(781) 283–2500
http://www.wellesley.edu/wcw/crwsub.html

The Center for Research on Women explores the diverse perspectives of women through research, action, training, and publications. It offers information and interdisciplinary studies on gender equity in education, sexual harassment in schools, child care, adolescent development, and adult roles in the home and the workplace. The center also seeks to offer innovative policy alternatives to a wide range of pressing societal concerns.

Corporate Diversity Search
P.O. Box 1086
Webster, NY 14580
(716) 787–0537
http://www.corpdiversitysearch.com/

Nationwide executive search firm specializing in the career placement of women and minorities. Founded in 1993, this organization caters to both the job candidate as well as the company having a job opening. Corporate Diversity Search is particularly helpful in recognizing the needs that exist between the home and the workplace.

Cultural Diversity Training Program
University of Sydney
A36, Faculty of Education
Sydney, Australia NSW 2006
(612) 351–6385
http://www.edfac.usyd.edu.au/centres/mcc/INDEX.HTM

Located at the University of Sydney, Australia, the Cultural Diversity Training Program is part of the University's Multicultural Centre, Faculty of Education. The program's mission is to develop and provide cross-cultural training, of the highest quality, for both the private and the public sectors.

Ethnic Studies Website
Waite Phillips Hall (WPH)
303 University of Southern California
Los Angeles, CA 90089–4033
(213) 740–2426
http://www.usc.edu/isd/archives/ethnicstudies/

The Ethnic Studies Website is maintained by the Doheny Reference Center at the University of Southern California. It provides access to research resources available through the Internet based on a global perspective of ethnicity and migration issues. The library resources are complimented by libraries, museums, and other organizations in the Southern California area which either specialize in an ethnic group or have very strong resources for ethnic studies.

Intercultural Center
Sonoma State University
1801 East Cotati Avenue
Rohnert Park, CA 94928–3609
(707) 664–2710
http://www.sonoma.edu/icc/

The mission of the Intercultural Center is to support the recruitment, retention, and graduation of a culturally diverse student body by identifying and supporting personal, academic, career, cultural, and educational development opportunities. The center seeks to enhance the awareness of cultural diversity by promoting cooperative planning among students, faculty, and staff.

Multicultural Advantage
600 W. Harvey Street, Suite A416
Philadelphia, PA 19144
(215) 849–0946
http://www.tmaonline.net/

A website that celebrates and promotes the cultural diversity of our society, particularly the importance and benefits of multiculturalism and unity. As part of its services, the Multicultural Advantage provides a rich assortment of resources, tools, and information that are career-related.

Chapter 3: Family Issues and Controversies
Family Planning
Alan Guttmacher Institute
120 Wall Street, 21st Floor
New York, NY 10005
(212) 248–1111
http://www.agi-usa.org/

The Alan Guttmacher Institute (AGI) is a nonprofit organization focused on sexual and reproductive health research, policy analysis, and public education. AGI publishes *Family Planning Perspectives, International Family Planning Perspectives,* The *Guttmacher Report* on Public Policy, and other reports on sexual and reproductive health and rights. The institute's mission is to protect the reproductive choices of all women and men in the United States and throughout the world.

American College of Obstetricians and Gynecologists
409 12th Street, SW
P.O. Box 96920
Washington, DC 20090–6920
(202) 863–4994
http://www.acog.com/

The American College of Obstetricians and Gynecologists (ACOG) was founded in 1951 in Chicago, Illinois. The ACOG today has over 43,000 members and is the nation's leading group of professionals providing health care for women. Now based in

Washington, DC, it is a private, voluntary, nonprofit membership organization.

American Society for Reproductive Medicine
1209 Montgomery Highway
Birmingham, AL 35216–2809
(205) 978–5000
http://www.asrm.com/

The American Society for Reproductive Medicine (ASRM) is an organization devoted to advancing knowledge and expertise in reproductive medicine and biology. The ASRM provides a wide assortment of literature on such topics as infertility, fertility, contraception, and reproductive technologies. The ASRM is a voluntary nonprofit organization.

National Family Planning and Reproductive Health Association
1627 K Street, NW, 12th Floor
Washington, DC 20006
(202) 293–3114
http://www.nfprha.org/

The National Family Planning and Reproductive Health Association (NFPRHA), founded in 1971, is a nonprofit, membership organization established to assure access to voluntary, comprehensive, and culturally sensitive family planning and reproductive health-care services. It also supports reproductive freedom. Members include private nonprofit clinics; state, county, and local health departments; Planned Parenthood Federation of America affiliates; and family planning councils and hospital-based clinics, along with international family planning agencies.

Planned Parenthood Federation of America
810 Seventh Avenue
New York, NY 10019
(212) 541–7800
http://www.plannedparenthood.com/index.html

Founded in 1916, Planned Parenthood is the world's largest and oldest voluntary family planning organization. Planned Parenthood believes in the fundamental rights of each individual, throughout the world, to manage his or her fertility, regardless of the individual's income, marital status, race, ethnicity, sexual orientation, age, national origin, or residence. Among its services, Planned Parenthood provides comprehensive reproductive and complementary health-care services, advocates public policies, provides sexuality education programs, and promotes research and the advancement of technology in reproductive health.

The Population Council
One Dag Hammarskjold Plaza
New York, NY 10017
(212) 339–0500
http://www.popcouncil.org/

This international organization seeks to improve the well-being and reproductive health of the population and to help achieve a humane, equitable, and sustainable balance between people and resources. It is a nonprofit institution that conducts research on three fronts: biomedical, social science, and public health. This research—and the information it produces—is designed to promote a better understanding of the problems related to reproductive health and population growth.

Reproductive Health Online
1615 Thames Street, Suite 200
Baltimore, MD 21231
(410) 955–8558
http://www.reproline.jhu.edu/index.htm

The Reproductive Health Online website provides a wide assortment of information and communication forums tailored to the needs of family planning and reproductive health educators. Members of this organization are located both in the United States and internationally. The organization places a special emphasis on increasing the number of qualified health professionals involved in family planning.

RESOLVE: The National Infertility Association
1310 Broadway
Sommerville, MA 02144
(617) 623–0744
http://www.resolve.org

RESOLVE is a nonprofit organization that provides timely support and information to people who are experiencing infertility and to increase awareness of infertility issues through public education and advocacy. The organization supports family building through a variety of methods, including appropriate medical treatment, adoption, surrogacy, and the choice of childfree living.

Society for the Study of Reproduction
1619 Monroe Street
Madison, WI 53711–2063
(608) 256–2777
http://www.ssr.org/ssr/brochure.htm

The Society for the Study of Reproduction (SSR) promotes the study of reproduction by fostering interdisciplinary communication among scientists, holding conferences, and publishing meritorious studies. The SSR consists of scientists, medical and veterinary physicians, trainees in graduate and professional schools, and others engaged in research, education, and training in fields relevant to reproductive biology. It is affiliated with colleges and universities, medical and veterinary schools, medical centers, research institutes, government agencies, and industry in some forty-seven countries.

Contemporary Parenthood

Administration for Children and Families
370 L'Enfant Promenade SW
Washington, DC 20447
(202) 205–7923
http://www.acf.dhhs.gov

The Administration for Children and Families (ACF) is a federal agency funding state, local, and tribal organizations to provide family assistance (welfare), child support, child care, Head Start, child welfare, and other programs relating to children and families. Actual services are provided by state, county, city, and tribal governments, and public and private local agencies. ACF assists these organizations through funding, policy direction, and information services.

Families Worldwide
5278 Pinemount Drive, Suite A-180
Salt Lake City, UT 84123
(801) 262–6878
http://www.fww.org

Families Worldwide emphasizes that the greatest resource in solving family problems lies within the family members themselves. The organization seeks to teach important family life skills and ways to nourish family bonds. A particularly strong emphasis is placed on such relationship-building principles as kindness, commitment, communication, choices, well-being, and spirituality.

Family Education Network
20 Park Avenue, 12th Floor
Boston, MA 02116
(800) 323–4776
http://family education.com/home/

This organization offers an online consumer network of the world's best learning and information resources, personalized to help parents, teachers, and students of all ages take control of their learning and make it part of their everyday lives. It is built on a strong foundation from leading educational publishers and technology companies. The network has business offices in San Francisco; New York City; Boston; Chicago; and Paramus, New Jersey.

National Center for Fathering
P.O. Box 413888
Kansas City, MO 64141
1–800–593–DADS
http://www.fathers.com

The mission of the National Center for Fathering is to inspire and educate men on how to be better fathers. In response to increases in fatherlessness in America, the center has developed a range of resources designed to prepare men for fathering. The center offers supportive assistance and advice through its nationwide radio program, as well as through its *Today's Father* magazine and regular newsletters.

National Council on Family Relations
3989 Central Avenue, NE, Suite 550
Minneapolis, MN 55421
(763) 791–9331
http://www.ncfr.com

The National Council on Family Relations (NCFR) provides a forum for family researchers, educators, and practitioners to share in the development and dissemination of knowledge about families and family relationships, establishes professional standards, and works to promote family well-being. The organization publishes two scholarly journals, *Journal of Marriage and Family* and *Family Relations*.

National Parenting Center
22801 Ventura Boulevard
Woodland Hills, CA 91364
(800) 753–6667
http://www.tnpc.com

The National Parenting Center promotes the concept of parenting education and seeks to enhance parenting skills and competencies. It publishes the newsletter *ParenTalk*, which features advice and guidance from child-rearing experts. The organization seeks to share the latest in medical, behavioral, and educational information.

National Partnership for Women and Families
1875 Connecticut Avenue, NW, Suite 650
Washington, DC 20009
(202) 986–2600
http://www.nationalpartnership.org

A nonprofit, nonpartisan organization that uses public education and advocacy to promote fairness in the workplace, quality health care, and policies that help women and men meet the dual demands of work and family. Founded in 1971 as the Women's Legal Defense Fund, the National Partnership has grown from a small group of volunteers into one of the nation's most powerful and effective advocates for women and families. Working with business, government, unions, nonprofit organizations, and the media, the National Partnership is a voice for fairness, a source for solutions, and a force for change.

Work and Family Life

Center for Families, Work, and Well-being
900 Mackinnon
University of Guelph, Ontario N1G 2W1
Canada
(519) 824–4120
http://www.worklifecanada.ca/

The Center for Families, Work, and Well-being was founded in 1998 at the University of Guelph in Canada. It is an interdisciplinary research and educational center responding to the importance of individual and family well-being as a foundation for both economic growth and strong communities. The center focuses on the interplay that exists in family patterns, paid work, and broader economic and political structures. The center also emphasizes the importance of research, policy development, and progressive practices that relate to the changing nature of work and family life.

Center for Work and the Family
5409 Thomas Avenue
Oakland, California 94618
(510) 527–0107
http://www.centerforworkandfamily.com

This organization seeks to bridge the gap between the needs of families and the world of work. Providing psycho-education and support services at the worksite, the center offers parent education, group facilitation, corporate consulting, counseling, and psychotherapy. Programming is designed with feedback mechanisms so that management can learn about employees' needs and experiences and so participants can provide constructive feedback to their companies.

Families and Work Institute
267 Fifth Avenue, Floor 2
New York, NY 10016
(212) 465–2044
http://www.familiesandwork.org

The Families and Work Institute (FWI) is a nonprofit center for research that provides data to inform decision-making on the changing workplace, the changing family, and the changing community. The institute is known for its nonpartisan research into emerging work-life issues; for its solutions-oriented studies addressing topics of vital importance to all sectors of society; and for its fostering connections among workplaces, families, and communities. Business and community leaders, policymakers, individual families, educators, and the media seek out its research, which has influenced decisions across the nation.

Kunz Center for the Study of Work & Family
Department of Sociology
University of Cincinnati
P.O. Box 210378
Cincinnati, OH 45221–0378
(513) 556–4733
http://asweb.artsci.uc.edu/sociology/kunzctr

The Kunz Center for the Study of Work & Family (KCSWF) exists within the Department of Sociology at the University of Cincinnati. The center conducts research and other programs on work, the family, and issues of interdependence between work and family. The center's work is interdisciplinary, and its programs and projects are open to all who share an interest in work and family issues.

Labor Project for Working Families
2521 Channing Way, #5555
Berkeley, CA 94720
(510) 643–7088
http://violet.berkeley.edu/~iir/workfam/home.html

A national advocacy and policy center providing technical assistance, resources, and education to unions and union members addressing family issues in the workplace including child care, elder care, flexible work schedules, family leave, and quality of life issues. The Labor Project publishes a quarterly labor-oriented newsletter on work and family. The project has an extensive database of work/family collective bargaining language from a range of industries. The Labor Project is funded by union contributions and private foundations.

NIH Work and Family Life Center
31 Center Drive, MSC 2205

Building 31, Room B3C15
Bethesda, MD 20892–2205
(301) 435–1619
http://wflc.od.nih.gov/

This organization seeks to help people balance the increasing demands of their work with their personal interests and responsibilities. The center strives to increase employee well-being, thereby improving the quality of work and the quality of life. To this end, the center stresses the development of workplaces where employees are given the resources, flexibility, and trust they need to exercise personal responsibility and self-discipline in managing their careers and their personal lives.

Work and Family Connection Site
5197 Beachside Drive
Minnetonka, MN 55343
(952) 936–7898
http://www.workfamily.com

An organization intent on creating a workplace that is both supportive and effective. It provides employers, and those that offer them products and services, with the most information possible. It offers training programs for employers as well a national news and information service that summarizes the latest trends and practices in the career world. The primary goals of this organization are to help employers see the value of a supportive, flexible workplace, see their own responsibility in achieving that goal, and learn how to be a force in transforming their culture.

Work in America Institute
700 White Plains Road
Scarsdale, NY 10583
(914) 472–9600
http://www.workinamerica.org

The mission of this organization is to advance productivity and the quality of working life through the principles of sound human resource practices which are applicable in all industries. The institute promotes policies and practices that address personnel development, employee security, life-long learning, training in basic and technical skills, and employee involvement. The institute's programming seeks to upgrade the productivity and the quality of working life for employees, employers, unions, government, and the nation as a whole.

Work-Family-Life Interactions
Children, Youth and Family Consortium
McNamara Alumni Center, Suite 207A
200 Oak Street Southeast
Minneapolis, MN 55455
(619) 625–7849
http://www.cyfc.umn.edu/work.html

Located at the University of Minnesota, this program offers a collection of information, research, and opinion on work and family issues. Work-Family-Life Interactions aims to provide parents, employers, and employees with ongoing electronic access to the information resources that assist in balancing work and personal lives.

Single-Parent Families

Children's Rights Council
Suite 401, 300 I Street NE
Washington, DC 20002
(202) 547–6227
http://www.info4parents.com/index.html

The Children's Rights Council (CRC) works to assure a child the frequent, meaningful, and continuing contact with two parents and an extended family that the child would normally have during a marriage. The organization strengthens families through education, favoring family formation, and family preservation. Unlike many other organizations with some of the same concerns, CRC is genderless; it is not a women's group nor a men's group. Rather, the CRC advocates what it believes to be in the best interests of children including the Children's Bill of Rights. The organization publishes a quarterly newsletter, meets with policy makers throughout the country, and generally educates people of the plight of our children due to prevalent practices in our courts and departments of human services.

Divorce Information
Alabama Family Law Center
3280 Morgan Drive

Birmingham, AL 35216
(205) 979–6960
http://www.divorceinfo.com

This organization provides a diversity of information to single parents, including financial issues, child-care challenges, social adjustments, and work responsibilities. The emphasis is on problems and issues that single parents face, as well as the opportunities that exist. Special consideration is given to legal, counseling, and mediation practices.

Parenting Coalition
1025 Connecticut Avenue, NW, Suite 415
Washington, DC 20036
(202) 530–0849
http://www.parentingcoalition.org

The Parenting Coalition is a nonprofit, membership-based organization whose goal is to build the profession of practitioners working to strengthen families. Its vision is to make tools, information, resources, and research easily accessible to all parents and caregivers enabling them to enhance their skills and attitudes for raising healthy, successful, and responsible children. Programs, initiatives, and services are designed to foster communication, promote professionalism, build partnerships, and enhance collaboration among individuals and organizations working with parents.

Parents Without Partners
1650 South Dixie Highway, Suite 510
Boca Raton, FL 33432
(561) 391–8833
http://www.parentswithoutpartners.org

Parents Without Partners provides single parents and their children with an opportunity for enhancing personal growth, self-confidence, and sensitivity toward others by offering an environment for support, friendship, and the exchange of parenting techniques. Parents Without Partners is the largest international, nonprofit membership organization devoted to the welfare and interests of single parents and their children. Single parents may be male or female, custodial or noncustodial, separated, divorced, widowed, or never-married.

Responsible Single Fathers
541 Knopp NE
Grand Rapids, MI 48909
(616) 447–0798
http://www.singlefather.org/

Responsible Single Fathers is an organization of men and women working to help children adjust to the difficulties often brought about by their parents' divorce, death, or other forms of relationship dissolution. The organization offers programming designed to help fathers better cope with their ability to nurture, love, support, and emotionally and financially care for their children.

Single Parent Resource Center
31 East 28th Street, 2d Floor
New York, NY 10016
(212) 951–7030
http://www.singleparentusa.com/

The Single Parent Resource Center (SPRC) was started in 1975 as a demonstration-project of the Community Service Society of New York. Today it exists as an independent, not-for-profit organization, supported by a variety of public and private funds from New York State, New York City, foundations, churches, and interested friends and supporters. It is a clearinghouse for information on single-parent organizations in the United States and around the world. Its goal is to enable single-parent groups and organizations to share information on program development, service models, and techniques.

Single Parents Association
4727 E. Bell Road, Suite 45, PMB 209
Phoenix, AZ 85032
(623) 581–7445
http://www.singleparents.org

Single Parents Association (SPA) is a nonprofit organization devoted to providing educational opportunities and supportive services. The SPA provides a wide range of single-parent educational information at its regular meetings as well as in its publication, the *SPA News*. Major programming themes are the promotion of self-growth and happiness among the members, their children, and the community at large.

Single Parents World
Parents World Productions
216 Queen Anne Pl. SE
Calgary, AB T2J 4S3
(403) 278–0950
http://www.parentsworld.com

This organization caters to the needs and interests of single parents and their children. Single Parents World provides access to an assortment of information and services, including books, articles, and newsletter archives. The organization also provides a discussion forum on single parenthood, child support advice and guidance, and valuable single-parenting links.

Families with Physical Disabilities and Chronic Illnesses

Center for Research in Chronic Disorders
University of Pittsburgh School of Nursing
460 Victoria Building
3500 Victoria Street
Pittsburgh, PA 15261
(412) 624–7838
http://crcd.nursing.pitt.edu/

The Center for Research in Chronic Disorders (CRCD) was founded in October 1994 and is located at the University of Pittsburgh School of Nursing. The center is designed to provide infrastructure support for the development of science in the area of chronic disorders, with particular emphasis on quality of life, functional status, cognitive function, and adherence to treatment regimens as they are impacted by and impact management of those disorders.

Center for Research on Chronic Illness
University of North Carolina at Chapel Hill
School of Nursing, Carrington Hall, CB #7460
Chapel Hill, NC 27599
(919) 966–0453
http://www.unc.edu/depts/crci

The Center for Research on Chronic Illness is one of nine centers funded by the National Institute of Nursing Research (NR) to promote excellence in nursing research. The center includes 13 federally funded research projects, a pilot study program, and a range of services to advance research on preventing and managing chronic illness in vulnerable people.

Children with Disabilities
Office of FirstGov
750 17th Street, NW, Suite 200
Washington, DC 20006–4634
(866) 347–7846
http://www.childrenwithdisabilities.ncjrs.org

Children with Disabilities is a government-sponsored organization. It offers families, service providers, and other interested individuals information about advocacy, education, employment, health, housing, recreation, technical assistance, and transportation covering a broad array of developmental, physical, and emotional disabilities.

Family Caregiver Alliance
690 Market Street, Suite 600
San Francisco, CA 94104
(415) 434–3388
http://www.caregiver.org

The Family Caregiver Alliance was the first community-based nonprofit organization in the country to address the needs of families and friends providing long-term care at home. The FCA is now a nationally recognized information center on long-term care. The FCA serves as a public voice for caregivers, illuminating the daily challenges they face, offering them the assistance they need, and championing their cause through education, services, research, and advocacy.

Henry J. Kaiser Family Foundation
2400 Sand Hill Road
Menlo Park, CA 94025
(650) 854–9400
http://www.kff.org

The Henry J. Kaiser Family Foundation is an independent philanthropy focusing on the major health-care issues facing the nation, including chronic illness and physical disabilities. It is an independent voice and source of facts and analysis for policymakers, the media, the health-care community, and the general public. The foundation is primarily an operating organization that develops and runs its own research and communications programs, often in partnership with outside organizations.

National Center for Health Statistics
Division of Data Services
6525 Belcrest Road
Hyattsville, MD 20782–2003
(301) 458–4636
http://www.cdc.gov/nchs

The National Center for Health Statistics (NCHS) is the federal government's principal vital and health statistics agency. To meet priority data needs for public health, NCHS works closely with other federal agencies as well as researchers and academic institutions. NCHS data systems include data on vital events as well as information on health status, lifestyle, exposure to unhealthy influences, the onset and diagnosis of illness and disability, and the use of health care. These data are used by policymakers in Congress and the administration, by medical researchers, and by others in the health community.

National Council on Disability
1331 F Street, NW, Suite 850
Washington, DC 20004
(202) 272–2004
http://www.ncd.gov

The National Council on Disability (NCD) is an independent federal agency making recommendations to the president and Congress on issues affecting 54 million Americans with disabilities. NCD is composed of 15 members appointed by the president and confirmed by the U.S. Senate. NCD's overall purpose is to promote policies, programs, practices, and procedures that guarantee equal opportunity for all individuals with disabilities, regardless of the nature or severity of the disability and to empower individuals with disabilities to achieve economic self-sufficiency, independent living, and inclusion and integration into all aspects of society.

The National Information Center for Children and Youth with Disabilities
P.O. Box 1492

Washington, DC 20013
(800) 695–0285
http://www.nichcy.org/#about

NICHCY is the national information and referral center that provides information on disabilities and disability-related issues for families, educators, and other professionals. Its special focus is children and youth (birth to age 22). NICHCY provides information and makes referrals in areas related to specific disabilities, early intervention, special education and related services, family issues, individualized education programs, and disability organizations and associations.

National Institute on Disability and Rehabilitation Research
400 Maryland Avenue, SW
Washington, DC 20202–2572
(202) 205–8134
http://www.ed.gov/offices/OSERS/NIDRR

The National Institute on Disability and Rehabilitation Research (NIDRR) provides leadership and support for a comprehensive program of research related to the rehabilitation of individuals with disabilities. All of its programmatic efforts are aimed at improving the lives of individuals with disabilities from birth through adulthood.

National Parent Network on Disabilities
1130 17th St, NW, Suite 400
Washington, DC 20036
(202) 463–2299
http://www.npnd.org/main.htm

NPND is a nonprofit organization dedicated to empowering parents. Located in Washington, DC, NPND has the unique capability to provide its members with the most up-to-date information on the activities of all three branches of government that affect individuals with disabilities. NPND's membership includes individuals and family members, as well as national, state, and local organizations that represent the interests of individuals with disabilities.

Gay and Lesbian Families

Association for Gay, Lesbian, and Bisexual Issues in Counseling

American Counseling Association
5999 Stevenson Avenue
Alexandria, VA 22304–3300
(703) 823–9800
http://www.aglbic.org/

The mission of the Association for Gay, Lesbian, and Bisexual Issues in Counseling is to educate mental health service providers about issues confronting gay, lesbian, bisexual, and transgender (GLBT) individuals. This organization believes that all individuals should be free to develop their full potential regardless of sexual orientation and gender identity and that professional counselors must understand the unique ways gays, lesbians, bisexuals, and transgendered individuals experience inequality and injustice resulting from discrimination and prejudice.

Gay and Lesbian Alliance Against Defamation
248 West 35th Street, 8th Floor
New York, NY 10001
(212) 629–3322
http://www.glaad.org/org/index.html

The Gay and Lesbian Alliance Against Defamation (GLAAD) is dedicated to promoting and ensuring fair, accurate, and inclusive representation of individuals and events in all media as a means of eliminating homophobia and discrimination based on gender identity and sexual orientation. GLAAD was formed in New York in 1985 and began by protesting blatantly offensive and sensationalized stories about HIV infection and AIDS. Its mission is to study and articulate cultural and media-specific trends, issues, and controversies and to educate the entertainment industry on the importance of accurate and realistic images and portrayals.

Gay, Lesbian, and Straight Education Network
121 West 27th Street, Suite 804
New York, NY 10001–6207
(212) 727–0135
http://www.glsen.org/templates/about/index.
  html?section=31

The Gay, Lesbian and Straight Education Network strives to assure that each member of every school community is valued and respected regardless of sexual orientation or gender identity/

expression. The organization believes that such an atmosphere engenders a positive sense of self, which is the basis of educational achievement and personal growth. Believing that homophobia and heterosexism undermine a healthy school climate, the organization works to educate teachers, students, and the public at large about the damaging effects these forces have on youth and adults alike.

Human Rights Campaign
919 18th Street, NW, Suite 800
Washington, DC 20006
(202) 628–4160
http://www.hrc.org

An organization that shares the latest on national political issues affecting gay, lesbian, bisexual, and transgender families. Among other functions, it provides information, support, and advice on adoption, aging, domestic partner agreements, money, parenting, powers of attorney, schools, and wills. It also seeks to educate the public on ending workplace discrimination, combating hate crimes, fighting HIV/AIDS, protecting families, and working for better health.

Lambda Legal Defense and Education Fund
120 Wall Street, Suite 1500
New York, NY 10005–3904
(212) 809–8585
http://lambdalegal.org/cgi-bin/iowa/index.html

The Lambda Legal Defense and Education Fund is a national organization committed to achieving full recognition of the civil rights of lesbians, gay men, and people with HIV/AIDS through impact litigation, education, and public policy work. Lambda pursues litigation in all parts of the country and in every area of the law, such as discrimination in employment, housing, public accommodations, and the military; HIV/AIDS-related discrimination; parenting and relationship issues; equal marriage rights; equal employment and domestic partnership benefits; immigration issues; anti-gay initiatives; and free speech and equal protection rights.

Lesbian and Gay Immigration Rights Task Force
350 West 31st Street, Suite 505
New York, NY 10001

(212) 714–2904
http://www.lgirtf.org/

The Lesbian and Gay Immigration Rights Task Force (LGIRTF) is a coalition of immigrants, attorneys, and other activists that addresses the widespread discriminatory impact of immigration laws on the lives of lesbians, gay men, and people with HIV through education, outreach, and advocacy, and by providing legal services, information, referrals, and support.

LesbiaNation
2800 Biscayne Boulevard, 8th Floor
Miami, FL 33137
(305) 572–9912
http://www.lesbianation.com

LesbiaNation is a leading online community dedicated to the celebration of lesbian culture and identity. As a global multimedia medium this website aims to enlighten, connect, educate, entertain, distribute goods and services, and provide borderless communication paths for its visitors.

National Gay and Lesbian Task Force
1700 Kalorama Road, NW
Washington, DC 20009–2624
(202) 332–6483
http://www.ngltf.org/

The National Gay and Lesbian Task Force (NGLTF) is a national progressive organization working for the civil rights of gay, lesbian, bisexual, and transgendered people, with the vision and commitment to building a powerful political movement. The NGLTF publishes original research, conducts unique analysis on existing data, engages in policy analysis, convenes roundtables of scholars and activists, and engages in public speaking and public education. NGLTF is a full participant in the public policy debates at the federal level, both in Congress and in the administration. It connects policy work at the federal level with local activists and pursues federal resources for state and local projects.

Parents, Families and Friends of Lesbians and Gays
1726 M Street, NW, Suite 400
Washington, DC 20036

(202) 467–8180

http://www.pflag.org

Parents, Families and Friends of Lesbians and Gays (PFLAG) is a national nonprofit organization with over 80,000 members and supporters and more than 460 affiliates in the United States. PFLAG promotes the health and well-being of gay, lesbian, bisexual, transgendered persons, and their families and friends through: support, to cope with an adverse society; education, to enlighten an ill-informed public; and advocacy, to end discrimination and secure equal civil rights.

Caring for Aging Family Members

Aging Parents and Adult Children Together
Consumer Response Center
Federal Trade Commission
Washington, DC 20580
(877) 382–4357
http://www.ftc.gov/bcp/conline/pubs/services/apact/

An outreach service sponsored by the Federal Trade Commission in partnership with AARP. Exposes the public to some of the more frequent eldercare issues and sheds light on the life options and decisions that can help maximize the independence, comfort, and quality of later life. Advice is offered by medical, legal, financial, and gerontology experts, as well as caregiver support organizations.

American Geriatrics Society
The Empire State Building
350 Fifth Avenue, Suite 801
New York, NY 10118
(212) 308–1414
http://www.americangeriatrics.org/

The American Geriatrics Society (AGS) is a professional organization of health-care providers dedicated to improving the health and well-being of all older adults. With an active membership of over 6,000 health-care professionals, the AGS has a long history of effecting change in the provision of health care for older adults. In the last decade, the AGS has become a pivotal force in shaping attitudes, policies, and practices regarding health care for older people.

American Society on Aging
833 Market Street, Suite 511
San Francisco, CA 94103–1824
(415) 974–9600
http://www.asaging.org/index.cfm

A professional organization uniting researchers, practitioners, educators, business people, and policymakers concerned with the physical, emotional, social, economic, and spiritual aspects of aging. Through its educational programming, publications, and training resources, the American Society on Aging acknowledges that the complexity of aging can only be addressed as a multidisciplinary whole.

Children of Aging Parents
1609 Woodbourne Road, Suite 302A
Levittown, PA 19057
(800) 227–7294
http://www.caps4caregivers.org/

Children of Aging Parents (CAPS) is a nonprofit, charitable organization whose mission is to assist the nation's nearly 23 million caregivers of the elderly with reliable information, referrals, and support, and to heighten public awareness that the health of the family caregivers is essential to ensure quality care of the nation's growing elderly population. CAPS writes, collects, and disseminates fact sheets on various topics. Also, it publishes a bimonthly newsletter filled with news and advice for caregivers. CAPS arranges conferences and workshops on issues vital to caregivers and professionals, shares new product information, and utilizes the media to improve the public's understanding of caregiving and issues of aging.

ElderWeb
1305 Chadwick Drive
Normal, IL 61761
(309) 451–3319
http://www.elderweb.com/

ElderWeb includes thousands of reviewed links to long-term care information, a searchable database of organizations, and an expanding library of articles and reports, news, and events. This website is designed to be a research site for both professionals and family members looking for information on eldercare and long-term care, and includes links to information on legal, financial, medical, and housing issues, as well as policy, research, and statistics.

Family Caregiver Alliance
690 Market Street, Suite 600
San Francisco, CA 94104
(415) 434–3388
http://www.caregiver.org

Founded in 1977, Family Caregiver Alliance (FCA) was the first community-based nonprofit organization in the country to address the needs of families and friends providing long-term care at home. FCA is recognized as a national information center on long-term care and the leading agency in California's system of Caregiver Resource Centers. FCA serves as a public voice for caregivers, illuminating the daily challenges they face, offering them the assistance they so desperately need and deserve, and championing their cause through education, services, research, and advocacy.

Gerontological Society of America
1030 15th Street, NW, Suite 250
Washington, DC 20005–1503
(202) 842–1275
http://www.geron.org/society.htm

A national organization that promotes the conduct of multi- and interdisciplinary research in aging by expanding and improving the quantity of gerontological research, and by increasing its funding resources. It also disseminates gerontological knowledge to researchers, to practitioners, and to decision and opinion makers. This organization publishes *The Gerontologist* and *The Journal of Gerontology*.

National Family Caregivers Association
10400 Connecticut Avenue, #500
Kensington, MD 20895–3944
(800) 896–3650
http://www.nfcacares.org

The National Family Caregivers Association (NFCA) supports family caregivers and speaks out publicly for caregivers' needs.

NFCA embraces a philosophy of self-advocacy and self-care that rests on the belief that caregivers who choose to take charge of their lives, and see caregiving as but one of its facets, are in a position to be happier and healthier individuals. Caregivers are then able to have a higher quality of life and to make a more positive contribution to the well-being of their care recipient, all of which has a positive impact on society and health-care costs.

National Institute on Aging
Building 31, Room 5C27 31
Center Drive, MSC 2292
Bethesda, MD 20892
(301) 496–1752
http: //www.nia.nih.gov/

The National Institute on Aging (NIA), one of the 25 institutes and centers of the National Institutes of Health, leads a broad scientific effort to understand the nature of aging and to extend the healthy, active years of life. The NIA provides leadership in aging research, training, health information dissemination, and other programs relevant to aging and older people.

Senior Solutions
60 Fenton Street, Suite 4
Livermore, CA 94550
(925) 443–3101
http://www.seniorsolutionsinc.com

Senior Solutions provides health, financial, and legal services to enhance the lives of elderly persons wishing to remain in their own homes. This organization supports assistance to families through an assortment of seminars, lectures, and continuing education programs. In addition, Senior Solutions works with health-care teams of physicians, therapists, and social workers to ensure continuous quality care for the elderly.

Families of Divorce

American Academy of Matrimonial Lawyers
150 N. Michigan Avenue, Suite 2040
Chicago, IL 60601
(312) 263–6477
http://www.aaml.org

This national legal organization seeks to encourage the study, improve the practice, elevate the standards, and advance the cause of matrimonial law, to the end that the welfare of the family and society are protected. Areas of specialization include divorce, prenuptial agreements, postnuptial agreements, annulment, child custody and visitation, property valuation and division, alimony, and child support.

American Bar Association Section of Family Law
750 N. Lake Shore Drive
Chicago, IL, 60611
(312) 988–5603
http://www.abanet.org/family

The Family Law Section was organized in 1958 to improve the administration of justice in the field of family law. The section recognizes that family law is a rapidly growing, complex area with an interstate and at times international character. Areas such as divorce, custody, adoption, alimony, and support are within the scope of the section, as are emerging issues such as third-party parental rights, child abduction, federal and interstate legislation, mediation, and such complicated areas as paternity, perinatal drug addiction, and genetic engineering.

Association for Conflict Resolution
1527 New Hampshire Avenue, NW, Third Floor
Washington, DC 20036
(202) 667–9700
http://www.mediators.org/

The Association for Conflict Resolution (ACR) is a professional organization dedicated to enhancing the practice and public understanding of conflict resolution. ACR represents and serves a diverse national and international audience that includes more than 7,000 mediators, arbitrators, facilitators, educators, and others involved in the field of conflict resolution and collaborative decision-making.

Children of Separation and Divorce
2000 Century Plaza, Suite 121
Columbia, MD 21044
(410) 740–9553
http://www.divorceABC.com

Children of Separation and Divorce (COSD) is a private non-profit organization serving as an advocate and liaison for families in transition. It seeks to help people of all ages and walks of life to adjust to the processes of separation, divorce, and remarriage. COSD offers a combination of professional and peer counseling services, community outreach and prevention programs, research efforts, and advocacy.

Coalition for Marriage, Family and Couples Education
5310 Belt Road, NW
Washington, DC 20015–1961
(202) 362–3332
http://www.smartmarriages.com/about_cmfce.html

The coalition (CMFCE) is an independent, nonpartisan, nondenominational, nonsectarian organization. It serves as a clearinghouse to help people find the information they need to strengthen their marriages and families. CMFCE serves to promote an educational approach to strengthening marriages and families, while it increases the availability of courses and programs in the community.

DivorceCare
P.O. Box 1739
Wake Forest, NC 27588–1739
(800) 489–7778
http://www.divorcecare.com

DivorceCare is a support program designed to assist individuals going through divorce and separation. It provides group support, encouragement, guidance, and access to resources and information designed to help with the healing process.

Divorcesource
P.O. Box 1580
Allentown, PA 18105–1580
(610) 820–8120
http://www.divorcesource.com

Divorcesource is a resource for divorce-related information as well as guidance and supportive services. This network is a guide to help individuals understand basic divorce-related information and laws that pertain to specific issues and specific locations throughout the United States and Canada. Divorcesource is available to educate persons prior to seeking professional services and/or products that may be required and/or needed.

Mediation Center
P.O. Box 51119
Eugene, OR 97405
(541) 345–1456

The Mediation Center provides information on the practical skills, strategies, and techniques necessary for effective mediation practice. It espouses theoretical foundations of conflict resolution, negotiation, and mediation theory, as well as ethical standards and policy considerations of mediation practice.

Rainbows
2100 Golf Road, Suite 370
Rolling Meadows, IL 60008–4231
(847) 952–1770
http://www.rainbows.org/mission.html

Rainbows is a not-for-profit, international organization that offers training and curricula for establishing peer support groups in schools, parenting groups, social agencies, churches, synagogues, or other groups. This supportive assistance is available to children, adolescents, and adults of all ages and walks of life who are grieving a death, divorce, or any other painful transition in their family.

Remarried Families

Bonus Families
1555 Riverlake Road, Suite D-120
Discovery Bay, CA 94514
(925) 516–2681
http://www.bonusfamilies.com/

Bonus Families is a website dedicated to the support, reassurance, and well-being of every stepfamily member. It offers visitors a wide range of services, from expert advice and informative articles to editorials and book reviews. The central theme of Bonus Families is to help individuals feel appreciated for who they are even though they're not biologically related to everyone in the family.

Center for Law and Social Policy
1015 15th Street, NW, Suite 400
Washington, DC 20005
(202) 906–8000
http://www.clasp.org/

This is a legal organization whose work is concentrated on family policy and access to civil legal assistance for low-income families. Family policy projects include welfare reform, workforce development, child care, child support enforcement, and reproductive health. The organization maintains an extensive network of state and local advocates; provides training and technical assistance to advocates and officials; and produces publications, newsletters, and periodic updates on new policy developments.

Children's Foundation
725 Fifteenth Street, NW, Suite 505
Washington, DC 20005–2109
(202) 347–3300
http://www.childrensfoundation.net

The Children's Foundation (CF), a private national educational nonprofit organization, seeks to improve the lives of children and those who care for them. Its mission is to provide a voice for caregivers, children, and their families on issues of critical concern. Through the National Child Care Advocacy Program and National Child Support Program, CF conducts research and provides information and training on child nutrition programs; quality child care; leadership development; health care; welfare-to-work programs; and enforcement of court-ordered child support.

Stepfamily Association of America
650 J Street, Suite 205
Lincoln, NE 68508
(800) 735–0329
http://www.saafamilies.org/

This association provides information, education, support, and advocacy for stepfamilies and those who work with them. It strives to develop and disseminate research-based information and materials and to develop opportunities for support and education. Additionally, the Stepfamily Association of America serves as an advocate for financial, institutional, political, and social changes that support stepfamilies.

Stepfamily Foundation
333 West End Avenue
New York, NY 10023
(212) 877–3244
http://www.stepfamily.org/

The Stepfamily Foundation provides counseling and information to create a successful step relationship. Founded in 1975, it gives guidance, supportive understanding, and training to forge happier and healthier stepfamilies. The foundation also offers an assortment of books, learning tools and information packets, seminars, and workshops.

Stepfamily inFormation
675 Lake Street, Suite 249
Oak Park, IL 60301
(708) 848–0909
http://sfhelp.org

Stepfamily inFormation is a nonprofit, research-based education website designed to build high-nurturance relationships and family resiliency. This website promotes both the teaching of important life skills and concepts and minimizing the problems often accompanying post-divorce life. It provides an array of helpful materials for co-parents, children, and helping professionals, online and by mail.

Stepfamily Network
555 Bryant Street, Suite 361
Palo Alto, CA 94301
(800) 487–1073
http://www.stepfamily.net

The Stepfamily Network is a nonprofit organization dedicated to helping stepfamily members achieve harmony and mutual respect in their family lives through education and support. This organization promotes the concept of stepfamily cohesion and solidarity so that each members' potential and needs can be achieved. It offers resources such as book reviews, child-care articles, and forums on important stepfamily issues.

Stepfamily Solutions
7215 Jackson Road, Suite G
Ann Arbor, MI 48103
(734) 669–7202
http://www.stepfamilysolutions.net

Stepfamily Solutions provides educational opportunities to enhance the rewards and satisfactions of stepfamily life. Their organizational philosophy it that the roles, rules, and relationships within the stepfamily do not mirror those of the nuclear family. To realign perceptions, Stepfamily Solutions offers couple counseling, premarital stepfamily counseling, group therapy, stepfamily workshops and classes, and training opportunities for professionals.

Abusive Family Relationships

Administration on Children, Youth and Families
U.S. Department of Health and Human Services
200 Independence Avenue, SW
Washington, DC 20201
(202) 619–0257
http://www.acf.dhhs.gov/programs/acyf

This organization oversees the major federal programs that support social services. It promotes the positive growth and development of children, youth, and their families by providing protective services and shelter for children and youth in at-risk situations. They also provide child care for working families and families on public assistance, and they help secure the adoption of children with special needs.

American Professional Society on the Abuse of Children
PO Box 26901
CHO 3B-3406
Oklahoma City, OK 73190
(405) 271–8202
http://www.apsac.org

This organization addresses all facets of the professional response to child maltreatment: prevention, assessment, intervention, and treatment. It represents all of the major disciplines responding to child abuse and neglect, including mental health, law, medicine, child protective services, and law enforcement. Its publications and training covers all aspects of child maltreatment, including emotional neglect and other forms of neglect, psychological maltreatment, and physical and sexual abuse.

Childhelp USA
15757 N. 78th Street
Scottsdale, AZ 85260
(480) 922–8212
http://www.childhelpusa.org

Childhelp USA focuses on the many faces of child abuse, from personal suffering to legal battles. Their programs include the National Child Abuse Hotline; residential treatment facilities in both California and Virginia; children's advocacy centers; foster care and group homes; and increasing education, community outreach, and public awareness.

Children's Institute International
711 S. New Hampshire Avenue
Los Angeles, CA 90005
(213) 385–5100
http://www.childrensinstitute.org

The Children's Institute International (CII) is a private, nonprofit organization dedicated to protecting, preserving, and strengthening the family through the provision of child-abuse prevention and treatment services for high-need, low-resource families, as well as through professional training, research, and advocacy. The CII offers programming that includes such areas as child and family assessment, sexual abuse treatment, domestic violence intervention, family treatment services, therapeutic day care, child health care, and substance abuse treatment and prevention services.

Family Violence and Sexual Assault Institute
FVSAI at Alliant International University
6160 Cornerstone Court East
San Diego, CA 92121
(858) 623–2777
http://www.fvsai.org/

This institute assists professionals in obtaining the latest information on the treatment of batterers. It offers therapy for children who have been exposed to violence or maltreatment and educates visitors about the need for research and evaluation in these areas. The organization also provides information, networking, training, education, and program evaluation for other agencies, practitioners, and organizations.

Family Violence Prevention Fund
383 Rhode Island Street, Suite 304
San Francisco, CA 94103–5133
(415) 252–8900
http://endabuse.org/index2.php3

The Family Violence Prevention Fund (FVPF) works to end domestic violence and help women and children whose lives are devastated by abuse. The FVPF is a national nonprofit organization committed to allied professionals, women's rights, civil rights, and other social justice organizations. It encourages children's groups to join the campaign through public education/ prevention, public policy reform, model training, advocacy programs, and concerted organization.

International Society for the Prevention of Child Abuse and Neglect
25 W. 560 Geneva Road, Suite L2C
Carol Stream, IL 60188
(630) 221–1311
http://www.ispcan.org/

The International Society for the Prevention of Child Abuse and Neglect is a multidisciplinary, international organization that brings together a worldwide cross-section of committed professionals to work toward the prevention and treatment of child abuse, neglect, and exploitation globally. The mission of this organization is to prevent the following from happening to children in every nation: their physical, sexual, and/or emotional abuse; their neglect; their living on the streets; their deaths; their involvement in prostitution; their displacement as a result of war; and their labor.

National Clearinghouse on Child Abuse and Neglect Information
330 C Street, SW

Washington, DC 20447
(800) 394–3366
http://www.calib.com/nccanch

The National Clearinghouse on Child Abuse and Neglect Information was established by the Child Abuse Prevention and Treatment Act of 1974. It provides information products and technical assistance services to help professionals locate information related to child abuse and neglect and related child welfare issues. Among the information available are statistics, state laws, and resources on such topics as prevention, child protection, and out-of-home care.

National Resource Center on Child Maltreatment
P.O. Box 441470
Aurora, CO 80044–1470
(303) 369–8008
http://www.gocwi.org/nrccm/

This center helps states and local agencies develop effective and efficient child protective services (CPS) systems. Jointly operated by the Child Welfare Institute and ACTION for Child Protection, the center responds to needs related to prevention, identification, intervention, and treatment of child abuse and neglect.

Violence Against Women Office, U.S. Department of Justice
810 7th Street, NW
Washington, DC 20531
(202) 307–6026
http://www.ojp.usdoj.gov/vawo

The Violence Against Women Office works with victim advocates and law enforcement in developing grant programs that support a wide range of services for women including: advocacy, emergency shelter, law enforcement protection, and legal aid. Additionally the Violence Against Women Office is leading efforts both nationally and internationally to intervene in and prosecute crimes of trafficking in women and children.

8

Print Resources

This chapter contains a comprehensive listing of recommended readings for those desiring more in-depth information on American families. For the dual purpose of convenience and organization, these print resources are presented according to their relevance to each of the chapters.

Chapter 1: History and Scope of American Families

Books

Benokraitis, Nijole V. 2001. *Marriages and Families*. 4th ed. Upper Saddle River, NJ: Prentice-Hall.

As a comprehensive and readable exploration of contemporary marriages and families, this book examines the diversity of American families, giving equal attention to all racial, ethnic, and other societal groups.

Brehm, Sharon S. 2002. *Intimate Relationships*. 3d ed. New York: McGraw-Hill.

Brehm presents important findings on intimate relationships, major theoretical perspectives, and some current controversies in the field. The practical relevance of close-relationship science is stressed, which serves to encourage thought and analysis.

Cherlin, Andrew J. 2001. *Public and Private Families: A Reader.* 2d ed. New York: McGraw-Hill.

As a cross-section of readings, this book looks at intimate personal concerns, such as whether to marry, as well as societal concerns, such as governmental policies that affect families.

Cowan, Carolyn P., and Philip Cowan. 2000. *When Partners Become Parents: The Big Life Change for Couples.* Mahway, NJ: Lawrence Erlbaum.

This is an excellent resource book for new parents and parents-to-be and a reference source containing well-researched information and recommendations for professionals who work with couples. This book offers reassuring, realistic information about how to survive—or help others survive—the change.

Lauer, Robert H., and Jeannette C. Lauer. 1999. *Marriage and Family: The Quest for Intimacy.* 4th ed. New York: McGraw-Hill.

The Lauers offer a very positive and practical approach to the study of marriage and family life, including a good blend of research and sociological theory. The strength of this book lies in its applied formulations of enhancing and maintaining intimacy within marriage and the family.

Schwartz, Mary Ann, and Barbara M. Scott. 2000. *Marriages and Families: Changes, Choices, and Constraints.* 3d ed. Upper Saddle River, NJ: Prentice-Hall.

Through its emphasis on diversity and changes, this text challenges students to examine both their personal belief systems and societal views of the many diverse forms that marriages and families have taken in the past and their evolution to the present.

Sussman, Marvin B., Suzanne K. Steinmetz, and Gary W. Peterson. 2000. *Handbook of Marriage and the Family.* 2d ed. New York: Plenum Press.

An impressive assortment of topics are presented by some of the noted scholars in marriage and family research. Among the issues are past, present, and future perspectives on family diversity; theory and methods of the family; changing family patterns and roles; the family and other institutions; and family dynamics and processes.

Tischler, Henry L., ed. 2001. *Debating Points: Marriage and Family Issues.* Upper Saddle River, NJ: Prentice-Hall.

This paperback provides a series of quality readings on eight major issues—arranged in pro/con format—regarding various aspects of marriage and the family. It is designed to highlight important issues and debates on marriage and family.

Vail, Ann. 2001. *Controversial Issues in Family and Personal Relationships.* New York: McGraw-Hill.

Vail gathers an interesting potpourri of issues worthy of consideration and debate. Among the topics are traditional assumptions related to marital life; challenges to successful relationships; parenthood; and relational conflict and dissolution.

Weiss, Jessica. 2000. *To Have and Hold: Marriage, the Baby Boom and Social Change.* Chicago: University of Chicago Press.

Weiss gives a thoughtful analysis of the dynamics of American families past and present. The seven chapters that make up the crux of the book investigate such topics as gender roles in the 1950s, the baby boom, the changing role of fathers in American families, divorce, and the rise of feminism.

Research Journals

American Journal of Sociology
http:/www.journals.uchicago.edu/AJS/home.html

This journal was established in 1895 and remains a leading voice for analysis and research in the social sciences, presenting work on the theories, methods, practices, and history of sociology. The journal also seeks the application of perspectives from other social sciences and publishes papers by psychologists, anthropologists, statisticians, economists, educators, historians, and political scientists.

Family and Consumer Sciences Research Journal
http://www.sagepub.co.uk/journals/details/j0085.html

This journal publishes original research concerned with the general well-being of families and individuals. It is a major vehicle for the dissemination of new knowledge generated by home economics researchers, focusing on such current issues as child development, family economics, and family relationships.

Family Relations
http://www.ncfr.com/

This journal is a quarterly publication of the National Council on Family Relations (NCFR). It is an applied scholarly journal that emphasizes relationships across the life cycle and research with implications for intervention, education, and public policy.

Gender and History
http://www.blackwellpublishers.co.uk/asp/journal.asp?ref=09535233

Gender and History is a major international journal for research and writing on the history of femininity, masculinity, and gender relations. It publishes scholarly and nonscholarly articles both on particular episodes in gender history and on broader methodological questions that have ramifications for the discipline as a whole.

Gender and Society
http://www.sagepub.co.uk/journals/details/j0135.html

This journal focuses on the social and structural study of gender as a basic principle of the social order and as a primary social category. Emphasizing theory and research, *Gender and Society* seeks to advance both the study of gender and feminist scholarship.

Journal of Historical Sociology
http://www.blackwellpublishers.co.uk/asp/journal.asp?ref=09521909

This journal operates on the belief that historical and social studies share a common subject matter and can benefit from the interchange of ideas and perspectives. Edited by an international panel of historians, anthropologists, geographers, and sociologists, it is both interdisciplinary in approach and innovative in content. In addition to its articles, the journal offers commentary designed to provoke discussion and debate.

Journal of the History of the Behavioral Sciences
http://www.interscience.wiley.com/jpages/0022–5061/

This quarterly, international journal is devoted to the scientific, institutional, and cultural history of the social and behavioral sciences. It publishes research articles, book reviews, and news and notes that cover the development of such core disciplines as psychology, anthropology, sociology, psychiatry, and communications.

Sociological Inquiry
http://www.utexas.edu/utpress/journals/jsi.html

Sociological Inquiry maintains a tradition of providing insight into the human condition by publishing leading theoretical and empirical research in sociology. This research publication is the official journal of Alpha Kappa Delta, the International Sociology Honor Society.

Sociological Quarterly
http://www.ucpress.edu/journals/tsq/

This quarterly is devoted to publishing research and theory in all areas of sociological inquiry. It publishes a variety of topics in sociological research in order to reach the widest possible audience. Founded in 1959, each issue is designed for efficient browsing and reading, and the articles are helpful for teaching and classroom use.

Chapter 2: Exploring the Diversity of Family Life

Books

Barry, Brian M. 2001. *Culture and Equality: An Egalitarian Critique of Multiculturalism.* Cambridge, MA: Harvard University Press.

A highly regarded scholar probes the dynamics groups that differ from the mainstream and from each other in religious beliefs, customary practices, or cultural ideas. He wrestles with how public policy should best respond to this diversity, particularly the multicultural legal controversies that are involved.

Bucher, Richard. 2000. *Diversity Consciousness: Opening Our Minds to People, Cultures, and Opportunities.* Upper Saddle River, NJ: Prentice Hall.

With a laudable effort, this book helps readers develop the ability to understand, respect, and value diversity. Bucher explores ways to raise "diversity consciousness" and demonstrates how opening one's mind to the views of other peoples and cultures is central for a quality education and successful career.

Coontz, Stephanie, Maya Parson, and Gabrielle Raley, eds. 1999. *American Families: A Multicultural Reader.* New York and London: Routledge.

This book is an examination of the variety of families that exist in the United States. Case studies are supplied to describe the wide array of family forms and values, gender roles, and parenting practices that have prevailed in different times and places for different population groups.

Ferrante, Joan, and Prince Brown, Jr., eds. 2001. *Social Construction of Race and Ethnicity in the United States.* 2d ed. Upper Saddle River, NJ: Prentice Hall.

This book gives special attention to the social construction of race and ethnicity in the United States. Of particular interest is the manner in which the concepts of race and ethnicity came into being and how they remain in modern times.

McAdoo, Hariette P., ed. 1999. *Family Ethnicity: Strength in Diversity.* 2d ed. Thousand Oaks, CA: Sage.

In this edited collection of essays, seven major areas of investigation are offered to the reader: an overview of ethnic American families; African American families; Latino families; Native American families; Muslim families; Asian-American families; and a review of social work practices with ethnic families.

Parekh, Bhikhu. C. 2000. *Rethinking Multiculturalism: Cultural Diversity and Political Theory.* Cambridge, MA: Harvard University Press.

The author provides clear accounts of why cultural differences have emerged and need to be better understood. This book stresses why diversity must be embraced, respected, and publicly affirmed, including tolerance and acceptance of those who are different.

Rosenblum, Karen E., and Toni-Michelle C. Travis, eds. 2000. *The Meaning of Difference: American Constructions of Race, Sex, and Gender, Social Class, and Sexual Orientation.* New York: McGraw-Hill.

Rosenblum and Travis detail the social construction of difference as it exists in such formulations as race, sex and gender, social class, and sexual orientation. The various authors also explore the interplay that exists between the perception of these differences and other master statuses such as disability and ethnicity or national-origin.

Schaefer, Richard T. 2001. *Race and Ethnicity in the United States.* 2d ed. Upper Saddle River, NJ: Prentice Hall.

This book clearly explains the concepts of race and ethnicity, and how levels of tolerance vary enormously from place to place. Schaeffer provides readers with Census 2000 data.

Susser, Ida, and Thomas C. Patterson, eds. 2001. *Cultural Diversity in the United States.* Williston, VT: Blackwell Publishers.

This book consists of 20 chapters that offer a wide range of perspectives about cultural diversity in the United States. Among other suggestions, readers are encouraged to rethink diversity, identity politics, and multiculturalism in the United States today.

Watson, C. W. 2000. *Multiculturalism.* Bristol, PA: Taylor and Francis.

Watson examines some of the debates associated with multiculturalism in the world today. In particular, arguments for and against multiculturalism are examined in the context of modern states that have different political and historical circumstances.

Research Journals

Cross-cultural Research
http://www.sagepub.co.uk/journals/details/j0072.html

This journal offers peer-reviewed articles that describe cross-cultural and comparative studies in all human sciences. It examines topics that span societies, nations, and cultures, providing strategies for the systematic testing of theories about human society and behavior. Research reports, review articles, methodological studies, bibliographies, and discussions are also included.

Cultural Critique
http://www3.oup.co.uk/jnls/list/cultur/

This journal investigates cultural topics from both multidisciplinary and international perspectives. It takes a broad approach to cultural criticism, covering literary, philosophical, anthropological, and sociological studies, while applying a range of theoretical perspectives.

Cultural Diversity and Ethnic Minority Psychology
http://www.apa.org/journals/cdp.html

This journal provides psychologists, social workers, psychiatrists, counselors, and other mental health professionals with the knowledge base and therapeutic tools to effectively assess and treat clients from diverse backgrounds. It emphasizes how multicultural factors such as age, ethnicity, gender, race, sexual orientation, socioeconomic status, language, religion, and political and social ideology can significantly impact the process and outcome of mental health treatment.

Cultural Studies
http://www.tandf.co.uk/journals/routledge/09502386.html

This international journal explores the relationships among cultural practices, everyday life, material, economic, political, geographical, and historical contexts. *Cultural Studies* seeks to foster analytical, critical, and political conversations by encouraging readers to actively explore the status of contemporary research in cultural studies.

Cultural Values
http://www.blackwellpublishers.co.uk/asp/journal.asp?ref=13625179

This research journal is dedicated to a multidisciplinary analysis of culture and its changing values. It addresses a broad range of related issues, encompassing both the theoretical nature of values and their social and historical consequences. *Cultural Values* publishes the latest thinking of leading international figures and the writing of scholars from around the globe.

Culture and Psychology
http://www.sagepub.co.uk/journals/details/j0160.html

This journal explores the twin forces of culture and psychology by drawing on research in anthropology, sociology, education, ethnography, linguistics, communication studies, and philosophy. It analyzes the social discourse of people in their culturally organized forms of life, and includes theoretically informed empirical work, as well as providing a forum for high quality debate and analysis.

Culture, Health & Sexuality
http://www.tandf.co.uk/journals/tf/13691058.html

Culture, Health & Sexuality is broad and multidisciplinary in focus, containing papers that deal with topics related to culture, health, and sexuality. It addresses methodological concerns as well as those that are empirical and conceptual in nature. The journal offers a forum for key debates on policy and practice, and adopts a practitioner's focus where appropriate.

Ethnic and Racial Studies
http://www.tandf.co.uk/journals/routledge/01419870.html

Ethnic and Racial Studies is one of the leading international journals for the analysis of race, ethnicity, and nationalism throughout the world. The journal provides an interdisciplinary academic forum for the presentation of research and theoretical analysis, drawing on sociology, social policy, anthropology, political science, economics, geography, international relations, history, social psychology, and cultural studies.

Gender and Society
http://www.sagepub.co.uk/journals/details/j0135.html

This journal focuses on the social and structural study of gender as a basic principle of the social order and as a primary social category. Emphasizing theory and research, this publication aims to advance both the study of gender and feminist scholarship. Each peer-reviewed article encourages the development of new knowledge and the analysis of social aspects of gender.

Multicultural Perspectives
http://www.erlbaum.com/Journals/journals/MUP/mup.htm

This publication promotes the philosophy of social justice, equity, and inclusion. It celebrates cultural and ethnic diversity as a national strength that enriches the fabric of society. The journal publishes a range of material from academic to personal perspectives that address or embody multicultural forms.

Chapter 3: Family Issues and Controversies
Family Planning
Books

Aronson, Diane. 2001. *Resolving Infertility.* Scranton, PA: HarperCollins.

This book offers a comprehensive analysis of infertility in a clear and understandable fashion. Case studies are used to highlight treatment options that include adoption, surrogacy, and donor pregnancy.

Becker, Gaylene. 2000. *The Elusive Embryo: How Women and Men Approach New Reproductive Technologies.* Los Angeles: University of California Press.

As another insightful look at infertility and the interventions available, this book will interest those considering reproductive technologies, as well as health professionals, cultural anthropologists, and general readers concerned with the developing relationship between technology and the human body.

Bentley, Gillian R., and C. G. Nicholas Mascie-Taylor. 2001. *Infertility in the Modern World: Present and Future Prospects.* Port Chester, NY: Cambridge University Press.

The authors spell out the medical, environmental, and social changes that have affected human reproduction. The strength of this book lies in its ability to provide an interdisciplinary perspective on the subject.

Glasier, Anna, Ailsa Gebbie, and Nancy Loudon, eds. 2000. *Handbook of Family Planning and Reproductive Healthcare.* Foreword by Sir Malcolm Macnaughton. Orlando, FL: Churchill Livingstone.

An excellent reference manual that is as readable as it is user-friendly. This handbook provides clear and concise information about uses, complications, contraindications, and other relevant contraception details.

Grant, George. 2000. *Grand Illusions: The Legacy of Planned Parenthood.* Nashville, TN: Cumberland House.

This is must reading for anyone interested in the evolution of Planned Parenthood. Grant has penned an engaging historical narrative, one that successfully captures the rise of this organization and the legal, moral, and religious controversy it created.

Jequier, Anne M. 2000. *Male Infertility.* Williston, VT: Blackwell.

This book is a clear and straightforward account of male infertility, including the causes and types of medical intervention available today. Chapters present topics such as semen analysis, micro-assisted fertilization, testicular disease, spinal cord injury, and donor insemination.

Keyzer, Amy, ed. 2000. *Family Planning Sourcebook.* Detroit, MI: Omnigraphics.

This book offers the reader considerable information on family planning issues and contraceptive choices. Among the topics are various categories of contraception, abortion, and future methods of birth control. Includes a glossary and an annotated list of helpful organizations.

Rosenthal, Masood S., and M. Sara Khatamee. 2001. *The Fertility Sourcebook.* Lincolnwood, IL: Lowell House.

This book is one of the more popular resource books on fertility. In addition to the latest in fertility treatments, the authors present topics unavailable in other books, such as issues for same-sex partners and the ethical considerations surrounding medical intervention.

Van Lunsen, R. H., V. Unzeitig, and G. Creatsas, eds. 2000. *Contraceptive Choices and Realities.* Pearl River, NY: Parthenon.

This book is a cross-section of topics related to birth control techniques. Particularly well done are sections dealing with sexually transmitted diseases, sexuality education and adolescent contraceptive behavior, emergency contraception, and family planning services.

Williams, Kara. 2000. *Fertility Technology: The Baby Debate.* New York: Rosen Publishing Group.

Williams presents much food for thought in this well-researched book on medical-ethics debates. Her book presents an overview of available fertility techniques followed by the ethics and morality of employing such measures.

Research Journals

Demographics
http://www.jstor.org/journals/00703370.html

Demographics is the official journal of the Population Association of America. It is an interdisciplinary, peer-reviewed periodical that publishes articles of general interest to population scientists. Fields represented in its contents include geography, history, biology, statistics, business, and public health, in addition to social scientific disciplines such as sociology, economics, psychology, and political science. Published quarterly, it includes theoretical and methodological articles, commentaries, and specialized research papers covering both developed and developing nations.

Family Planning Perspectives
http://www.jstor.org/journals/00147354.html

This journal serves researchers, policy makers, and family planning program providers. Its many subjects include contraceptive practice; fertility levels; adolescent pregnancy; abortion; public policies and legal issues affecting childbearing; program operation, development, and evaluation; information, education, and communication activities; sexually transmitted diseases; and reproductive, maternal, and child health. The journal also contains staff-written material summarizing research from other journals, discussing policy issues and providing coverage of conferences.

Fertility and Sterility
http://www.elsevier.com/locate/fertilsteril

This is an international journal for obstetricians, gynecologists, reproductive endocrinologists, urologists, basic scientists, and others who treat and investigate problems of infertility and human reproductive disorders. The journal publishes articles in clinical and laboratory research relevant to reproduction, contraception, and related topics.

International Family Planning Perspectives
http://uk.jstor.org/journals/01903187.html

International Family Planning Perspectives is published by the Alan Guttmacher Institute, a nonprofit organization that focuses its energies on sexual and reproductive-health issues. This peer-reviewed research journal concentrates its energy on research conducted in Africa, Asia, and Latin America. The publication serves researchers, policy makers, and family planning program providers.

Population and Development Review
http://www.popcouncil.org/pdr/default.asp

This review explores a wide variety of topics related to the population, including issues related to public policy. It contains articles on advances in theory and application, sociographic studies, and critical assessments of recent research; notes and commentaries on current population questions and policy developments; data and perspectives on new statistics and their interpretation; archives with a resonance for current debate on population issues; book reviews; and documents and official voices on population matters from around the world.

Population Studies
http://www.lse.ac.uk/depts/pic/

This journal seeks to capture major advances in the methods and findings of population research. It publishes articles that make a significant contribution to the literature of population science, whether the focus is historical or contemporary, qualitative or quantitative, an advance in theory or technique, or an application to policy.

United Nations Population Information Network
http://www.un.org/popin/about.htm

Founded in 1981, this publication seeks to identify, establish, strengthen, and coordinate population information activities at international, regional, and national levels. It also seeks to facilitate and enhance the availability of population information to the reading public. The network provides a forum for the exchange of experiences among developed and developing countries on population information issues.

ZPG Reporter
http://www.zpg.org

The *ZPG Reporter* explores the many issues surrounding zero population growth, with a special emphasis on achieving a sustainable balance between the Earth's people and its resources. Articles and public forum pieces explore how to protect the environment and ensure a high quality of life for present and future generations. ZPG's education and advocacy programs aim to influence public policies, attitudes, and behavior on national and global population issues and related concerns.

Contemporary Parenthood
Books

Ambert, Anne-Marie. 2001. *The Effect of Children on Parents.* Binghamton, NY: Haworth Press.

The title of this book says it all. Ambert describes how children affect parents positively and negatively in many areas, from employment and finances to marital relations and life plans.

Baker, Robin, and Elizabeth Oram. 2000. *The Baby Wars: The Dynamics of Family Conflict.* Scranton, PA: HarperTrade.

The authors' premise is that even the happiest of families endure periods of intense conflict and emotional strife. From sibling rivalry to temper tantrums, this eye-opening book sheds considerable light on the disharmony that punctuates most households.

Balter, Lawrence. 2000. *Parenthood in America: An Encyclopedia.* Santa Barbara, CA: ABC-CLIO.

An A-to-Z encyclopedia that covers virtually every aspect of parenthood in the United States. This important reference book is multidisciplinary and mixes psychology, health, sociology, anthropology, and family history. Each entry is accompanied by suggestions for further reading.

Brubaker, Timothy. 2000. *Family Relations.* Thousand Oaks, CA: Sage.

A noted authority in the field offers a life-span perspective on family life, particularly how various dimensions of societal change have impacted the family dynamics and processes. The ability of the family to adapt to change and crisis is explored, and several intervention strategies to assist the family in dealing with challenges are reviewed.

Ferrucci, Piero. 2001. *What Our Children Teach Us: Lessons in Joy, Love, and Awareness.* Boston: Little, Brown.

The author shares how the journey of parenthood represents a succession of experiences that can enrich and transform adults like few other experiences. Ferruci explores how each moment of parenting, no matter how trivial or challenging, holds hidden surprises and opportunities for change.

Hauswirth, Katherine. 2000. *Things My Mother Told Me: Reflections on Parenthood.* New York: Trafford Publishing.

Filled with amusing and captivating anecdotes, Hauswirth reflects on the trials and tribulations of parenthood. She does so in a feisty and poignant way, in the process imparting wisdom and intelligence born of direct experience.

Irvine, William B. 2001. *Doing Right by Children: Reflections on the Nature of Childhood and Obligations of Parenthood.* La Vergne, TN: Publisher Resources.

This book is a probing and sobering look at our changing views on the obligations of parenthood. Irvine tackles a number of important issues, such as what family structure best serves the interest of children as well as what characteristics are deemed desirable in parents.

Jeffers, Susan. 2001. *I'm Okay, But You're a Brat: Freeing Yourself from the Guilt of Parenthood.* Gordonsville, VA: Renaissance Books.

This is must reading for any parent who has ever generated feelings of guilt or failure. Sections of the book are cleverly written to admonish negative self-appraisals, such as "climbing off the ladder of distress," "dropping the heavy baggage," and "finding beauty in the land of tears."

Ryder, Verdene. 2000. *Parents and Their Children.* Scranton, PA: HarperTrade.

Ryder supplies insight into the many adaptations and adjustments accompanying parenthood. In addition to describing parenthood's many challenges, attention is focused on how to successfully balance the needs of children and those originating from within the marital relationship.

Westman, Jack. 2001. *Parenthood in America.* Green Bay: University of Wisconsin Press.

This book is aimed at what Westman calls the complex and demanding vocation of parenthood, and the supportive assistance it deserves. He urges employers, communities, government, and society to take strides to better understand the complex needs of today's parents and to provide meaningful support where and when needed.

Research Journals

Attachment & Human Development
http://www.tandf.co.uk/journals/routledge/14616734.html

Attachment & Human Development presents an academic vehicle for the presentation and discussion of scientific theories related to emotional and cognitive development, internal representations, and social processes. The journal addresses the growing demand from the domains of psychology, psychiatry, psychotherapy, and related disciplines including nursing and social work, for a clear presentation of ideas, methods, and research based on attachment theory.

Child Development

http://www.blackwellpublishers.co.uk/asp/journal.asp?ref=
0009–3920

This journal, founded in 1930, publishes articles, essays, reviews, and tutorials on various topics in the field of child development. Spanning many disciplines, the journal provides the latest research, not only for researchers and theoreticians, but also for child psychiatrists, clinical psychologists, psychiatric social workers, specialists in early childhood education, educational psychologists, special education teachers, and other researchers.

Childhood

http://www.sagepub.co.uk/journals/details/j0077.html

This publication is an interdisciplinary forum for child research that spans divisions between geographical regions, disciplines, social and cultural contexts, and applied and basic research. *Childhood* acknowledges the growing need for new forms of international and cross-disciplinary research committed to increasing our understanding of children and childhood. It seeks to answer this need by exploring the changing nature of childhood in diverse regions and social contexts and by illuminating the complex, globally articulated risks and possibilities that affect children today.

Children and Society

http://www.interscience.wiley.com/jpages/0951–0605/

This journal informs all those who work with and for children—as practitioners, managers, researchers, teachers, or concerned individuals—about significant developments and research findings as they affect the lives of children and young people. Among the topics explored are child health, children's rights, child protection, and international perspectives. The articles both reflect and contribute to research, and seek to promote improvement in policy and practice.

Children's Health Care

http://www.erlbaum.com/Journals/journals/CHC/chc.htm

This journal publishes empirically based articles addressing theoretical, clinical, programmatic, training, and professional practice issues relevant to the family-centered, developmental, and psychosocial aspects of children's health care. It directs itself toward articles involving parent-professional collaboration and multidisciplinary efforts including nursing, child life, psychology, social work, and related disciplines.

Infancy
http://www.erlbaum.com/Journals/journals/IN/in.htm

This journal emphasizes the research on normal and aberrant infant development during the first two years. Both human and animal research are included. In addition to articles, the journal includes commentaries and debates. The audience includes those involved in psychology, child development, pediatrics, nursing, and education.

Infant and Child Development
http://www.interscience.wiley.com/jpages/1522–7227/

Infant and Child Development publishes empirical, theoretical, and methodological papers dealing with psychological development during infancy and childhood up to and including adolescence. Areas covered include caregiver-child interaction, cognitive development, emotional development, infant perception, motor development, parenting and development, play and development, language development, and socialization.

Infant Mental Health Development
http://www3.interscience.wiley.com/cgi-bin/jtoc?ID=33748

This journal publishes peer-reviewed research articles, literature reviews, program descriptions/evaluations, clinical studies, and book reviews that focus on infant social-emotional development, caregiver-infant interactions, cultural influences on infant and family development, and all conditions that place infants and/or their families at risk for less than optimal development. The journal is dedicated to an interdisciplinary approach to the optimal development of infants and their families.

Work and Family Life
Books

Balswick, Jack, and Judith Balswick. 1999. *The Two-Paycheck Marriage.* New York: McGraw-Hill.

This book is an interesting study of dual-earner homes, most notably the perceived rewards and sacrifices. The authors conclude that the advantages of dual-earner households outweigh the drawbacks: Mothers with careers were happier and had more cheerful and competent children, and fathers were generally more engaged in family life.

Barnett, Rosalind, and Caryl Rivers. 1998. *She Works/He Works: How Two-Income Families Are Happy, Healthy, and Thriving.* Cambridge, MA: Harvard University Press.

The results of a four-year study of 300 middle-class and working-class couples are published in this book. In general, the study debunked the myth of the overwrought working mother with her insensitive husband and neglected children. The researchers report that "collaborative couples," busy as they are, thrive in their diverse roles and inspire competence and confidence in their children.

Campbell, Bebe Moore. 2000. *Successful Women, Angry Men.* East Rutherford, NJ: Berkley Publishing.

In this thought-provoking book, Campbell seeks to answer some tough questions about today's two-income couples: Who comes first in a marriage of equals? Whose job determines a family move? Who is responsible for the household duties and care of the children? Based on more than 100 interviews, the book provides some interesting answers as well sound advice for today's dual-earner couples.

Deutsch, Francine M. 1999. *Halving It All: How Equally Shared Parenting Works.* Cambridge, MA: Harvard University Press.

A clever play on words tells us that the best way to have it all—both a full family life and a career—is to "halve" it all. Family studies expert Francine Deutsch downplays the grim story of lopsided domestic workloads and maintains that equality based on shared parenting is possible and is emerging all around us.

Galinsky, Ellen. 2000. *Ask the Children: The Breakthrough Study That Reveals How to Succeed at Work and Parenting.* Scranton, PA: HarperTrade.

This is a landmark book written by Ellen Galinsky, president of the Families and Work Institute. Galinsky based her research on interviews with more than 1,000 children from the third to the twelfth grades. The results illuminate the fascinating interplay that children see between the home and the workplace.

Gill, Gurjeet K. 1998. *Third Job Employed Couples' Management of Household Work Contradictions.* Brookfield, VT: Ashgate Publishing.

A number of interesting issues regarding work and family life emerge in this book. Readers will likely enjoy Gill's multilayered analyses of housework, as well as the tension that often exists between traditional images of husbands and wives and the division of household labor actually required.

Hertz, Rosanna, and Nancy Marshall, eds. 2001. *Working Families: The Transformation of the American Home.* Los Angeles, CA: University of California Press.

This book is a highly informative snapshot of the intricate fabric of work and family in the nation today. With selections written by leading scholars, the authors shed light on how families manage to juggle career and household responsibilities.

Hochschild, Arlie R. 2000. *The Time Bind: When Work Becomes Home and Home Becomes Work.* Gordonsville, VA: Henry Holt.

Hochschild offers a penetrating analysis of dual-earner homes, most notably employee perceptions and images of the workplace. Among the topics are employee interpretations of "family friendly" employment options, devotion to the company, and job security.

Marshack, Kathy. 1998. *Entrepreneurial Couples: Making It Work at Work and at Home.* Palo Alto, CA: Consulting Psychologist Press.

Marshack gives a look at how couples can make their personal and professional lives work together. The book is filled with practical advice and suggestions, particularly for those about to launch their own home-based business.

Shellenbarger, Susan. 1999. *Work and Family.* New York: Random House.

This book is one of the best narratives about the delicate balance that exists between work and home. Shellenbarger captures the triumphant accomplishments of the two worlds as well as the resounding thuds, with no mixing of words in-between—a must reading for the two-paycheck home.

Research Journals

Gender, Work and Organization
http://www.blackwellpublishers.co.uk/journals./GWAO/descript.htm

This journal highlights the role that gender plays in the field of work and organization. It brings to the forefront wide-ranging research on this theme from a variety of academic disciplines into an international forum for debate and analysis. Dedicated to advancing theory, research and analytically driven applications concerning gender relations at work, the organization of gender, and the gendering of organizations.

Journal of Business and Psychology
http://www.wkap.nl/prod/j/0889–3268

This journal publishes empirical research, case studies, and literature reviews dealing with psychological concepts and services implemented in business settings. Written by psychologists, behavioral scientists, and organizational specialists employed in business, industry, and academia, articles deal with all aspects of psychology that apply to the career world.

Journal of Career Development
http://www.wkap.nl/prod/j/0894–8453

This publication offers professionals, the public, and policy makers the latest in career development theory, research, and practice, while focusing on the impact of theory and research on clinical practice. Among the topics covered are career education, adult career development, balancing work and family life, and career development of special needs populations. The journal provides up-to-date coverage of contemporary issues and identifies trends impacting the future of the world.

Journal of Economic Psychology
http://www.elsevier.nl/inca/publications/store/5/0/5/5/8/
9/index.htt

This journal aims to present research that will improve our understanding of the behavioral aspects of economic phenomena and processes. It seeks to be a channel for the increased interest in using behavioral science methods for the study of economic behavior, in the process stimulating new approaches and new theorizing about economic affairs.

Journal of Education and Work
http://www.tandf.co.uk/journals/carfax/13639080.html

The *Journal of Education and Work* offers an international forum for academic research and policy analysis, focusing on the inter-play that exists between the education and career spheres. Regarding the educational arena, attention is given to how knowledge, skills, values, and attitudes about work and employ-ment are developed. From the world of work, the focus is on those economic and industrial components that have a direct bearing on education and training.

Work and Occupations
http://www.sagepub.co.uk/journals/details/j0195.html

This journal publishes rigorous social science research on the human dynamics of the workplace, employment, and society from an international, interdisciplinary perspective. It provides a broad perspective on the workplace, examining international approaches to work-related issues as well as insights from schol-ars in a variety of fields, including demography, education, his-tory, management, psychology, and sociology.

Work & Stress
http://www.tandf.co.uk/journals/tf/02678373.html

Work & Stress is an international, multidisciplinary quarterly, pre-senting refereed academic papers relating to stress, health and safety, and performance (empirical reports, reviews, case studies, and theoretical papers), as well as articles of concern to the policy makers, managers, and trades unionists who have to deal with such issues. It presents individual, social, organizational, and soci-etal issues in relation to the nature of stress and its management.

Work Study
http://www.emeraldinsight.com/ws.htm

Work Study explores new developments in work study techniques and practice designed to improve individual and organizational performance. Self-improvement, at individual, team, and organizational levels receives a special focus, particularly as it relates to competitiveness and performance standard. This journal systematically explores the topic of working practices, most notably performance, efficiency, productivity, and profitability.

Single-Parent Families

Books

Hetherington, E. Mavis, ed. 2000. *Coping with Divorce.* Mahwah, NJ: Lawrence Erlbaum.

Hetherington, an accomplished child development and family studies expert, examines divorce and its effects in a risk and resiliency approach. She analyzes many angles of family functioning and child adjustment, including the complexity of problems and solutions alike.

Hoerner, Thomas. 1999. *Bachelor Parents and Their Disfunctional Families: A Guide to Successful Parenting for the Single Male.* Grand Prarie, TX: Hoerner Publishing.

This book is written entirely for single fathers who have custody or are active in their children's lives. The author employs a readable writing style, sprinkled with wit and loaded with practical advice and guidance.

Isenhart, Dawn. 2000. *Surviving Single Parenting.* Gordonsville, VA: Universe Publishers.

Isenhart offers insight into the world of raising a child on your own. Whether you are a single mother or single father, this book strives to offer advice, wisdom, and courage.

Karst, Patrice. 2000. *The Single Mother's Survival Guide.* New York: Crossing Press.

Patrice Karst, a single mother, covers a wide range of topics that concern the modern single mother, showing how it's possible not only to survive but to triumph. The book is loaded with helpful tips and practical information.

Mackall, Dandi. 2000. *Just One of Me*. Gordonsville, VA: Universe Publishers.

Just One of Me is a fitting title for the multiple stresses of being a single parent—being both father and mother, playmate and authority, bottle-washer, and financial provider. The author knows the ups and downs of such multiple roles and provides readers with valuable advice on achieving stability and sanity.

Marindin, H. 2000. *Handbook for Single Adoptive Parents*. Tucson, AZ: Communication Skill Builders.

This book is a rare find on an increasingly popular topic. It offers abundant expert information to single parents coping with the challenges of daily life, from managing finances to handling work demands.

Neely, Margery A., and Vera S. Maass. 2000. *Counseling Single Parents*. New York: Springer.

Neely and Maass examine the process of counseling single parents. The authors' central theme is that single parents have resilience but little time to recognize it, thus prompting need for therapeutic intervention.

Paterson, W. A. 2001. *The Unbroken Home*. Binghamton, NY: Haworth Press.

Countering gloomy portraits of single-parent households, this book champions the cause of single mothers, particularly the resiliency and strength they bring to their families. Case studies are used to capture the resourcefulness used in the face of adversity.

Strong, Dina. 1999. *Singular Ingenuity: Reflections on Being a Single Parent*. Chicago: ACTA Publishers.

Strong argues that the responsibilities of parenting can weigh heavily on a single parent, but one must not lose track of the rewards and satisfactions. Single parenthood often serves to tap inner reserves, in the process revealing hidden talents and capacities.

Varon, Lee. 2000. *Adopting on Your Own.* New York: Farrar, Straus, and Giroux.

This book has good coverage of adoption and its many sides. The author provides information and advice on such issues as the various stages attached to the adoption process, financial considerations, the advantages of international versus domestic adoption, choosing an agency, transracial adoption, the legal rights of gays and lesbians to adopt, and the evolving attitudes of agencies and social workers toward single-parent adoptions.

Research Journals

Child and Adolescent Social Work Journal
http://www.wkap.nl/journalhome.htm/0738–0151

This journal features original articles that focus on clinical social work practice with children, adolescents, and their families. The journal addresses current issues in the field of social work drawn from theory, direct practice, research, and social policy, as well as focusing on problems affecting specific populations in special settings.

Child and Family Social Work
http://www.uea.ac.uk/menu/acad_depts/swk/research/publications/cfsw/cfsw.htm

This journal, a forum where researchers, practitioners, policy makers, and managers can exchange knowledge, increases understanding and develops notions of good practice. In its promotion of research and practice, which is both disciplined and articulate, the journal is dedicated to advancing the well-being and welfare of children and their families throughout the world.

Child: Care, Health and Development
http://www.blacksci.co.uk/~cgilib/jnlpage.asp?Journal=cchd&File=cchd

As an international, multidisciplinary, peer-reviewed journal, it seeks to inform people from all disciplines working in child health. The journal publishes papers dealing with all aspects of the health and development of children and young people. It particularly encourages the submission of studies related to those who are disadvantaged by physical, developmental, emotional, and social problems.

Child Welfare
http://www.allenpress.com/cgi-bin/test-cat.cgi?journal=child_welfare

As a journal of policy, practice, and program devoted essentially to the needs and goals of personnel associated with the field of child welfare, it covers all phases of child welfare that affect the health, education, and social needs of children, offering theoretical concepts as well as practical ideas and strategies. It reports on innovations in practice, agency administration, and board functions, staffing designs and staff education, legislation, research, and community development.

Early Child Development and Care
http://www.tandf.co.uk/journals/gb/03004430.html

As a multidisciplinary publication, this journal serves psychologists, educators, psychiatrists, pediatricians, social workers, and other professionals who deal with research, planning, and the education and care of infants and young children. The periodical offers descriptive and evaluative articles on social, educational, and preventive medical programs for young children; experimental and observational studies; critical reviews; and summary articles. In addition to scientific papers, the periodical contains book reviews, reports on conferences, and other items of interest.

Early Childhood News
http://www.earlychildhood.com/community/news/cache_community_news_news_index_asp.htm

This publication has appeal to all parents of all young children. It is published six times a year and delivered to parents of young children, infants to age 8. In addition to its Professional Development Program with the University of Wisconsin-Stout, *Early Childhood News* provides its readers with articles on developmentally appropriate activities, behavior, health, child care, and safety issues.

Infant Behavior and Development
http://www.elsevier.nl/inca/publications/store/6/2/0/1/9/7/index.htt

As a journal that publishes empirical, theoretical, methodological, and review papers, this journal also releases brief reports dealing with behavioral development during infancy (up to 3 years). Areas covered by the journal include cognitive development, emotional development, parent-infant interaction, perception, motor development, and socialization.

Journal of Child and Family Studies
http://kapis.www.wkap.nl/journalhome.htm/1062–1024

The *Journal of Child and Family Studies* is an international forum for topical issues pertaining to the mental well-being of children, adolescents, and their families. The journal translates the latest research developments into practical applications by addressing all facets of emotional disorders, including issues associated with identification, diagnosis, treatment, rehabilitation, and prevention. Original papers detail basic and applied research, program evaluation, and policy issues on emotional or behavioral disorders, child abuse and neglect, respite care, foster care, mental health care financing, homelessness, family stress, AIDS, and substance abuse.

Journal of Parenting Research
http://truth.boisestate.edu/jpr/index2.html

This journal publishes original empirical and theoretical work in all areas of the scientific study of parenting and family influence on child and adolescent environment. Topics of interest include, but are not limited to, parent interventions, parent-child communication, parenting styles, parenting training, single parenting, teenage parenting, and methodological issues in parenting research.

Families with Physical Disabilities and Chronic Illnesses
Books

Ahamad, Waqar I., and C. Husband, eds. 2000. *Ethnicity, Disability and Chronic Illness.* Dallas, TX: Taylor Publishing.

This book is an excellent resource for readers seeking information on the interplay between ethnicity and physical disability or chronic illness. It describes the various ethnic strategies used in developing skills for coping with disability or chronic illness.

Ayrault, Evelyn. 2001. *Beyond a Physical Disability: The Person Within.* New York: International Publishing.

Ayrault brings keen understanding and wisdom to the sensitive topic of a child with a physical disability. She reveals how both parent and child can develop resiliency and effective coping skills, often by sharing how others have fared in physically challenging situations.

Bernstein Hyman, Ruth, and Juliet M. Corbin, eds. 2000. *Chronic Illness.* New York: Springer.

This books is a collection of key articles on research, theory, and concepts in chronic illness. The gathered articles cover a complexity and range of problems, including multiple sclerosis, skin disease, and heart disease.

Donoghue, Paul, and M. E. Siegel. 2000. *Sick and Tired of Feeling Sick and Tired.* New York: Norton.

The authors present advice on living with Invisible Chronic Illness (ICI), which they define as conditions which rarely show outward signs of disability. Examples include chronic fatigue syndrome, endometriosis, fibromyalgia, irritable bowel syndrome, lupus Lyme disease, and migraine headaches.

Duff, Kat. 2000. *The Alchemy of Illness.* Westminster, MD: Crown.

The author, who suffered from chronic fatigue syndrome, reflects on her illness and how it shaped her life. Her writing style is as captivating as her inner spirit, which is inspirational and stirring.

Fletcher, Todd V., and Candace S. Bos, eds. 2000. *Helping Individuals with Disabilities and Their Families.* Tempe, AZ: Bilingual Review Press.

One of the many strengths of this book is its emphasis on multicultural family perspectives. The authors also take an active stance in promoting policy changes and supportive practices for individuals with disabilities.

Funk, Sandra G., et al., eds. 2001. *Key Aspects of Preventing and Managing Chronic Illness.* New York: Springer.

This book represents a compendium of current research on the topic of chronic illness. It includes an overview of important issues in chronic illness as well as ways to apply research to practice.

Kaschak, Ellyn, ed. 2001. *Minding the Body.* Binghamton, NY: Haworth Press.

Kaschak offers both theoretical views and personal accounts of illness. She and a host of contributors describe ways that therapists can help clients cope with the pain, fear, and stigma of a serious disease.

Smart, Julie. 2000. *Disability, Society and the Individual.* Gaithersburg, MD: Aspen Publishers.

This book covers disability in a cultural context, comparing and contrasting the experience of disability from individual and social perspectives. It enables readers to define disability, to better understand social responses to disability, and to appreciate the individual experiences of a person with disabilities.

Wells, Susan M. 2000. *A Delicate Balance: Living Successfully with Chronic Illness.* Scranton, PA: Perseus.

Wells gives a sensitive, hopeful exploration of maximizing the quality of one's life while living with chronic illness or physical disability. She points out that while such conditions take their toll on every aspect of a person's life, there are ways to live successfully and manage life's challenges.

Research Journals

Contemporary Long-term Care
http://www.cltcmag.com/contemporarycare/index.jsp

This publication is primarily directed toward long-term care managers, including owners, administrators, and directors of nursing in for-profit and not-for-profit nursing homes, assisted living facilities, hospital-based skilled nursing units, retirement communities, and other long-term care facilities. A particular emphasis is placed on sharing the latest news and trends in key areas including legislation, regulations, patient care, staff management, and revenue sources.

Disability and Rehabilitation
http://www.tandf.co.uk/journals/tf/09638288.html

As an international, multidisciplinary journal, *Disability and Rehabilitation* seeks to encourage a better understanding of all aspects of disability and to promote the rehabilitation process. The journal publishes review articles, experimental and clinical research papers, case studies, clinical commentaries, reports on rehabilitation in practice, rehabilitation engineering, and major book reviews that span a range of issues including the severity and magnitude of disability, clinical medicine including gerontology, psychosocial adjustment, social policy issues, and vocational and educational training.

Disability and Society
http://www.tandf.co.uk/journals/carfax/09687599.html

As an international journal this publication provides a focus for debate about such issues as human rights, discrimination, definitions, policy, and practices. The contents of this journal appear against a background of change in the ways in which disability is viewed and managed. A particular emphasis is placed on community care and integration, with a critical eye on everyday practices and policy changes. While publishing articles that represent all professional perspectives, the journal also provides an opportunity for consumers of professional services to give their thoughts and perceptions.

Exceptionality
http://www.erlbaum.com/Journals/journals/EX/ex.htm

This journal provides a forum for presentation of current research and professional scholarship in special education. Topics include various research designs examining persons with exceptionalities, as well as reviews of the literature, discussion pieces, invited works, position papers, theoretical papers, policy analyses, and research syntheses. The editorial board seeks to publish a cross-section of all areas of special education and exceptionality, to further the knowledge base, and to improve services to both individuals with disabilities and individuals with gifted and talented behavior.

Health and Social Work
http://www.naswpress.org/publications/journals/health/hswintro.html

Health and Social Work is a professional research journal committed to improving social work practice and extending knowledge into the fields of physical and mental health. The journal carries articles on practice, social policy and planning, legislative issues, innovations in health care, and research.

Health Care for Women International
http://www.tandf.co.uk/journals/tf/07399332.html

This international publication provides an interdisciplinary approach to health care and related topics that concern women. Focusing on the latest research, theories, and issues, the journal spans health care, psychology, sociology, gender studies, family systems, and anthropology. Among the topics are cultural differences, alternative lifestyles, wife abuse, problems of aging, psychological challenges, child rearing and childbearing, and ethical issues.

Health Psychology
http://www.apa.org/journals/hea.html

This journal is devoted to furthering an understanding of scientific relationships between behavioral principles and physical health and illness. The journal is intended for those who have a broad range of backgrounds, interests, and specializations, often interdisciplinary in nature. Most articles focus on empirical research, most notably the relationships that exist between behavior and physical health. Examples of subject areas are factors that may contribute to disease or its prevention; methods used in the diagnosis, treatment, or rehabilitation of disorders; and techniques that could reduce disease risk.

Journal of the American Medical Association
http://jama.ama-assn.org/

JAMA, which began publication in 1883, is an international, peer-reviewed general medical journal. Its purpose is to promote the science and art of medicine and the betterment of public health. To achieve this, JAMA strives to improve public health internationally by elevating the quality of medical care, disease prevention, and research provided by an informed readership. It also seeks to foster responsible and balanced debate on controversial issues that affect medicine and health care.

Pain Research and Management
http://www.pulsus.com/Pain/Instruct.htm

This research journal publishes articles on scientific aspects of pain, namely basic science and animal studies, and clinical topics, including epidemiological, social, psychological, and psychiatric aspects, as well as reviews and case reports. Management topics, the economic aspects of pain, and historical studies are also offered.

Gay and Lesbian Families
Books

Bain, Jerald, and Phyllis Bruce. 2000. *So Your Child Is Gay.* Scranton, PA: HarperCollins.

A sensitive and empathetic book written for parents, siblings, friends, medical professionals, and gay people themselves. This compassionate guide helps families cope with their fears and concerns, shattering the myths associated with sexual orientation and offering advice and recent information on the topic.

Barret, Robert L., and Bryan E. Robinson. 2000. *Gay Fathers: Encouraging the Hearts of Gay Dads and Their Families.* San Francisco: Jossey-Bass.

Barret and Robinson present a collection of real-life stories on gay fatherhood from two family studies experts. This informative and engaging text also offers current data concerning gay fatherhood as well as practical guidance and information.

Brill, Stephanie A. 2001. *The Queer Parent's Primer: A Lesbian and Gay Family's Guide to Navigating the Straight World.* Oakland, CA: New Harbinger.

The challenges that accompany lesbian and gay parenting can be difficult. Brill's innovative contributions are one of the more important ones and includes finding culturally sensitive child care and schools, making decisions about spirituality and family celebrations, and understanding the legal aspects of protecting gay and lesbian families.

Drucker, Jane. 2001. *Lesbian and Gay Families Speak Out: Understanding the Joys and Challenges of Diverse Family Life.* Scranton, PA: Perseus.

This is another book that offers a frank and honest exploration of the issues faced by lesbian and gay families: from interpersonal relationships and sexual and psychological development, to coming out, dealing with prejudice, and finding a spiritual foundation. Drucker mixes real-life stories of gay fathers and lesbian mothers raising children in a wide variety or settings and styles.

Herdt, Gilbert, and Bruce Koff. 2001. *Something to Tell You: The Road Families Travel When a Child is Gay.* New York: Columbia University Press.

The authors recount the stories of 50 families whose lives have been touched by the discovery that a child is lesbian or gay. These revealing and moving stories show how sexual orientation disclosure affects and influences perceptions of children and even changes the self-image of parents themselves. .imposed by society.

Kaeser, G., P. Gillespie, K. Weston, and A. Martin. 1998. *Love Makes a Family: Portraits of Lesbian, Gay, Bisexual, and Transgendered Parents and Their Families.* Boston: University of Massachusetts Press.

A combination of interviews and photographs are used to document the experiences of lesbian, gay, bisexual, and transgender parents and their children. Included are people from diverse racial, ethnic, and economic backgrounds, representing a wide range of family structures.

Laird, Joan, and Robert Green, eds. 1996. *Lesbians and Gays in Couples and Families: A Handbook for Therapists.* San Francisco, CA: Jossey-Bass.

The focus of this informative book is on clinical work with lesbians and gays in family relationships. It contains case studies as well as recommendations and suggestions for working with gay couples and families.

Savin-Williams, Ritch C. 2001. *Mom, Dad, I'm Gay: How Families Negotiate Coming Out.* Washington, DC: American Psychological Association.

This critically acclaimed book provides insight into the world of nonheterosexual youths and the challenges they face in coming to terms with their sexual orientation. Readers will discover how these young people have negotiated healthy relationships with their families and the empowerment that resulted.

Sullivan, T. Richard, ed. 2000. *Queer Families, Common Agendas: Gay People, Lesbians, and Family Values.* Binghamton, NY: Haworth Press.

This is a timely and informative book about the nature, challenges, and advantages of gay and lesbian parenting. It is readable and filled with sensitive observations and sensible advice.

Switzer, David K. 2000. *Pastoral Care of Gays, Lesbians, and Their Families.* Minneapolis, MN: Fortress Press.

Written by a pastoral theologian with considerable experience in counseling gay and lesbian individuals and their families, this book assists both pastoral caregivers and congregations in examining and enhancing their pastoral care of homosexuals and their families.

Research Journals

Harrington Gay Men's Fiction Quarterly
http://www.haworthpress.com/

Special thematic issues of this journal will focus on fiction concerning AIDS, coming out, relationships, sexuality, religion, and family. This quarterly strives to be a leader in the growing genre of gay fiction and, in addition to scholarly studies and library collections, is intended for a general gay readership interested in the latest writing on the subject.

Harrington's Lesbian Fiction Quarterly
http://www.haworthpressinc.com/

This international journal focuses on lesbian writing in such areas as women's studies, sociology, psychology, gender studies, and alternative cultures. In addition to literature, the journal features artwork, graphics, and photography reflecting the themes of lesbian life experiences. The journal is diverse in its scope, presenting writers and researchers of all interests, ethnic backgrounds, and ages who can bring varied experiences and points of view to this forum of lesbian literature.

Journal of Bisexuality
http://www.haworthpressinc.com/

This professional quarterly publishes both professional articles and serious essays on bisexuality and its meaning for the individual, the community, and society. Topics include bisexual issues in therapy; growth of the bisexual movement; bisexuality and the media; differences from the straight, lesbian, and gay communities; and variations in the bisexual lifestyle.

Journal of Gay and Lesbian Psychotherapy
http://www.haworthpressinc.com/

As a clinical, multidisciplinary, professional forum for the exposition, discussion, and exchange of practical information about lesbian and gay psychotherapy, the primary editorial goal of this journal is to present the data of clinical psychotherapy with lesbian and gay patients/clients. Among the therapeutic interventions discussed are cognitive, behavioral, individual, and couples therapy; psychopharmacological intervention; and alcohol and substance abuse treatment modes.

Journal of Gay and Lesbian Social Services
http://www.haworthpressinc.com/

This journal is dedicated to the development of knowledge which meets the practical needs of lesbians, gays, and bisexuals in their social context. It provides contemporary research on such topics as ethnic and racial minorities, health and medical services, mental health services, foster care and child welfare agencies, juvenile and adult corrections, and services for the elderly. A particular focus is also placed on victims of social problems such as poverty, hate crimes, domestic violence, and physical disabilities.

Journal of Gender Studies
http://www.tandf.co.uk/journals/carfax/09589236.html

The *Journal of Gender Studies* is an interdisciplinary journal that publishes articles relating to gender from a feminist perspective covering a wide range of subject areas, including diversity of cultural backgrounds and differences in sexual orientation.

Journal of Homosexuality
http://www.haworthpressinc.com/

This journal gathers scholarly research on homosexuality, including sexual practices and gender roles and their cultural, historical, interpersonal, and modern social contexts. In addition to research on human sexuality, articles in the journal also explore the political, social, and moral implications of research on sexual orientation. Unique perspectives from the disciplines of law, history, and the humanities serve to further broaden the scope of the journal.

Journal of Lesbian Studies
http://www.haworthpressinc.com/

As a vehicle for the promotion of scholarship and commentary on lesbianism from an international and multicultural perspective, this journal features articles which focus primarily on women who identify as lesbians, alternating between informative, practical, research-based, and theoretical approaches.

Sexualities
http://www.sagepub.co.uk/journals/details/j0065.html

This international journal publishes articles, reviews, and scholarly comment on the shifting nature of human sexuality. *Sexualities* adopts a broad, interdisciplinary perspective covering the whole of the social sciences, cultural history, cultural anthropology, and social geography, as well as feminism, gender studies, cultural studies, and lesbian and gay studies.

Caring for Aging Family Members
Books

Abrams, Robert, et al. 2000. *Boomer Basics: Everything That You Need to Know about the Issues Facing You, Your Children, and Your Parents.* New York: McGraw-Hill.

This is must reading for anyone of the baby boomer generation. Among other topics, it explores the multiple demands of caring for aging parents as well as grown children, offering readers a wealth of information and wise suggestions.

Applegate, Barbara, and Jean Thorne. 2000. *Parent Care: A Survival Guide for Adult Children of Aging Parents.* New York: A.G.E. Consultants Press.

The authors are very thorough in their analysis of the stresses facing adult caregivers of aging parents, including physical, emotional, psychological, and financial pressures. A very compassionate and practical reference book.

Berman, Raeann. 2001. *How to Survive Your Aging Parents: So You and They Can Enjoy Life.* Chicago, IL: Surrey Books.

This is a comforting, anecdotal book that addresses issues regarding the health of both caregiver and care recipient, finances, living arrangements, communication, and emotional hurdles. It contains many valuable references and resources.

Bigby, Christine. 2000. *Moving on Without Parents.* Baltimore, MD: Paul H. Brookes Publishing.

This book offers a new twist to the topic of caring for aging parents. Bigby shares the results of a qualitative study that looks retrospectively at the lives of a group of adults and examines what they've experienced since their parents relinquished care.

Greenberg, Vivian. 2000. *Children of a Certain Age: Adults and Their Aging Parents.* Missoula, MT: University Press.

Greenberg gives a sensitive and captivating narrative of the journey most of us face during our adult lives. She supplies uplifting accounts of how elderly parents and their middle-aged children can interact with new levels of mutuality and reciprocity, in the process mending fences and healing old wounds.

Ilardo, Joseph A., and Carole R. Rothman. 2001. *Are Your Parents Driving You Crazy? How to Resolve the Most Common Dilemmas with Aging Parents*. Acton, MA: Vanderwyk and Burnham.

Do you have an aging parent who refuses to stop driving or will not see a doctor and ignores medical advice? Do you have a spouse who never offers to help with caregiving assistance and resents the time you spend caring for your parent? If you answered yes to either of these questions, you need to read this book.

Pipher, Mary. 2000. *Another Country: Navigating the Emotional Terrain of Our Elders*. East Rutherford, NJ: Berkley Publishing.

Renowned psychiatrist and author Mary Pipher takes us on a journey into old age, sharing with readers what our elders are going through, why we have trouble dealing with them, and how we can make old age a more pleasant experience for all concerned. Pipher brings her usual insight, candor, and wit to this project, providing a literary masterpiece to be savored and remembered.

Roberts, Suzanne, and N. Osa. 2000. *Coping in New Territory: A Guide for Adult Children of Aging Parents*. Chicago: Cheltenham Press.

This is another wise and practical book on how to best weather the strains of caregiving. The authors present a realistic view of the potential problem areas, but temper the sacrifices with the many positive dimensions of caregiving.

Robertson, Betty B. 2000. *TLC for Aging Parents: A Practical Guide*. Kansas City, MO: Beacon Hill Press.

Robertson does a credible job in not only describing the complexities of caregiving but also offering helpful advice and solutions to problematic areas. One of the better self-help books on the market.

Rubin, Lillian B. 2000. *Tangled Lives: Daughters, Mothers, and the Crucible of Aging.* Westminster, MD: Beacon Press.

Rubin skillfully examines the lives of women as they grow from daughters into mothers and move on into the intimidating territory of old age. At the heart of this book is how women struggle to forge their identity through middle age into late adulthood.

Research Journals

Abstracts in Social Gerontology
http://www.sagepub.co.uk/journals/details/j0007.html

This reference source provides abstracts and bibliographies of major articles, books, reports, and other materials on all aspects of social gerontology. Among the many topics are demography, economics, family relations, government policy, health, institutional care, physiology, psychiatric dysfunctions, psychology, societal attitudes, work, and retirement.

Alliance for Aging Research
http://www.agingresearch.org/aboutus.html

The Alliance for Aging Research was founded in 1986 to promote and disseminate medical research on aging. Since then, it has become the nation's leading citizen advocacy organization for improving the health and independence of older Americans through public and private research. The journal releases studies and surveys that examine important medical, behavioral, and social issues associated with aging.

American Journal of Geriatric Psychiatry
http://www.appi.org/

This journal contains peer-reviewed articles on a variety of topics, including the diagnosis and classification of the psychiatric disorders of later life. Innovative treatment strategies—including psychodynamic and other psychotherapeutic approaches in the treatment of elderly patients—are also included. Regular features include clinical concepts and case reports, editorials and perspectives, book reviews, and abstracts.

Gerontology News
http://www.geron.org/newsletter/news.htm

This journal is a publication of the Gerontological Society of America (GSA), a professional association in the field of aging with more than 5,000 members in thirty countries worldwide. It reports on policy issues, legislative actions, research results, and recently released major reports on aging.

Illness, Crisis and Loss
http://www.sagepub.co.uk/journals/details/j0227.html

This journal focuses on the fields of life-threatening illness and thanatology. It brings together the expertise of many and varied professionals, including those in sociology, social work, nursing, and counseling and publishes peer-reviewed articles, editorials, book reviews, and essays on psychosocial and ethical issues associated with life-threatening illnesses, traumatic human crises, and grief and loss.

Journal of Aging and Health
http://www.sagepub.co.uk/journals/details/j0100.html

The *Journal of Aging and Health* deals with social and behavioral factors relating to aging and health, emphasizing quality of life. Among the topics included are life expectancy, diet, nutrition, chronic illness, disease prevention, ethics in health care, and long-term care.

Journal of Aging and Identity
http://www.wkap.nl/prod/j/1087–3732

The *Journal of Aging and Identity* is designed to examine the phenomenon of aging as it is presented in literature, popular culture, and the arts. Articles address a wide range of issues, including attitudes toward aging as depicted in the writing and art of various people. The journal provides a forum for interdisciplinary dialogue with contributions from experts in the humanities and the biomedical, behavioral, and social sciences.

Journal of Applied Gerontology
http://www.sagepub.co.uk/journals/details/j0094.html

The *Journal of Applied Gerontology* provides an international forum for information that has clear and immediate applicability to the health care and quality of life of older persons. Among the topics receiving attention are caregiving, exercise, death and dying, health, leisure activities, mental health, retirement planning, and sexuality.

Psychology and Aging
http://www.apa.org/journals/pag.html

Psychology and Aging publishes a wide variety of articles on adult development and aging. Research topics may be applied, bio-behavioral, clinical, educational, methodological, or psychosocial psychology. Although the emphasis in this journal is on original research investigations, occasional theoretical analyses of research issues, practical clinical problems, or policy may appear, as well as critical reviews of a content area in adult development and aging.

Research on Aging
http://www.sagepub.co.uk/journals/details/j0142.html

This journal presents a diversity of articles that are both broad in scope and detailed in coverage. The articles encourage development of new knowledge and analysis and the current state of gerontology is frequently examined through a range of critical and review articles. Among the features are debates on current gerontological issues, practical applications of research findings, editorials, and future directions in the field.

Families of Divorce

Books

Benedek, Elissa P., and Catherine F. Brown. 2001. *How to Help Your Child Overcome Divorce: A Support Guide for Families.* New York: Newmarket Press.

This book provides the latest information on helping divorced parents raise their children to be happy, well-adjusted individuals. It offers practical advice along with numerous case examples to illustrate specifics.

Beyer, Roberta, and Kent Winchester. 2001. *Speaking of Divorce: How to Talk with Your Kids and Help Them Cope.* Minneapolis, MN: Spirit Publishing.

Talking with children about divorce is no easy task. However, these authors supply plenty of sound advice on how to ease the transition and keep the channels of communication open.

Booth, James. 2000. *Divorce and Remarriage.* Gordonsville, VA: Universe Publications.

Booth gives a solid overview to divorce and remarriage in clear and concise language. He explains how family dynamics change before, during, and after divorce, and how the family functioning process is at work in remarried households.

Kleeman, Robert E. and James Aderling. 1999. *The Handbook for Divorce Valuation.* New York: Wiley.

The authors give practical coverage of every aspect of business valuation in the context of a divorce. This comprehensive guide shows practitioners how to provide the highest level of service in divorce litigation.

Lawson, Erma Jean, and Aaron Thompson. 2001. *Black Men and Divorce.* Thousand Oaks, CA: Sage.

This book is an important addition to the research on divorces and diversity. The authors argue that the social construction of race has important implications for black marriages, and they examine the belief system by which black men are stigmatized and socially marginalized as debased individuals.

Margulies, Samuel. 2001. *Getting Divorced without Ruining Your Life.* New York: Simon and Schuster.

A highly regarded divorce attorney and mediator shares his knowledge and insight on the subject. He places an emphasis on achieving a "good" divorce, one that will leave a person and family members as financially and emotionally sound as possible.

McKay, Matthew, et al. 2001. *The Divorce Book.* Edited by Kirk and Susan Johnson. Oakland, CA: New Harbinger.

Written by two psychologists, a lawyer, and a relationship expert, this book offers answers and techniques to help negotiate the emotional, legal, and child-care issues of divorce in the clearest way possible. It is a practical and compassionate guide.

Staal, Stephanie. 2001. *The Love They Lost: Living with the Legacy of Our Parents' Divorce.* New York: Dell.

Staal's book is an interesting variation of the existing divorce literature. In it, she provides a forum for those who have grown up in divorce. She connects the observations of more than 100 adult children of divorce, knitting their stories together into a web of experience.

Teyber, Edward. 2001. *Helping Children Cope with Divorce.* San Francisco: Jossey-Bass.

This book provides specific guidelines to help parents deal with the issues that emerge during the divorce process. Teyber touches on a wide range of important topics, such as how parents can minimize the distress for children, how to best explain the divorce to the children, and how to shield children from parental conflict.

Wallerstein, Judith S., Julia Lewis, and Sandra Blakeslee. 2000. *The Unexpected Legacy of Divorce: A Twenty-Five Year Landmark Study.* Westport, CT: Hyperion.

In this important work, family studies expert the authors track the experiences of one group of children through a quarter century, identifying the difficulties that they faced growing up. The central message is that divorce has a more lasting effect on people than was previously thought.

Research Journals

American Journal of Family Therapy
http://www.brunner-routledge.co.uk/

The *American Journal of Family Therapy* continues to be the incisive, authoritative, independent voice in the therapeutic profession. It contains the latest techniques for treating families; theory on normal and dysfunctional family relationships; research on sexuality and intimacy; the effects of traditional and alternative family styles; and community approaches to family intervention.

Counseling Psychologist
http://www.sagepub.co.uk/journals/details/j0178.html

The *Counseling Psychologist* showcases new or developing areas of practice and research on topics of immediate interest to counseling psychologists. The journal defines the field and communicates this definition to the profession as well as to those in other disciplines. A sampling of the topics includes counseling HIV-infected clients, counseling lesbian and gay clients, ethics, and multicultural training.

Family Process
http://www.familyprocess.org/

As a peer-reviewed, international journal in the field of family therapy and research, it presents the latest therapy methods, newest strategies, and current research findings. *Family Process* is one of the most referenced journals in the field and is vital reading for family researchers, social workers, family therapists, nurses, psychologists, physicians, clergy, rehabilitation specialists, patient and family advocates, and medical ethicists.

Journal of Counseling Psychology
http://www.apa.org/journals/cou.html

The *Journal of Counseling Psychology* publishes empirical research in the areas of counseling activities, career development, diversity, and underrepresented populations in relation to counseling activities, the development of new measures to be used in counseling activities, and professional issues in counseling psychology. In addition, the journal often contains conceptual or empirical contributions about methodological issues in counseling psychology research.

Journal of Family Therapy
http://www.blackwellpublishers.co.uk/asp/journal.asp?ref=01634445

This journal advances the understanding and treatment of human relationships constituted in systems such as couples, families, professional networks, and wider groups, by publishing articles on theory, research, clinical practice, and training. A wide variety of topics are covered, reflecting the many perspectives of its international contributors.

Journal of Marriage and Family
http://www.ncfr.com/authors/index.htm

The *Journal of Marriage and Family* has been one of the leading research journals in the family field for 60 years. It features original research and theory, research interpretation and reviews, critical discussion concerning all aspects of marriage and family, and book reviews.

Journal of Sex and Marital Therapy
http://www.tandf.co.uk/journals/pp/0092623X.html

This respected research journal focuses on important developments in the United States and abroad. Among its major specialties are therapeutic techniques and outcomes, special clinical and medical problems, the theoretical parameters of sexual functioning, and marital relationships. Among the topics are sexual dysfunctions, atypical sexual behaviors, theoretical issues, marital relationships, and sexual abuse.

Sexual and Relationship Therapy
http://www.tandf.co.uk/journals/carfax/14681994.html

This international journal is for every professional concerned with sexual and marital function. Its readers include academics and researchers, clinicians, therapists, and counselors. The journal recognizes that sexual and marital difficulties, and their alleviation, are an increasing part of the workload of professionals from many different disciplines, including medicine, psychology, psychotherapy, nursing, counseling, and social work.

Remarried Families
Books

Berger, Roni. 1998. *Stepfamilies: A Multi-Dimensional Perspective.* New York: Haworth Press.

Berger shows helping professionals how to avoid stereotypes surrounding stepfamilies, and gives guidelines on how to offer supportive assistance to stepfamilies. A particular strength of this book are perspectives on ethnically and culturally different stepfamilies.

Bray, James, and John Kelly. 1999. *Stepfamilies.* Shelter Island, NY: Broadway Books.

This book offers suggestions on easing the conflicts of stepfamily life and healing the scars of divorce. The authors provide reasons why some stepfamilies fail while others succeed.

Burns, Cherie. 2001. *Stepmotherhood: How to Survive Without Feeling Frustrated, Left Out, or Wicked.* New York: Crown.

This is a sensitive, realistic handbook for the large population of stepmothers. Burns offers excellent advice to her audience in a practical, applied fashion.

Clapp, Genevieve. 2000. *Divorce and New Beginnings: A Complete Guide to Recovery, Solo Parenting, Co-Parenting and Stepfamilies.* New York: Wiley.

Clapp utilizes case studies and skillful advice to help readers better understand divorce and the challenges it creates. Her ability to describe uncharted and potentially troubling waters provides those facing new life roles with confidence as well as reassurance.

James, John W., Russell Friedman, and Leslie L. Matthews. 2001. *When Children Grieve: For Adults to Help Children Deal with Death, Divorce, Pet Loss, Moving, and Other Losses.* New York: HarperCollins.

In terms of divorce, the authors provide ways to empower children with positive, effective methods of dealing with loss. However great the feeling of loss, this thoughtful book helps the child at any stage of grieving.

Lofas, Jeanette. 1998. *Family Rules: Helping Stepfamilies and Single Parents Build Happy Homes.* East Rutherford, NJ: Kensington.

A recognized authority on divorce, remarriage, and blended families supplies straightforward, no-nonsense advice and guidance. This book is loaded with worthwhile tips and ways to bring stability and tranquility to the home front.

Marsolini, Maxine. 2000. *Blended Families: Creating Harmony as You Build a New Home Life.* Chicago, IL: Moody Press.

In this book, a good writing style converges with the author's supportive insight. Marsolini stresses that while remarried couples face unique and sometimes confusing challenges, there are ways to bring unity out of adversity and diversity.

Norwood, Perdita, and Teri Wingender. 1999. *The Enlightened Stepmother: Revolutionizing the Role.* New York: William Morrow.

Becoming a stepmother is a life-altering event in any woman's life. The issues facing stepmothers are often extraordinarily complex and many women are overwhelmingly unprepared. The authors gather the experiences from stepmothers of all ages, occupations, and lifestyles and share what works and what doesn't.

Shimberg, Elaine M. 1999. *Blending Families: A Guide for Parents, Stepparents, Grandparents, and Everyone Building a Successful New Family.* East Rutherford, NJ: Berkley Publishing.

This problem-solving guide offers practical advice against the backdrop of real-life stories from families who've been through the adjustment process. Topics include emotional, financial, disciplinary, territorial, and interpersonal issues.

Wright, Janet M. 1998. *Lesbian Stepfamilies: An Ethnography of Love.* New York: Haworth Press.

This unique title shows how amazingly ordinary yet extraordinarily different two-mother families can be. The reader is introduced to five different real-life lesbian families and explores the different kinds of steprelationships and types of stepmothering that exist in lesbian stepfamilies.

Research Journals

Children and Youth Services Review
http://www.childwelfare.com/kids/cysr.htm

Children and Youth Services Review offers a scientific and scholarly knowledge base for the child-welfare field. It is published eight times per year and provides in-depth coverage of such topics as child welfare, foster care, single parents, divorced and remarried families, adoptions, child abuse and neglect, income support, mental health services, and social policy.

Families, Systems & Health
http://www.fsh.org/call.html

Families, Systems & Health focuses on the collaboration that exists among all types of families, mental health professionals, and health-care providers. This journal publishes articles that describe and evaluate a holistic, systemic view of health, illness, and model of health care in the United States and other countries. The journal is particularly interested in new models of collaboration with families and among health-care professionals in different communities and health-care settings.

Family Futures
http://www.familyfutures.co.uk/

Family Futures is an international organization that seeks innovative ways of dealing with a variety of family crises and challenges. Services are directed toward everyone in the family and include such techniques as systemic family therapy, analytic concepts, creative arts, and parenting skills. The guidance is nonjudgmental, supportive, and rooted in the theory of positive attachment formation set in the context of family relationships.

Journal of Family and Economic Issues
http://www.wkap.nl/prod/j/1058–0476

This journal is an interdisciplinary publication that explores the intricate relationship between the family and its economic environment. Important topics and issues are explored, including issues in family management, household division of labor and productivity, relationships between economic and noneconomic decisions, and interrelations between work and family life. The journal features original and applied research, critical reviews, integrative theoretical articles, and reviews of significant books in the field.

Journal of Family Communication
http://www.erlbaum.com/Journals/journals/JFC/jfc.htm

This journal publishes articles on all aspects of communication in families, including communication in family systems and relationships, and how families manage communication with societal systems such as mass media, education, health care, and law and policy. Each issue contains research articles, theoretical essays, family communication education, and reviews of books and other resources (websites and instructional video/audio tapes).

Journal of Family Issues
http://www.sagepub.co.uk/frame.html?http://www.sagepub.co.uk/journals/details/j0179.html

This journal is devoted to the issues and problems related to marriage and family life and to theoretical and professional issues of current interest to those who work with and study families. It examines professional issues, research developments, and practical applications from an interdisciplinary perspective, encompassing such areas as family violence, gender studies, psychology, social work, sociology, social gerontology, and multiculturalism.

Journal of Family Psychology
http://www.apa.org/journals/fam.html

The *Journal of Family Psychology* is devoted to the study of the family systems and focuses on such topics as the following: marital and family processes, the outcome and process of marital and family treatment, the development and evaluation of family-focused prevention programs, families in transition (separation, divorce, and single parenting; remarriage and the stepfamily; adoption; and death and bereavement), family violence and abuse, work and family life, and multicultural variations.

Journal of Marital and Family Therapy
http://www.aamft.org/resources/Product_Events/jmft_menu.htm

The *Journal of Marital and Family Therapy* is published quarterly by the American Association for Marriage and Family Therapy (AAMFT), one of the leading professional associations in the field of marriage and family therapy. It is recognized around the world as the preeminent family therapy journal, focusing on a variety of social issues and problems related to marriage and family life.

Journal of Social and Personal Relationships
http://www.sagepub.co.uk/journals/details/j0036.html

The *Journal of Social and Personal Relationships* publishes empirical and theoretical papers and draws material from the fields of social psychology, communications, developmental psychology, and sociology. This bimonthly journal explores such diverse topics as family systems, dating, divorce, remarriage, jealousy, family processes, loneliness, deception, therapeutic relationships, loss of close relationships, attachment, and the transitions of parenthood.

Abusive Family Relationships
Books

Braun-Haley, Ellie, and Shawn D. Haley, S. D. 2001. *War on the Home Front: An Examination of Wife Abuse.* Herndon, VA: Berghahn Books.

This book explores factors that help and hinder our efforts to better understand and alleviate wife abuse. The magnitude of the problem is detailed by the authors along with interventions for future consideration.

Corby, Brian. 2000. *Child Abuse: Towards a Knowledge Base.* Bristol, PA: Taylor and Francis.

Corby analyzes child abuse from historical, social, and political contexts and in so doing provides a solid, multidisciplinary knowledge base. His book is a valuable reference source that can help us better understand the ways that we respond to this nagging social problem.

Hobbs, Christopher, and Jane Wynne. 2001. *Physical Signs of Child Abuse.* Philadelphia, PA: W. B. Saunders.

As a full-color, photographic atlas, this book illustrates all the major forms of child abuse and neglect. Each photograph is accompanied by a brief caption to guide the reader on borderline clinical signs, and case histories are given where appropriate.

Jones, Ann. 2000. *Next Time She'll Be Dead: Battering and How to Stop It.* Westminster, MD: Beacon Press.

This is a revised and updated edition of a critically acclaimed book on domestic violence. The author supplies new information on the effect of the 1994 Violence Against Women Act, examines resources on the Internet, and details what individuals can do to help stop and prevent battering.

Knauer, Sandy. 2000. *No Ordinary Life: Parenting the Sexually Abused Child and Adolescent*. Springfield, IL: Charles C. Thomas.

Knauer treats an important topic with great sensitivity, insight, and skill. She tells parents how to help their children through the healing process while creating a safe, supportive family environment.

Monteleone, James A. 2000. *Child Maltreatment: Identifying, Interpreting and Reporting Child Abuse*. St. Louis, MO: G. W. Medical Publishing.

This authoritative reference graphically depicts and details the signs and symptoms of child abuse. It covers both physical and emotional aspects of abuse and discusses how abuse can affect children physically, psychologically, socially, and developmentally.

Reece, Robert. M. 2000. *Treatment of Child Abuse*. Baltimore, MD: Johns Hopkins University Press.

This book consists of contributions on the topic of child abuse from pediatricians, psychiatrists, child advocates, social workers, and legal scholars. In addition to discussing the major types of child abuse, this volume also gives consideration to the treatment of offenders, the treatment of resistant families, and the research of child abuse treatments.

Straus, Murray A., and Denise A. Donnelly. 2000. *Beating the Devil Out of Them: Corporal Punishment in American Children*. New Brunswick, NJ: Transaction Publishers.

Two leading authorities on domestic violence raise important issues related to corporal punishment including the nature of spanking, myths about corporal punishment, the conspiracy of silence that often exists behind closed doors, gender variations in corporal punishment, and depression and suicide.

Van Dam, Carla. 2000. *Identifying Child Molesters.* Binghamton, NY: Haworth Press.

Van Dam Clearly spells out the techniques that child sexual molesters employ to charm adults into giving them access to children. The author contends that when these strategies are seen and understood, adults can take much more direct responsibility for preventing child sexual abuse than was previously possible.

Wallace, Harvey. 2001. *Family Violence.* Needham Heights, MA: Allyn and Bacon.

As one of the more popular books on domestic violence, this book successfully explores this complicated and multifaceted topic, particularly the family dynamics and processes in operation. It is ideal for social workers, law enforcement professionals, health-care professionals, and educators.

Research Journals

Aggression and Violent Behavior
http://www.elsevier.nl/inca/publications/store/3/0/8/4/3/index.htt

Aggression and Violent Behavior is a multidisciplinary journal that publishes substantive and integrative reviews, as well as summary reports of innovative ongoing clinical research programs on a wide range of topics on aggression and violent behavior. The journal publishes a large variety of issues, populations, and domains, including homicide, atypical behavior, child and youth violence, family violence, genetic predispositions, and the physiological basis of aggression and violence.

Aggressive Behavior
http://www3.interscience.wiley.com/cgi-bin/jtoc?ID=32356

This journal examines the manner in which fields such as psychiatry, psychology, sociology, anthropology, and ethology relate to either overt or implied conflict behaviors. It features articles exploring the underlying mechanisms or influencing behaviors generally regarded as aggressive and the physiological and/or behavioral consequences of such behaviors.

Child Abuse and Neglect
http://www.elsevier.nl/inca/publications/store/5/8/6/586.
pub.htt

Child Abuse and Neglect supplies international, multidisciplinary coverage of all aspects of child abuse and neglect, with special emphasis on prevention and treatment. Coverage is also extended to those facets of life which either favor or hinder optimal family interaction. Contributions are from the fields of psychology, psychiatry, social work, medicine, nursing, law, law enforcement, legislation, education, and anthropology.

Child Abuse Review
http://www3.interscience.wiley.com/cgi-bin/jtoc?ID=5060

This review is a forum for all professionals working in the field of child protection, giving them access to the latest research findings, practice developments, training initiatives, and policy issues. It covers all forms of maltreatment, whether they occur inside or outside of the family environment.

Journal of Family Violence
http://www.wkap.nl/prod/j/0885-7482

The *Journal of Family Violence* is an interdisciplinary forum for all forms of family violence and its precursors, including spouse-battering, child abuse, sexual abuse of children, incest, abuse of the elderly, marital rape, domestic homicide, the alcoholic marriage, and general family conflict. The gathered research is from a broad range of disciplines: clinical and counseling psychology, sociology, psychiatry, public health, criminology, law, marital counseling, and social work.

Journal of Interpersonal Violence
http://www.sagepub.co.uk/journals/details/j0015.html

This journal offers coverage of the concerns and activities of professionals and researchers working in domestic violence, child sexual abuse, rape and sexual assault, physical child abuse, and violent crime. Focusing on both victims and perpetrators, it examines theoretical links between all types of interpersonal violence, exploring the similarities and differences between these types of crimes.

Sexual Abuse: A Journal of Research and Treatment
http://www.wkap.nl/prod/j/1079–0632

Sexual Abuse: A Journal of Research and Treatment provides a forum for the latest original research and scholarly reviews on both clinical and theoretical aspects of sexual abuse. The journal thoroughly investigates its causes, consequences, and treatment strategies. The in-depth studies provide essential data for those working in both clinical and academic environments, including psychologists, psychiatrists, social workers, and therapists/counselors, as well as corrections officers and allied professionals in children's services.

Violence Against Women
http://www.sagepub.co.uk/journals/details/j0062.html

Violence Against Women publishes empirical research as well as historical and cross-cultural analyses on all aspects of the problem of violence against women. Topics include sexual assault and coercion, domestic violence, incest, sexual harassment, female infanticide, and female sexual slavery. A primary goal of this journal is to encourage dialogue on these topics among those working in various fields, as well as in agencies and other settings.

9

Nonprint Resources

This chapter contains a comprehensive listing of educational videotapes on American families. The videotape listing is organized according to the text's table of contents. Sources, including complete mailing addresses, are provided for each videotape and all of the recommended titles are in VHS format and are in color. At the end of this chapter, the reader will find a separate, additional listing of family life websites. The links presented there are designed to complement the issues and controversies presented in this book and to supply the reader with additional sources of information.

Videos

Chapter 1: History and Scope of American Families

The Changing Family and Its Implications
Length: 50 minutes
Date: 1996
Cost: $89.95
Source: Films for the Humanities and Sciences
P.O. Box 2053
Princeton, NJ 08543–2053
Phone: 800–257–5126
Fax: 609–275–3767
http://www.films.com

This video analyzes those forces responsible for changing today's family and the implications for parents as well as children.

Family
Length: 52 minutes
Date: 1998
Cost: $129
Source: Films for the Humanities and Sciences
P.O. Box 2053
Princeton, NJ 08543–2053
Phone: 800–257–5126
Fax: 609–275–3767
http://www.films.com

In this video, the concept of family is viewed from around the world and down through time. Historians and family-studies experts discuss various aspects of family change.

Family and Survival
Length: 52 minutes
Date: 1995
Cost: $89.95
Source: Films for the Humanities and Sciences
P.O. Box 2053
Princeton, NJ 08543–2053
Phone: 800–257–5126
Fax: 609–275–3767
http://www.films.com

This video focuses on the evolution of the family into its present-day structures and forms. Among the topics are divorce, dual-earner families, and single-parenting.

Family Matters: The Importance of Families
Length: 26 minutes
Date: 1999
Cost: $89.95
Source: Magna Systems
95 West County Line Rd.
Barrington, IL 60010
Phone: 800–203–7060
Fax: 815–459–4280
http://www.magnasystemsvideos.com

While introducing the strengths and resiliencies of family structures, this video highlights teenage families, single-parent families, and blended families.

Theories of Development
Length: 30 minutes
Date: 1997
Cost: $139
Source: Insight Media
2162 Broadway
New York, NY 10024–0621
Phone: 800–233–9910
Fax: 212–799–5309
http://www.insight-media.com

This video explores the work of major contributors to human development and family studies, including many of the researchers explored in Chapter 5 of this book.

What Is Family? Defining the Tie That Binds
Length: 45 minutes
Date: 2000
Cost: $89.95
Source: Films for the Humanities and Sciences
P.O. Box 2053
Princeton, NJ 08543–2053
Phone: 800–257–5126
Fax: 609–275–3767
http://www.films.com

As an interesting analysis of the family structure, the video includes sociological forces shaping the family's formation and psychological dynamics between its members.

Chapter 2: Exploring the Diversity of Family Life

Diversity: Contrasting Perspectives
Length: 30 minutes
Date: 1996
Cost: $89.95
Source: Magna Systems
95 West County Line Rd.
Barrington, IL 60010

Phone: 800–203–7060
Fax: 815–459–4280
http://www.magnasystemsvideos.com

The need to understand and respect cultural diversity is examined when exploring parent-child relations.

I'm Normal, You're Weird: Understanding Other Cultures
Length: 23 minutes
Date: 1997
Cost: $139
Source: Insight Media
2162 Broadway
New York, NY 10024–0621
Phone: 800–233–9910
Fax: 212–799–5309

This video is a creative and engaging analysis of the complexities attached to different cultures.

In My Country: An International Perspective on Gender
Length: 90 minutes
Date: 1993
Cost: $129
Source: Insight Media
2162 Broadway
New York, NY 10024–0621
Phone: 800–233–9910
Fax: 212–799–5309

As it explores cultural attitudes toward gender, this video includes an analysis of such topics as household labor, child rearing, and care of the elderly.

The Latino Family
Length: 28 minutes
Date: 1998
Cost: $149
Source: Films for the Humanities and Sciences
P.O. Box 2053
Princeton, NJ 08543–2053
Phone: 800–257–5126

Fax: 609–275–3767
http://www.films.com

As an investigation of the contemporary Latino family, this video focuses special attention on how cultural traditions have evolved over time.

Race and Ethnicity
Length: 30 minutes
Date: 1991
Cost: $139
Source: Insight Media
         2162 Broadway
         New York, NY 10024–0621
Phone: 800–233–9910
Fax: 212–799–5309

This video explores the concept of minority by discussing theories of race, racism, and ethnicity. It also highlights the concepts of prejudice and discrimination.

A World of Diversity
Length: Each part is 20 minutes
Date: 1996
Cost: $199 for each part
Source: Insight Media
         2162 Broadway
         New York, NY 10024–0621
Phone: 800–233–9910
Fax: 212–799–5309

This two-part presentation focuses on cultural differences and what individuals can do to overcome such interpersonal obstacles as stereotypes and communication difficulties.

Chapter 3: Family Issues and Controversies
Family Planning
Birth: Eight Women's Stories
Length: 70 minutes
Date: 1999
Cost: $149

Source: Films for the Humanities and Sciences
P.O. Box 2053
Princeton, NJ 08543–2053
Phone: 800–257–5126
Fax: 609–275–3767
http://www.films.com

This portrayal shows eight women giving birth in a variety of circumstances, such as natural childbirth, home birth, Cesarean, and water birth.

Human Reproductive Biology
Length: 35 minutes
Date: 1998
Cost: $149
Source: Films for the Humanities and Sciences
P.O. Box 2053
Princeton, NJ 08543–2053
Phone: 800–257–5126
Fax: 609–275–3767
http://www.films.com

This video covers the normal pregnancy processes and the physical hindrances that can prevent them. It includes the topic of infertility and the reproductive technologies described in this book.

Infertility
Length: 30 minutes
Date: 1991
Cost: $149
Source: Aquarius Health Care Videos
5 Powderhouse Lane, P.O. Box 1159
Sherborn, MA 01770
Phone: 888–440–2963
Fax: 508–650–4216
http://www.aquariusproductions.com

As this video examines infertility, it includes the range of treatment options available including hormones, surgery, and reproductive technologies. It also addresses the financial and ethical issues related to infertility and treatment possibilities.

Population Six Billion
Length: 57 minutes
Date: 1994
Cost: $129
Source: Films for the Humanities and Sciences
P.O. Box 2053
Princeton, NJ 08543–2053
Phone: 800–257–5126
Fax: 609–275–3767
http://www.films.com

This video provides a sobering look at overpopulation and the implications for the world's resources. It presents a good foundation for the topic of family planning.

Pregnancy and Birth: Caring and Preparing for the Life Within
Length: 26 minutes
Date: 1996
Cost: $89.95
Source: Magna Systems
95 West County Line Rd.
Barrington, IL 60010
Phone: 800–203–7060
Fax: 815–459–4280
http://www.magnasystemsvideos.com

Pregnancy and the birth process are examined, including such topics as medical monitoring, testing, and intervention.

Prenatal Development: A Life in the Making
Length: 26 minutes
Date: 1996
Cost: $89.95
Source: Magna Systems
95 West County Line Rd.
Barrington, IL 60010
Phone: 800–203–7060
Fax: 815–459–4280
http://www.magnasystemsvideos.com

Prenatal life is overviewed, including the nature of growth and development in the embryo and fetus. The video includes a look at those maternal, paternal, and environmental factors that impact intrauterine life.

The Reproductive Tug of War: A Pregnancy Paradox
Length: 50 minutes
Date: 2000
Cost: $129
Source: Films for the Humanities and Sciences
P.O. Box 2053
Princeton, NJ 08543–2053
Phone: 800–257–5126
Fax: 609–275–3767
http://www.films.com

This video considers important medical complexities and problems that have the potential of disrupting the course of pregnancy.

Contemporary Parenthood

Basic Parenting Skills
Length: 50 minutes
Date: 1990
Cost: $89.95
Source: Magna Systems
95 West County Line Rd.
Barrington, IL 60010
Phone: 800–203–7060
Fax: 815–459–4280
http://www.magnasystemsvideos.com

An overview of what parenthood embraces is given with particular emphasis on effective parent-child discipline, communication, and promoting self-esteem in children.

Child in the Family
Length: 37 minutes
Date: 1993
Cost: $89.95
Source: Magna Systems
95 West County Line Rd.
Barrington, IL 60010

Phone: 800–203–7060
Fax: 815–459–4280
http://www.magnasystemsvideos.com

A child impacts couples' lives, including various adjustments and adaptations of both mother and father. This video includes several interviews with parents.

Early Adulthood: Parenthood
Length: 29 minutes
Date: 1999
Cost: $89.95
Source: Magna Systems
           95 West County Line Rd.
           Barrington, IL 60010
Phone: 800–203–7060
Fax: 815–459–4280
http://www.magnasystemsvideos.com

An introduction to the topic of parenthood is provided with special emphasis on the myths and misconceptions common to our culture. It also includes coverage of adoptive parents.

Family Affair: Educating Today's Parents
Length: 25 minutes
Date: 1998
Source: Aquarius Health Care Videos
           5 Powderhouse Lane, P.O. Box 1159
           Sherborn, MA 01770
Phone: 888–440–2963
Fax: 508–650–4216
http://www.aquariusproductions.com

Parenthood's many sides and the coping strategies needed to resolve issues and problems are examined. A particular emphasis is placed on parent-support groups and how they offer support and learning opportunities.

Family Influences
Length: 30 minutes
Date: 1992
Cost: $139

Source: Insight Media
 2162 Broadway
 New York, NY 10024–0621
Phone: 800–233–9910
Fax: 212–799–5309

This video explores different styles of child rearing and the potential impact of each on child development. It also considers the role of siblings and birth order on family dynamics.

Right from the Start
Length: 60 minutes
Date: 1983
Cost: $119
Source: Insight Media
 2162 Broadway
 New York, NY 10024–0621
Phone: 800–233–9910
Fax: 212–799–5309

The importance of bonding and attachment between parents and infants is considered, including which child-rearing practices encourage or hinder bonding and attachment.

Shaking, Hitting, Spanking: What to Do Instead
Length: 30 minutes
Date: 1998
Cost: $85
Source: Child Development Media
 5632 Van Nuys Blvd., Suite 286
 Van Nuys, CA 91401
Phone: 800–405–8942
Fax: 818–994–0153
http://www.childdevmedia.com/index.cfm

This video examines positive nurturing parenting techniques that promote healthy, desirable behavior in children.

Siblings: Why Do They Fight and What Can We Do About It?
Length: 60 minutes
Date: 1996
Cost: $40

Source: Child Development Media
5632 Van Nuys Blvd., Suite 286
Van Nuys, CA 91401
Phone: 800–405–8942
Fax: 818–994–0153
http://www.childdevmedia.com/index.cfm

This video provides an illuminating look at the dynamics between brothers and sisters and the rivalry that can develop between them.

Your Place in the Family
Length: 20 minutes
Date: 1998
Cost: $90
Source: Child Development Media
5632 Van Nuys Blvd., Suite 286
Van Nuys, CA 91401
Phone: 800–405–8942
Fax: 818–994–0153
http://www.childdevmedia.com/index.cfm

Birth order shapes individual behavior of the child as well as family interactions and dynamics.

Work and Family Life

Child Care Puzzle
Length: 27 minutes
Date: 1998
Cost: $60
Source: Aquarius Health Care Videos
5 Powderhouse Lane, P.O. Box 1159
Sherborn, MA 01770
Phone: 888–440–2963
Fax: 508–650–4216
http://www.aquariusproductions.com

Geared to the needs of dual-earner homes, this video helps parents make informed choices about child-care arrangements for their youngsters.

Double Shift
Length: 47 minutes
Date: 1995
Cost: $149
Source: Films for the Humanities and Sciences
P.O. Box 2053
Princeton, NJ 08543–2053
Phone: 800–257–5126
Fax: 609–275–3767
http://www.films.com

This videotape concerns itself with those women who have careers and raise families. Special attention is given to the many demands facing working women and the balance that must be struck between the home and workplace.

Early Adulthood: The World of Work
Length: 29 minutes
Date: 1999
Cost: $89.95
Source: Magna Systems
95 West County Line Rd.
Barrington, IL 60010
Phone: 800–203–7060
Fax: 815–459–4280
http://www.magnasystemsvideos.com

The nature of work in modern society and the challenges it poses are presented. Of particular interest are the issues faced by dual-career couples.

Juggling Family and Work
Length: 56 minutes
Date: 1996
Cost: $89.95
Source: Films for the Humanities and Sciences
P.O. Box 2053
Princeton, NJ 08543–2053
Phone: 800–257–5126
Fax: 609–275–3767
http://www.films.com

An insightful portrayal of fathers who effectively balance family and career responsibilities is given, including interviews with fathers.

Not Just a Job: Career Planning for Women
Length: 35 minutes
Date: 1997
Cost: $150
Source: Cambridge Documentary Films
P.O. Box 390385
Cambridge, MA 02139–0004
Phone: 617–484–3993
Fax: 617–484–0754
http://www.cambridgedocumentaryfilms.org

The different ways women think about and plan their careers is investigated. Eight women are shown exploring their individual values, interests, and skills.

Working Parents: Balancing Kids and Careers
Length: 25 minutes
Date: 1998
Cost: $90
Source: Aquarius Health Care Videos
5 Powderhouse Lane, P.O. Box 1159
Sherborn, MA 01770
Phone: 888–440–2963
Fax: 508–650–4216
http://www.aquariusproductions.com

This video looks at the many challenges and pressures of combining a job, housework, and parenthood. It includes interviews with dual-earner couples, single parents, and experts in the field.

Single-Parent Families

And Baby Makes Two: Single Motherhood
Length: 30 minutes
Date: 1996
Cost: $89.95
Source: Films for the Humanities and Sciences
P.O. Box 2053
Princeton, NJ 08543–2053

Phone: 800–257–5126
Fax: 609–275–3767
http://www.films.com

This video shows how many women are voluntarily choosing to have and rear their children as single parents.

Chris and Bernie
Length: 25 minutes
Date: 1992
Cost: $99
Source: New Day Films
Department CA, 22-D Hollywood Avenue
Hohokus, NJ 07423
Phone: 888–367–9154
Fax: 201–652–1973
http://www.newday.com

Two single mothers share the responsibilities and challenges of family and career.

Family in Crisis
Length: 28 minutes
Date: 1993
Cost: $89.95
Source: Films for the Humanities and Sciences
P.O. Box 2053
Princeton, NJ 08543–2053
Phone: 800–257–5126
Fax: 609–275–3767
http://www.films.com

Single-parent families facing economic disadvantage and deprivation are the focus of this video.

Fatherless in America
Length: 26 minutes
Date: 1998
Cost: $149
Source: Films for the Humanities and Sciences
P.O. Box 2053
Princeton, NJ 08543–2053
Phone: 800–257–5126

Fax: 609–275–3767
http://www.films.com

This video investigates the implications of fatherless homes in America, including such effects as poverty and violence.

Single Families
Length: 28 minutes
Date: 1999
Cost: $89.95
Source: Magna Systems
          95 West County Line Rd.
          Barrington, IL 60010
Phone: 800–203–7060
Fax: 815–459–4280
http://www.magnasystemsvideos.com

The challenges facing families with one custodial parent are addressed. Among the topics presented are child-rearing issues, financial needs, and career challenges.

Families with Physical Disabilities and Chronic Illnesses

disAbility Awareness
Length: 20 minutes
Date: 1999
Cost: $139
Source: Insight Media
          2162 Broadway
          New York, NY 10024–0621
Phone: 800–233–9910
Fax: 212–799–5309

An exploration of what disabilities are and how to enhance communication skills with disabled persons is given.

Family Challenges: Parenting with a Disability
Length: 25 minutes
Date: 1998
Cost: $195
Source: Aquarius Health Care Videos
          5 Powderhouse Lane, P.O. Box 1159
          Sherborn, MA 01770

Phone: 888–440–2963
Fax: 508–650–4216
http://www.aquariusproductions.com

Family dynamics that occur when a parent has a disability is explored, including adjustments, adaptations, and role realignments.

My Body Is Not Who I Am
Length: 35 minutes
Date: 1993
Cost: $150
Source: Aquarius Health Care Videos
5 Powderhouse Lane, P.O. Box 1159
Sherborn, MA 01770
Phone: 888–440–2963
Fax: 508–650–4216
http://www.aquariusproductions.com

Individuals openly share the struggles and triumphs they have experienced living in a body that is physically disabled or chronically ill.

Nurturing the Families of Chronically Ill or Disabled Children
Length: 86 minutes
Date: 1995
Cost: $150
Source: Child Development Media
5632 Van Nuys Blvd., Suite 286
Van Nuys, CA 91401
Phone: 800–405–8942
Fax: 818–994–0153
http://www.childdevmedia.com/index.cfm

This video focuses attention on the special skills employed by families who have a special needs youngster. It includes interviews with parents and their children who have a chronic illness or physical disability.

Pain Management
Length: 30 minutes
Date: 2000
Cost: $129

Source: Insight Media
2162 Broadway
New York, NY 10024–0621
Phone: 800–233–9910
Fax: 212–799–5309

This video looks at pain management and control, including interviews with medical experts in the field.

Promoting Family Collaboration
Length: 25 minutes
Date: 1997
Cost: $129
Source: Insight Media
2162 Broadway
New York, NY 10024–0621
Phone: 800–233–9910
Fax: 212–799–5309

The parents' role in the care of a disabled child as well as becoming the child's advocate is emphasized, including how therapists and medical practitioners can help promote parental sensitivity and involvement.

Raising Kids with Special Needs
Length: 21 minutes
Date: 1998
Cost: $80
Source: Child Development Media
5632 Van Nuys Blvd., Suite 286
Van Nuys, CA 91401
Phone: 800–405–8942
Fax: 818–994–0153
http://www.childdevmedia.com/index.cfm

This videotape provides an intimate look into the lives of parents of special needs children. Interviews with parents shed light on challenges, concerns, and the importance of social support.

Without Pity: A Film about Abilities
Length: 56 minutes
Date: 1999
Cost: $129

Source: Insight Media
      2162 Broadway
      New York, NY 10024–0621
Phone: 800–233–9910
Fax: 212–799–5309

This video examines how disabled persons can lead full, productive lives. A cross-section of disabled individuals are included, paying close attention to their resiliency and determination.

Gay and Lesbian Families

Beauty before Age: Growing Older in Gay Culture
Length: 22 minutes
Date: 1997
Cost: $79
Source: New Day Films
      Department CA, 22-D Hollywood Avenue
      Hohokus, NJ 07423
Phone: 888–367–9154
Fax: 201–652–1973
http://www.newday.com

The impact of youth and beauty in the gay community is explored. Interviews with a diverse group of gays focus on fears of growing old alone.

Choosing Children
Length: 45 minutes
Date: 1997
Cost: $140
Source: Cambridge Documentary Films
      P.O. Box 390385
      Cambridge, MA 02139–0004
Phone: 617–484–3993
Fax: 617–484–0754
http://www.cambridgedocumentaryfilms.org

This video looks at the issues faced by women who decide to become parents after coming out as lesbians.

Gay Couples: The Nature of Relationships
Length: 50 minutes

Date: 1998
Cost: $149
Source: Films for the Humanities and Sciences
P.O. Box 2053
Princeton, NJ 08543–2053
Phone: 800–257–5126
Fax: 609–275–3767
http://www.films.com

Gay and lesbian relationships are investigated by using a case-study approach. Among the areas explored are communication, conflict resolution, gender roles, and career involvement.

Gender and Relationships
Length: 30 minutes
Date: 1990
Cost: $139
Source: Insight Media
2162 Broadway
New York, NY 10024–0621
Phone: 800–233–9910
Fax: 212–799–5309

The concepts of human interaction and attachment are explored, with a special emphasis on affection, sexual attraction, and love. This video is useful as an introduction to the topic of sexual orientation.

Mother and Eve: Breaking the Silence
Length: 53 minutes
Date: 2000
Cost: $149
Source: Films for the Humanities and Sciences
P.O. Box 2053
Princeton, NJ 08543–2053
Phone: 800–257–5126
Fax: 609–275–3767
http://www.films.com

Four middle-aged women speak about how they came to redefine their sexual orientation, including interviews with their ex-spouses and children.

Caring for Aging Family Members

Age Happens
Length: 28 minutes
Date: 2000
Cost: $139
Source: Insight Media
2162 Broadway
New York, NY 10024–0621
Phone: 800–233–9910
Fax: 212–799–5309

Aging, including physical, social, and psychological processes are examined. Special emphasis is placed on those factors helping elderly persons to maintain health and well-being.

Ageless America
Length: 52 minutes
Date: 1997
Cost: $89.95
Source: Films for the Humanities and Sciences
P.O. Box 2053
Princeton, NJ 08543–2053
Phone: 800–257–5126
Fax: 609–275–3767
http://www.films.com

Growing old is analyzed, with a special emphasis on family caregiving. The video includes both the process and problems of aging.

Grandparenting
Length: 27 minutes
Date: 2000
Cost: $95.00
Source: Magna Systems
95 West County Line Rd.
Barrington, IL 60010
Phone: 800–203–7060
Fax: 815–459–4280
http://www.magnasystemsvideos.com

This video has particular appeal for a number of reasons, particularly since so many grandparents today have grandchildren living in their homes. Of special interest is how the grandparent role has changed over the years.

Late Adulthood: Retirement and Options for Living
Length: 30 minutes
Date: 2001
Cost: $89.95
Source: Magna Systems
95 West County Line Rd.
Barrington, IL 60010
Phone: 800–203–7060
Fax: 815–459–4280
http://www.magnasystemsvideos.com

The topic is explored by examining the challenges and realties of growing old in America. Late adulthood is presented against the backdrop of life satisfaction and well-being throughout the life-span, as well as maintaining a sense of control and independence throughout the later years.

Oldest Victims: Elder Abuse
Length: 45 minutes
Date: 2000
Cost: $129
Source: Films for the Humanities and Sciences
P.O. Box 2053
Princeton, NJ 08543–2053
Phone: 800–257–5126
Fax: 609–275–3767
http://www.films.com

A number of elder abuse topics are explored, such as embezzlement of elders' funds by family members, criminal neglect, and physical abuse.

Midlife Crisis?
Length: 28 minutes
Date: 2000
Cost: $139
Source: Insight Media
2162 Broadway
New York, NY 10024–0621

Phone: 800–233–9910
Fax: 212–799–5309

This video is useful, particularly in light of the many challenges facing middle-age caregivers of elderly parents. It examines how such challenges are part of the midlife transition and how we can better understand its many sides.

Families of Divorce

Children of Divorce
Length: 28 minutes
Date: 1996
Cost: $89.95
Source: Films for the Humanities and Sciences
P.O. Box 2053
Princeton, NJ 08543–2053
Phone: 800–257–5126
Fax: 609–275–3767
http://www.films.com

The various effects that divorce has on children is investigated. Interviews with divorce experts are included.

Divorce and the Family: When Parents Divorce
Length: 24 minutes
Date: 1995
Cost: $89.95
Source: Magna Systems
95 West County Line Rd.
Barrington, IL 60010
Phone: 800–203–7060
Fax: 815–459–4280
http://www.magnasystemsvideos.com

This video gives a frank and realistic portrayal of divorce and its many sides. It covers custody, alimony, mediation, child support, and visitation rights.

Early Adulthood: Love, Marriage, and Divorce
Length: 29 minutes
Date: 1996
Cost: $90

Source: Aquarius Health Care Videos
5 Powderhouse Lane, P.O. Box 1159
Sherborn, MA 01770
Phone: 888–440–2963
Fax: 508–650–4216
http://www.aquariusproductions.com

Various aspects of intimate relationships are presented, including dissolution and the factors responsible for divorce.

Joint Custody
Length: 56 minutes
Date: 1992
Cost: $99
Source: New Day Films
Department CA, 22-D Hollywood Avenue
Hohokus, NJ 07423
Phone: 888–367–9154
Fax: 201–652–1973
http://www.newday.com

This video shows three portraits of the rewards and difficulties of shared parenting and extended family relationships after divorce.

Why Don't the Kids Have a Voice?
Length: 42 minutes
Date: 2000
Cost: $89.95
Source: Films for the Humanities and Sciences
P.O. Box 2053
Princeton, NJ 08543–2053
Phone: 800–257–5126
Fax: 609–275–3767
http://www.films.com

This video looks at divorce law and the manner in which child custody is perceived. It raises the issue of revising custody rules and procedures.

Remarried Families

An American Stepfamily
Length: 26 minutes
Date: 1997
Cost: $89.95
Source: Films for the Humanities and Sciences
P.O. Box 2053
Princeton, NJ 08543–2053
Phone: 800–257–5126
Fax: 609–275–3767
http://www.films.com

The nature of today's blended families is examined and coverage of such issues as conflicting loyalties and rivalries, as well as dealing with former spouses, is offered.

Blended Families
Length: 28 minutes
Date: 1999
Cost: $89.95
Source: Magna Systems
95 West County Line Rd.
Barrington, IL 60010
Phone: 800–203–7060
Fax: 815–459–4280
http://www.magnasystemsvideos.com

Issues surrounding divorce and remarriage in modern society are reviewed. Topics include stepparent and stepsibling dynamics, freedom, domestic boundaries, and tips for successful adjustment.

Family of Choice
Length: 27 minutes
Date: 1999
Cost: $89.95
Source: Magna Systems
95 West County Line Rd.
Barrington, IL 60010
Phone: 800–203–7060
Fax: 815–459–4280
http://www.magnasystemsvideos.com

This video is an overview of how a new family of choice, such as one formed through remarriage, rebuilds and extends itself to others and nurtures a supportive and safe haven for family members.

Healing Wounded Hearts
Length: 28 minutes
Date: 1996
Cost: $125
Source: Aquarius Health Care Videos
5 Powderhouse Lane, P.O. Box 1159
Sherborn, MA 01770
Phone: 888–440–2963
Fax: 508–650–4216
http://www.aquariusproductions.com

Issues associated with parental divorce and remarriage are explored, including the impact of divorce on children and the intervention available from mental health professionals and divorce mediators.

Who's Raising Our Children?
Length: 29 minutes
Date: 1996
Cost: $89.95
Source: Films for the Humanities and Sciences
P.O. Box 2053
Princeton, NJ 08543–2053
Phone: 800–257–5126
Fax: 609–275–3767
http://www.films.com

This video looks at changing family structures and parental roles, including those shaped by divorce and blended families.

Abusive Family Relationships

Breaking the Cycle: Child Abuse
Length: 30 minutes
Date: 1993
Cost: $159
Source: Insight Media
2162 Broadway
New York, NY 10024–0621

Phone: 800–233–9910
Fax: 212–799–5309

The emphasis of this video is how families can prevent child abuse from being perpetuated across generations. It includes the role of therapeutic intervention, support groups, and home visits.

Defending Our Lives
Length: 42 minutes
Date: 1994
Cost: $160
Source: Cambridge Documentary Films
P.O. Box 390385
Cambridge, MA 02139–0004
Phone: 617–484–3993
Fax: 617–484–0754
http://www.cambridgedocumentaryfilms.org

This Oscar-winning documentary is about the magnitude and severity of domestic violence in America. Interviews with battered women are at the foundation of this production.

Family Violence: Private Business, Public Price
Length: 30 minutes
Date: 1995
Cost: $199
Source: Insight Media
2162 Broadway
New York, NY 10024–0621
Phone: 800–233–9910
Fax: 212–799–5309

Domestic abuse is explored from all sides, including the characteristics of the victims, abusers, and therapeutic assistants.

Horror and the Healing
Length: 33 minutes
Date: 1995
Cost: $199
Source: Insight Media
2162 Broadway
New York, NY 10024–0621

Phone: 800–233–9910
Fax: 212–799–5309

This video analyzes how victims of domestic violence begin the healing process. It provides case studies of violent acts and the manner in which the path to recovery is found.

Reporting Child Abuse: A Personal Responsibility
Length: 28 minutes
Date: 1997
Cost: $150
Source: Child Development Media
      5632 Van Nuys Blvd., Suite 286
      Van Nuys, CA 91401
Phone: 800–405–8942
Fax: 818–994–0153
http://www.childdevmedia.com/index.cfm

This video is designed to explore the procedures in reporting child abuse. It is especially suited for educators and health and public safety professionals.

Secret Wounds: Working with Child Observers of Family Violence
Length: 32 minutes
Date: 1998
Cost: $95
Source: Child Development Media
      5632 Van Nuys Blvd., Suite 286
      Van Nuys, CA 91401
Phone: 800–405–8942
Fax: 818–994–0153
http://www.childdevmedia.com/index.cfm

Issues regarding children living in domestically violent families is explored. Among the topics are the child's self-concept, social isolation, fear, and anger.

Sexual Abuse of Children: Victims and Abusers
Length: 28 minutes
Date: 1998
Cost: $199

Source: Insight Media
2162 Broadway
New York, NY 10024–0621
Phone: 800–233–9910
Fax: 212–799–5309

The many effects of child sexual abuse are examined. Video includes candid interviews with therapists, victims, and recovering offenders.

Understanding the Six Forms of Emotional Child Abuse
Length: 25 minutes
Date: 1999
Cost: $199
Source: Insight Media
2162 Broadway
New York, NY 10024–0621
Phone: 800–233–9910
Fax: 212–799–5309

This video provides an illuminating look at exploitation, rejection, terrorization, corruption, isolation, and neglect.

Violence Prevention: What Every Parent Should Know
Length: 28 minutes
Date: 1995
Cost: $99
Source: Magna Systems
95 West County Line Rd.
Barrington, IL 60010
Phone: 800–203–7060
Fax: 815–459–4280
http://www.magnasystemsvideos.com

The focal points of this video are consequences of domestic violence and what parents can do to prevent abusive tendencies. Three sections are included: crisis avoidance, conflict resolution, and problem solving.

Web Resources

Family Health and Well-Being

American Academy of Pediatrics
http://www.aap.org

The mission of the American Academy of Pediatrics is to attain optimal physical, mental, and social health and well-being for all infants, children, adolescents, and young adults. The academy will accomplish this mission by addressing the needs of children, their families, and their communities, and by supporting academy members through advocacy, education, research, service, and improving the systems through which they deliver pediatric care.

American Medical Association
http://www.ama-assn.org

The American Medical Association's (AMA) work includes the development and promotion of standards in medical practice, research, and education; strong advocacy agenda on behalf of patients and physicians; and the commitment to providing timely information on matters important to the health of America. The AMA strives to serve as the voice of the American medical profession.

American Psychological Association
http://www.apa.org

The American Psychological Association (APA) is a scientific and professional organization that represents psychology in the United States. With more than 155,000 members, APA is the largest association of psychologists worldwide. Its primary objective is to advance psychology as a science and profession and as a means of promoting human welfare.

American School Health Association
http://www.ashaweb.org/

The American School Health Association unites the many professionals working in schools who are committed to safeguarding the health of school-aged children. The association, a multidisciplinary organization of administrators, counselors, dentists, health educators, physical educators, school nurses, and school physicians advocates high-quality school health instruction, health services, and a healthful school environment.

Center for Mental Health Services
http://www.mentalhealth.org

The Center for Mental Health Services (CMHS) is charged with leading the national system that delivers mental health services. The goal of this system is to provide the support services needed by adults with mental disorders and children with serious emotional problems. CMHS administers programs and provides assistance with treatment, employment, housing, transportation, and other aspects of community participation.

Children's Health Council
http://www.chconline.org

The Children's Health Council (CHC) provides quality mental health, special education, and developmental services for children and adolescents. These programs serve children with specific behavioral and developmental difficulties as well as children and families facing common everyday challenges. The CHC team consists of specialists in child psychiatry, psychology, speech and language pathology, occupational therapy, social work, special education, and child development.

Cross-cultural Health Care Program
http://www.xculture.org

This organization addresses broad cultural issues that impact the health of individuals and families in ethnic minority communities in Seattle and nationwide. Through a combination of support services, the CCHCP serves as a bridge between communities and health-care institutions to ensure full access to quality health care that is culturally and linguistically appropriate.

Facts for Health
http://www.factsforhealth.org

Facts for Health promotes excellence in medical education and research. The organization seeks to develop and disseminate innovative approaches to educating both professionals and the general public about medical disorders and their treatment. The website offers individuals and families medical information, treatment resources, and educational opportunities.

Federation of Families for Children's Mental Health
http://www.ffcmh.org

The Federation of Families for Children's Mental Health is a national advocacy organization for families of children and youth with mental health needs. The organization has more than 120 state organizations, chapters, and representatives in all states as well as in Ontario, Canada. The organization represents children, youth, and families from diverse cultures and backgrounds.

Food and Nutrition Information Center
http://www.nal.usda.gov/fnic

The Food and Nutrition Information Center (FNIC) is a leader in on-line global nutrition information. It was established in 1971 and exists as part of the National Agricultural Library (NAL). Its mission is to collect and disseminate information about food and human nutrition.

KidsHealth
http://www.kidshealth.org

KidsHealth is a medical website providing doctor-approved health information about children from before birth through adolescence. Created by the Nemours Foundation's Center for Children's Health Media, KidsHealth provides families with accurate, up-to-date, understandable, and practical health information.

National Center for Children in Poverty
http://cpmcnet.columbia.edu/dept/nccp

This national organization seeks to identify and promote strategies that prevent child poverty in the United States and that improve the lives of low-income children and their families. It emphasizes how both the public and private sectors must work together in reducing child poverty while simultaneously investing in families.

National Center for Education in Maternal and Child Health
http://www.ncemch.org/

This center provides national leadership to the maternal and child-health community in three areas: program development, policy analysis and education, and a strong knowledge base. The organization strives to improve the health and well-being of the nation's children and families and works to help federal, state, and local policymakers, public health professionals, and the public make informed decisions about maternal and child-health services, programs, and policies.

National Center for Health Statistics
http://www.cdc.gov/nchs

The National Center for Health Statistics (NCHS) is the federal government's principal vital and health statistics agency. The NCHS provides data on vital events as well as information on health status, lifestyle and exposure to unhealthy influences, the onset and diagnosis of illness and disability, and the use of health care. The NCHS is a part of the Centers for Disease Control and Prevention in the U.S. Department of Health and Human Services.

National Resource Center for Health and Safety in Child Care
http://nrc.uchsc.edu/

The National Resource Center for Health and Safety in Child Care (NRC) is located at the University of Colorado Health Sciences Center in Denver, Colorado, and is funded by the Maternal and Child Health Bureau, U.S. Department of Health and Human Services, HRSA. NRC's primary mission is to promote health and safety in out-of-home child-care settings throughout the nation.

National SAFE KIDS Campaign
http://www.safekids.org

The National SAFE KIDS Campaign is a national organization dedicated solely to the prevention of unintentional childhood injury—the number one killer of children ages 14 and under. Presently, 300 state and local SAFE KIDS coalitions in all 50 states, the District of Columbia, and Puerto Rico comprise the campaign.

National Training Institute for Child Care Health Consultants
http://www.sph.unc.edu/courses/childcare/

This institute is a cooperative undertaking of the Department of Maternal and Child Health and the Frank Porter Graham Child Development Center, both of the University of North Carolina at Chapel Hill. The purpose of the institute is to support the health and safety of young children in child-care settings through the development of a national child-care health consultant training program.

World Health Organization
http://www.who.ch

The fundamental objective of the World Health Organization (WHO) is the attainment by all people of the highest possible level of health and well-being. WHO proposes conventions, agreements, regulations, and makes recommendations about international nomenclature of diseases, causes of death, and public health practices. It also develops, establishes, and promotes international standards concerning foods and biological, pharmaceutical, and similar substances.

Family Policy

Advocates for Youth
http://www.advocatesforyouth.org

Advocates for Youth is dedicated to creating programs and advocating for policies that help young people make informed and responsible decisions about their reproductive and sexual health. The organization's mission rests on the importance of teaching rights, respect, and responsibility. Advocates for Youth provides information, training, and strategic assistance to youth-serving organizations, policy makers, youth activists, and the media.

Center for Law and Social Policy
http://www.clasp.org

The Center for Law and Social Policy (CLASP) is a national nonprofit organization with expertise in both law and policy affecting the poor. Through education, policy research, and advocacy, CLASP seeks to improve the economic security of low-income families with children and to secure access to our civil justice system for low-income persons.

Center for Youth Development and Policy Research
http://www.aed.org/us/youth.html

This center is dedicated to helping youths become productive and involved citizens. It maintains that too many children and youth are at the risk of poor outcomes because opportunities are too few, too fragmented, too problem-focused, and too distant from family and neighborhood. The center's central mission is to strengthen and support local systems in order to build a comprehensive youth development infrastructure.

Child Advocate
http://www.childadvocate.net

The Child Advocate is a national organization that serves the medical, mental health, educational, and legal needs of children and their families. The professional staff is entirely volunteer, with all resources and contributions going directly to supporting children and families in need. The organization also supports local, state, and national legislative action for children.

Child Welfare League of America
http://www.cwla.org

The Child Welfare League of America (CWLA) is an association of more than 1,100 public and private nonprofit agencies that assists over 3.5 million abused and neglected children and their families each year with a wide range of services. The CWLA is the nation's oldest and largest membership-based child welfare organization. The organization is committed to engaging people everywhere in promoting the well-being of children, youth, and their families, and protecting every child from harm.

Children Now
http://www.childrennow.org

Children Now is a nonpartisan, independent voice for America's children. The organization employs innovative communications strategies that inform and educate the public regarding the status of children, while it advocates policy positions to bring about change in government, business, and communities. Particular attention is focused on the needs of children who are poor or at risk, as well as improving conditions for all children by making them a top priority across the nation.

Children's Partnership
http://www.childrenspartnership.org

The Children's Partnership is a national nonprofit, nonpartisan organization whose mission is to inform leaders and the public about the needs of America's 70 million children and to engage them in ways that benefit children. The partnership undertakes research and policy analysis, publishes reports and multimedia materials, and forges new alliances among parents, policymakers, and the private sector to achieve tangible gains for children.

Connect for Kids
http://www.connectforkids.org/

Connect for Kids, a multimedia project of the Benton Foundation, helps adults make their communities better places for families and children. The website offers a place on the Internet for adults—parents, grandparents, educators, policymakers, and others—who want to become more active citizens, from volunteering to voting with the welfare and rights of children in mind.

Families Worldwide
http://www.fww.org

The mission of Families Worldwide is to strengthen families through programs based on six principles: kindness, commitment, communication, choices, well-being, and spirituality. The organization strives to teach families the practical, applied skills necessary to strengthen internal resources and resiliency. It offers information and various types of support, including group classes that teach parenting effectiveness.

Family Support America
http://www.familysupportamerica.org/content/home.htm

Family Support America is a nationally recognized movement to strengthen family support, adaptation, and resiliency. The organization strives to accomplish this by identifying and connecting individuals and organizations that have contact with families; by providing technical assistance, training and education, conferences, and publications; and by promoting the voice of families. Family Support America seeks to emerge as a national strategy for ensuring the well-being of our children and families.

Human Services Policy Center
http://www.hspc.org/

The Human Services Policy Center (HSPC)'s mission is to improve the well-being of children, families, and communities. The center conducts policy and data analysis and provides training, technical assistance, and consultation to further this mission. Core funding is provided by the Stuart Foundations (other local and national foundations support various HSPC initiatives). It is located at the University of Washington in Seattle.

Institute for Child Health Policy
http://www.ichp.edu/

The Institute for Child Health Policy focuses its attention on issues of access, utilization, cost, quality, and family involvement in both policy and program development and health services research. Its primary goal is to research, evaluate, formulate, and advance health policies, programs, and systems that promote the health and well-being of children and youth.

Institute for Women's Policy Research
http://www.iwpr.org/

The Institute for Women's Policy Research (IWPR) is a public policy research organization dedicated to identifying and researching issues of critical importance to women and their families. The IWPR focuses on such issues as poverty and welfare, employment and earnings, work and family issues, the economic and social aspects of health care and domestic violence, and women's civic and political participation.

National Association of Child Advocates
http://www.childadvocacy.org

The National Association of Child Advocates (NACA) is a national organization devoted to building the capacity of state and local child advocacy organizations. Founded in 1984, the NACA shares ideas and exchanges information, formulates joint efforts and coordinate strategies, and increases the impact of the child advocacy movement. The NACA establishes links between state and local child advocates and national experts and provides a clearinghouse of information on issues affecting children and effective advocacy.

National Economic Development and Law Center
http://www.nedlc.org

This center is a multidisciplinary legal and planning resource center whose mission is to contribute to the abilities of low-income persons, families, and communities to realize their full potential. It does this by collaborating with community organizations to develop integrated community-building skills, indigenous leadership, and community-building creativity in order to build local capacity and achieve greater economic, social, and cultural development.

National Families in Action
http://www.emory.edu/NFIA

National Families in Action is a national drug education, prevention, and policy center based in Atlanta, Georgia. The organization focuses on preventing drug use, abuse, addiction, and death, and it serves as a link between science, law, and the public. Its central mission is to help families and communities prevent drug abuse among children by promoting policies based on science.

National Women's Law Center
http://www.nwlc.org

The National Women's Law Center protects and advances the progress of women and girls at work, in school, and in virtually every aspect of their lives. The center offers expertise in the major areas of family economic security, health, employment, and education. It uses a variety of tools to maximize its impact by bringing women's concerns to public policy makers, advocates, and the public alike. The center performs public policy research, monitoring, and analysis; litigation, advocacy, and coalition-building; and public education.

Stand for Children
http://www.stand.org

Stand for Children is a nationwide grassroots voice for children.

Its mission is to build a powerful citizen voice to ensure all children have the opportunity to grow up healthy, educated, and safe. Stand for Children strives to educate parents, provide high quality child care and educational experiences, ensure adequate medical care, and build safe communities.

Government Agencies Serving Families

Afterschool.gov
http://www.afterschool.gov

This website provides access to government resources that support after school programs. It offers information on how to understand the issues that children and adolescents face, as well as how to fund, start, and operate an after school program. Research studies, news, and publications are added to this website as they are released to keep users up to date on what is happening in the field of after school programs.

Child Care Bureau
http://www.acf.dhhs.gov/programs/ccb/

The Child Care Bureau is dedicated to enhancing the quality, affordability, and availability of child care for all families. The Child Care Bureau administers federal funds to states, territories, and tribes to assist low-income families in accessing quality child care for children when the parents work or participate in education or training.

Children's Bureau
http://www.acf.dhhs.gov/programs/cb

The Children's Bureau is responsible for assisting states in the delivery of child welfare services designed to protect children and strengthen families. The bureau provides grants to states, tribes, and communities to operate a range of child welfare services including child protective services (child abuse and neglect), family preservation and support, foster care, adoption, and independent living. In addition, the agency makes major investments in staff training, technology, and innovative programs.

Division of Violence Prevention
http://www.cdc.gov/ncipc/dvp/dvp.htm

The Division of Violence Prevention is part of the Centers for Disease Control and Prevention (CDC). The Division of Violence Prevention has four priority areas for violence prevention: youth violence, family and intimate violence, suicide, and firearm injuries. Program activities focus on primary prevention of violence through a public health approach that complements the approaches used by criminal justice, education, and the many other disciplines that work in this area.

Family and Youth Services Bureau
http://www.acf.dhhs.gov/programs/fysb

The Family and Youth Services Bureau (FYSB) is a federal agency dedicated to supporting young people and strengthening families. The bureau does so by providing runaway and homeless youth service grants to local communities. In addition, the bureau offers a network of support that includes a national hotline and referral system for runaway and homeless youth; conferences, trainings, and onsite consultations; documentation of effective practices; and distribution of information.

Healthy Schools, Healthy Communities
http://www.bphc.hrsa.dhhs.gov/hshc/hshc1.htm

Healthy Schools, Healthy Communities is a community-based, prevention focused program established in 1994. It provides family-centered, community-based primary care, as well as mental health and dental services. The program also promotes the concept of school health centers as an effective way to improve access to health services for vulnerable children and adolescents.

National Child Care Information Center
http://nccic.org/

The National Child Care Information Center (NCCIC), a project of the Child Care Bureau, Administration for Children and Families (ACF), U.S. Department of Health and Human Services, is a national resource that links information and people to complement, enhance, and promote the child-care delivery system. The primary mission of NCCIC is working to ensure that all children and families have access to high-quality comprehensive services.

National Institute of Child Health and Human Development
http://www.nichd.nih.gov

This organization seeks to assure that every individual is born healthy and wanted, that women suffer no adverse consequence from the reproductive process, and that all children have the opportunity to fulfill their potential for a healthy and productive life unhampered by disease or disability. The organization conducts and supports research on the processes that determine and maintain the health of children, adolescents, and adults.

National Institutes of Health
http://www.nih.gov

The National Institutes of Health (NIH) mission is to uncover new knowledge that will lead to better health for everyone. The NIH is one of eight health agencies of the Public Health Services which, in turn, is part of the U.S. Department of Health and Human Services. The primary goal of NIH research is to acquire new knowledge to help prevent, detect, diagnose, and treat disease and disability, from the rarest genetic disorder to the common cold.

Office of Community Services
http://www.acf.dhhs.gov/programs/ocs

The Office of Community Services works in partnership with states, communities, and other agencies to provide a range of human and economic development services and activities that assist those in need. The aim of these services and activities is to increase the capacity of individuals and families to become self-sufficient, to revitalize communities, and to build the stability and capacity of children, youth, and families so that they become able to create their own opportunities.

Office of Family Assistance
http://www.acf.dhhs.gov/programs/ofa

The Office of Family Assistance (OFA) is located in the United States Department of Health and Human Services, Administration for Children and Families. The OFA provides assistance and work opportunities to needy families by granting states the federal funds and wide flexibility to develop and implement their own welfare programs.

Office of Family Planning
http://www.hhs.gov/progorg/opa/titlex/ofp.html

The National Family Planning Program was created in 1970 as Title X of the Public Health Service Act. It provides individuals with the information and means to exercise personal choice in determining the number and spacing of their children. Grants provide funding for comprehensive family planning and preventive reproductive health services.

Social Security Administration
http://www.ssa.gov/

The Social Security Administration (SSA) is the nation's primary income security agency. It administers the federal retirement, survivors, and disability insurance programs, as well as the program of supplemental security income (SSI) for the aged, blind, and disabled, and performs certain functions with respect to the black lung benefits program. SSA also directs the aid to the aged, blind, and disabled in Guam, Puerto Rico, and the Virgin Islands.

U.S. Department of Health and Human Services
http://www.dhhs.gov

The U.S. Department of Health and Human Services is the government's principal agency for protecting the health of all Americans and providing essential human services. It includes more than 300 programs, covering a wide spectrum of activities, from medical and social science research to financial assistance and services for low-income families. It is also the largest grant-making agency in the federal government, providing some 60,000 grants per year.

U. S. Department of Labor Women's Bureau
http://www.dol.gov/dol/wb

The U.S. Department of Labor Women's Bureau, established by Congress in 1920, is the only federal agency mandated to represent the needs of wage-earning women in the public policy process. For over 80 years, it has been meeting that mandate—identifying the issues working women care about most and vigorously pioneering research and remedies to address them.

U. S. Government Printing Office
http://www.access.gpo.gov/

The U. S. Government Printing Office produces and distributes federal government information products. Whether providing public access to government information online or producing and procuring printed publications, the U. S. Government Printing Office combines conventional technology with modern methods for supporting nearly all the information needs of Congress, federal agencies, and the American public.

National Family Organizations

About Our Kids
http://www.aboutourkids.org

About Our Kids is a multidisciplinary team of professionals dedicated to advancing the field of mental health for children and their families through evidence-based practice, science, and education. Located at New York University's Child Study Center, this organization offers psychiatric and psychological services for children and families, with emphasis on early diagnosis and intervention.

Center for the Child Care Workforce
http://www.ccw.org/

The Center for the Child Care Workforce (CCW) was founded in 1978 as the Child Care Employee Project. The CCW strives to promote the link between good jobs for child-care teachers and providers and good care for young children. It has provided significant research on the professional importance of early childhood education, including documentation, advocacy, and training and organizing around the issues of better compensation and working conditions for teachers.

Child Care Action Campaign
http://www.childcareaction.org

A leading voice and national resource advocating quality, affordable child care for all families. The organization communicates innovative ideas for improving child care; stimulates investment in child care by employers; encourages partnerships among communities, schools, and business leaders to improve child care and early education; and advocates public policies that support families.

Child Care Aware
http://www.childcareaware.org/index.htm

Child Care Aware is a nonprofit initiative committed to helping parents find the best information on locating quality child care and child-care resources in their community. The organization does this by raising the visibility of child-care resources and referral agencies nationwide and by connecting parents with the local agencies best equipped to serve their needs.

Children's Defense Fund
http://www.childrensdefense.org

The Children's Defense Fund (CDF) is a private, nonprofit organization supported by foundations, corporation grants, and individual donations. The CDF provides a strong, effective voice for all the children of America who cannot vote, lobby, or speak for themselves. The CDF pays particular attention to the needs of poor and minority children and those with disabilities.

Children's Foundation
http://www.childrensfoundation.net

The Children's Foundation (CF) is a private national educational nonprofit organization that strives to improve the lives of children and those who care for them. Its mission is to provide a voice for caregivers and children and their families on issues of critical concern. The CF conducts research and provides information and training on child nutrition programs; quality child care; leadership development; health care; welfare-to-work programs; and enforcement of court-ordered child support.

Children's Resources International
http://www.childrensresources.org/about.html

Children's Resources International (CRI) is a nonprofit educational organization dedicated to improving the quality of educational experiences and opportunities for children and their families in the United States and internationally. Among other services the CRI writes curriculum guides, activity books, training materials, and college courses for educators, administrators, caregivers, and parents.

Council for Exceptional Children
http://www.cec.sped.org

The Council for Exceptional Children (CEC) is the largest international professional organization dedicated to improving educational outcomes for individuals with exceptionalities, students with disabilities, and/or gifted students. CEC advocates for appropriate governmental policies, sets professional standards, provides continual professional development, advocates for newly and historically underserved individuals with exceptionalities, and helps professionals obtain conditions and resources necessary for effective professional practice.

Council on Contemporary Families
http://www.contemporaryfamilies.org

The Council on Contemporary Families (CCF) is a nonprofit organization dedicated to enhancing the national conversation about what contemporary families need and how these needs can best be met. The organization seeks to heighten public awareness of the contemporary family and its needs through educational materials, media coverage, conferences, and seminars.

Fathers Network
http://www.fathersnetwork.org

The Fathers Network, through its more than 100 regional and national programs, provides powerful and positive supports for fathers, families, and providers. The organization offers information that will provide insight on the challenges of raising a child with special needs. Resources include conferences, award-winning monographs, videos, and newsletters.

Federal Interagency Coordinating Council
http://www.fed-icc.org/

This resource organization identifies the needs of young children with and at risk for disabilities and the needs of their families and it works energetically with all in an open process for policies addressing those needs. It also seeks the best information about the existing system of services.

The Future of Children
http://www.futureofchildren.org

The primary purpose of The Future of Children is to disseminate timely information on major issues related to children's well-being. A special emphasis is placed on providing objective analysis and evaluation, translating existing knowledge into effective programs and policies, and promoting constructive institutional change.

Institute for Youth, Education, and Families
http://www.nlc.org/nlc_org/site/programs/institute_for_youth_education_and_families/index.cfm

The Institute for Youth, Education, and Families helps municipal leaders take action on behalf of the children, youth, and families in their communities. The institute focuses on five core program areas: education, youth development, early childhood development, safety of children and youth, and family economic security. The organization compiles and disseminates information and builds networks of officials working on similar issues and concerns.

National Adoption Information Clearinghouse
http://www.calib.com/naic

The clearinghouse is a national resource for information on all aspects of adoption for professionals, policy makers, and the general public. Clearinghouse services include technical assistance to professionals and policy makers, a library collection, publications, databases on adoption resources, and information on federal and state legislation.

National Black Child Development Institute
http://www.nbcdi.org

Established in 1970, the National Black Child Development Institute (NBCDI) is a nonprofit organization that has provided and supported programs, workshops, and resources for African American children, their parents, and their communities. Focus areas include early health and education, elementary and secondary education, child welfare, and parenting.

National Center for Health Statistics
http://www.cdc.gov/nchs/

The National Center for Health Statistics (NCHS) is the federal government's principal vital and health statistics agency. Since 1960, when the National Office of Vital Statistics and the National Health Survey merged to form NCHS, the agency has provided a wide variety of data with which to monitor the nation's health. To meet priority data needs for public health, the NCHS works closely with other federal agencies as well as researchers and academic institutions.

National Center for Community Education
http://www.nccenet.org

The National Center for Community Education has been in operation since 1962 to promote community education by providing leadership training to people who are interested in community schools, as well as leadership training to further the development and skills of those implementing community education. Training includes recognizing the important bridge that exists between families and schools.

National Information Center for Children and Youth with Disabilities
http://www.nichcy.org

This national information and referral center provides information on disabilities and disability-related issues for families, educators, and other professionals. It offers a special focus on children and youth from birth to age 22. Among the focus areas are early intervention, individualized education programs, disability organizations, professional associations, and educational rights.

National Resource Center for Family Centered Practice
http://www.uiowa.edu/~nrcfcp/new/starts.shtml

The National Resource Center for Family Centered Practice provides technical assistance, staff training, research and evaluation, and library research on family-based programs and issues to public and private human services agencies in states, counties, and communities across the United States. The center offers expertise in such areas as child welfare, mental health, juvenile justice, community action, county extension, Head Start, and job training programs.

National School Age Care Alliance
http://www.nsaca.org

The National School Age Care Alliance (NSACA) is a national organization representing all public, private, and community-based providers of after school programs. NSACA has over 8,000 members and 36 affiliated state organizations. It promotes national standards of quality school-age care for children and youth from ages 5 to 14 and grants accreditation to programs meeting the standards.

National Youth Development Information Center
http://www.nydic.org

The National Youth Development Information Center provides practice-related information about youth development to national and local youth-serving organizations at low cost or no cost. Among the available youth development services are research and evaluation, projects and programs, policies and regulations, foundation and federal funding opportunities, and career development information.

North American Council on Adoptable Children
http://www.nacac.org

The North American Council on Adoptable Children strives to meet the needs of waiting children and the families who adopt them. The mission of the NACAC is that every child has the right to a permanent family. The council advocates the right of every child to a permanent, continuous, nurturing, and culturally sensitive family, and the council presses for the legal adoptive placement of any child denied that right.

Zero to Three
http://www.zerotothree.org

Zero to Three is a national nonprofit organization. Its mission is to promote the healthy development of the nation's infants and toddlers by supporting and strengthening families, communities, and those who work on their behalf. The organization is dedicated to advancing current knowledge; promoting beneficial policies and practices; communicating research and the best practices to a wide variety of audiences; and providing training, technical assistance, and leadership development.

Family Life Research Sites

Bureau of Labor Statistics
http://www.bls.gov

The Bureau of Labor Statistics (BLS) is the principal fact-finding agency for the federal government in the broad field of labor economics and statistics. The BLS produces timely and accurate data relevant to the needs of its users and to the social and economic conditions of the nation, its workers, its workplaces, and its workers' families.

Center for Health Services Research and Policy
http://www.gwu.edu/~chsrp

The Center for Health Services Research and Policy (CHSRP) conducts sponsored health services research and policy analysis on complex health policy issues, including those impacting the family. The CHSRP identifies, monitors, and analyzes emerging issues in federal and state health law and policy and evaluates the effects of changing federal policies on health-care access, quality, and cost at the state and local levels.

Child Trends
http://www.childtrends.org

Child Trends is a nonprofit, nonpartisan research organization dedicated to studying children, youth, and families through research, data collection, and data analyses. Among the focus areas are the teenage pregnancy and childbearing rates; the effects of welfare and poverty on children; and the issues related to parenting, family structure, and family processes.

ChildStats.gov
http://www.childstats.gov

This website offers easy access to federal and state statistics and reports on children and their families including: population and family characteristics, economic security, health, behavior and social environment, and education. It also provides reports of the Federal Interagency Forum on Child and Family Statistics including "America's Children: Key National Indicators of Well-Being," the annual federal monitoring report on the status of the nation's children, and Nurturing Fatherhood.

FedStats

http://www.fedstats.gov/aboutfedstats.html

FedStats provides the full range of official statistical information available to the public from the federal government. It enables visitors to use the Internet's linking and searching capabilities to track economic and population trends, including data related to family life.

FirstGov

http://www.firstgov.gov/

FirstGov is a public-private partnership, led by a cross-agency board and administered by the Office of FirstGov in the General Services Administration's Office of Governmentwide Policy. This reference source transcends the traditional boundaries of government and its vision is global—connecting the world to all U.S. government information and services.

Foundation for Child Development

http://www.ffcd.org

The Foundation for Child Development (FCD) is dedicated to the principle that all families should have the social and material resources to raise their children to be healthy, educated, and productive members of their communities. The foundation seeks to understand children, particularly the disadvantaged, and to promote their well-being. To this end, the foundation supports basic and policy-relevant research about the factors that promote and support the optimal development of children and adolescents.

Library of Congress

http://www.lcweb.loc.gov/

The Library of Congress is the nation's oldest federal cultural institution. Its primary mission is serving the research needs of institutions, businesses, and the general public. The library's global collections cover all languages, topics, and types of material, including family life in the United States.

MCH Policy Research Center

http://www.mchpolicy.org

The Maternal & Child Health Policy Research Center specializes in health-care issues affecting children, including those with special health-care needs and those from low-income families. Through the analysis of existing large national databases and its own surveys, this research organization provides timely and reliable analytic reports on a variety of issues of national, state, and local significance.

National Research Council
http://www.nas.edu/nrc/

The National Research Council was organized by the National Academy of Sciences in 1916. Functioning in accordance with general policies determined by the academy, the National Research Council serves to further our nation's knowledge and make research available to the government, the public, and the scientific communities.

National Women's Health Information Center
http://www.4women.gov/about/index.htm

Provides a gateway to the vast array of federal and other women's health research and resources. This website can help the user link to, read, and download a wide variety of women's health-related research developed by the Department of Health and Human Services, other federal agencies, and private-sector research.

Population Reference Bureau
http://www.prb.org/

The Population Reference Bureau (PRB) provides timely and objective information on U.S. and international population trends and their implications. The PRB informs policymakers, educators, the media, and concerned citizens working in the public interest around the world through a broad range of activities, including publications, information services, seminars and workshops, and technical support.

Research and Training Center on Family Support
http://www.rtc.pdx.edu

The Research and Training Center on Family Support is dedicated to promoting effective community-based, culturally competent, family-centered services for families and their children who are, or may be affected by mental, emotional, or behavioral disorders. This goal is accomplished through collaborative research partnerships with family members, service providers, policy makers, and other concerned persons.

Research Forum on Children, Families and the New Federalism
http://www.researchforum.org

The Research Forum encourages collaborative research and informed policy on welfare reform, child and family well-being, and community/neighborhood issues. This website, updated on a regular basis, features a searchable database of summaries of large- and small-scale research projects, key topics pages, resources pages, and lists of recent publications related to these issues.

United States Census Bureau
http://www.census.gov

The United States Census Bureau is the preeminent collector and provider of timely, relevant, and quality data about the people and economy of the United States, including that related to family life. The primary goal of the Census Bureau is to provide the best mix of timeliness, relevancy, quality, and cost for the data it collects and services it provides.

Internet Search Engines

If you cannot find what you are looking for in this and other chapters with your current internet search engine, we recommend the following:

About.com
http://www.about.com/

Alta Vista
http://www.altavista.digital.com

DejaNews
http://www.dejanews.com/

Dogpile
http://www.dogpile.com/

Excite!
http://www.excite.com/

Google
http://www.google.com/

HotBot
http://www.hot.com/

InfoSeek
http://www.infoseek.com

MetaCrawler
http://www.go2net.com/search.html

Northern Light
http://www.northernlight.com/

Snap
http://www.snap.com/

WebCrawler
http://www.webcrawler.com/

Yahoo!
http://www.yahoo.com/

Glossary

adoption   The act of legally becoming the parent of a child not biologically one's own.

annulment   Invalidation of a marriage on the basis of some reason existing at the beginning of that marriage, such as fraud, being underage, or duress.

artificial insemination   A form of reproductive technology in which donor sperm, carefully screened for genetic defects and other problems, is used to fertilize the female egg.

assisted reproductive technologies   Medical interventions used to help women become pregnant. Such technologies include in-vitro fertilization, artificial insemination, surrogate motherhood, and embryo transfer.

behavior modification theory   Style of child rearing that emphasizes the parental use of positive and negative reinforcement.

bilateral descent   Tracing lineage on both sides of the family.

blended family   A family that results when a divorced parent with custody of children remarries. Also called the *compound* or *reconstituted family*, this household consists of parent, children, and stepparent.

child sexual abuse   Sexual contact between an adult and a child who are in no way related. Interactions between a child and an adult where the youngster is being used for the sexual stimulation of that adult or another person.

chronic illness   A progressive disorder caused by a nonreversible condition that often leaves the person with some type of disability.

civil union   A legal institution parallel to marriage that provides the same rights, benefits, and protections to same-sex couples (e. g., adoption, medical care, taxes, inheritance).

crude divorce rate The number of divorces per 1,000 members of the population in a given year.

culture Everything individuals do or have as members of society. Culture serves to identify, organize, and unify people who share a common way of life.

democratic theory Style of child rearing proposed by Dreikurs. Emphasis is placed on integrating children as fully as possible into the family network so that they can benefit from everyone's observations, feedback, and encouragement.

developmental-maturational theory Child-rearing theory emphasizing the importance of childhood's developmental sequences and the need to adjust parental demands and expectations accordingly.

divorce The legal dissolution of marriage.

divorce mediation A conflict resolution process in which the disputants meet with a third-party mediator whose role is that of a facilitator and an impartial guide to negotiation.

egalitarian power structure A power structure emphasizing the sharing of marital power between husband and wife.

embryo transfer Form of reproductive technology in which a female is designated to become impregnated with the father's sperm. After several days, the fertilized egg is removed from her womb and placed within the mother's uterus.

employment discrimination The unfair and unequal treatment of a person based on her or his sex.

endogamy Marrying from within one's own social group. For instance, an African American marries an African American, or a Catholic marries a Catholic.

equal rights amendment An amendment drafted in 1972 that states in essence that sex has no effect on equality of rights under the law. It passed both houses of Congress. At the time of this publication, 35 of the required 38 states had ratified the amendment. It is annually re-introduced into the Congress.

exogamy Marrying outside one's particular social group. For example, a Native American marries an Asian American (called an interracial marriage), or a Catholic marries a Protestant (called an interfaith marriage).

extended family A household consisting of parents and offspring as well as other relatives such as grandparents, aunts, and uncles living in a single residence. Also called the *consanguine family* or the *family of kinship*.

family of orientation The family into which one is born.

family of procreation The family established through marriage and parenthood.

family planning Voluntary planning how many children are wanted, when, or if they are wanted at all.

fertility The number of births a woman will have during her reproductive life.

in-vitro fertilization A type of reproductive technology in which the female's ovum is surgically removed from the womb, fertilized by the male sperm, and then placed in the uterus. Sometimes called "test-tube fertilization."

incest Sexual contact between close blood relatives. Interactions between a child and adult where the youngster is being used for the sexual stimulation of that adult or another person.

infertility The inability to conceive and carry pregnancies to live birth.

joint custody Mutual sharing of parental rights and responsibilities after a divorce has taken place.

legal separation A contract between two marriage partners that focuses on the issues that have to be resolved before a divorce is granted, such as property division or child custody.

matriarchal power structure A pattern of authority in which the wife dominates family decisionmaking.

matrilineal descent Tracing lineage on the wife's side of the family.

matrilocal residency Establishment of residency with or near the wife's relatives.

miscegenation The technical name given to interracial marriages.

modified extended family A household having a nuclear structure, but members live in geographically dispersed locations. It is considered a modified version of the extended family because the family maintains an ongoing network of interaction.

monogamy The marriage of one man to one woman. This is the characteristic form of marriage in the United States, and the only type that is legal.

multiculturalism A recognition of the cultural diversity that exists in all societies and an effort to promote the equality of all cultural traditions.

negative population growth A demographic trend that occurs when a nation's population decreases.

neolocal residency A neutral living arrangement for married couples; that is, the geographical location is not based on ties originating from either the husband's or the wife's family.

no-fault divorce   Divorce legislation that does not accuse either party of causing the divorce.

nuclear family   A family consisting of the mother, father, and children living in a home or residence of their own. Sometimes called the *conjugal family.*

parent effectiveness training   Style of child-rearing emphasizing, among other techniques, active listening, reflecting positive images back to children, and mutual problem solving.

patriarchal power structure   A pattern of authority in which the husband dominates family decisionmaking.

patrilineal descent   Tracing lineage on the husband's side of the family.

patrilocal residency   Establishment of residency with or near the husband's relatives.

permissive parenting approach   Child-rearing approach emphasizing greater levels of freedom with children.

physical disability   An impairment of body structure and function, including mobility impairments, amputations, skeletal deformities, and disfigurements.

polyandry   The marriage of one woman to two or more men.

polygamy   A plural marriage arrangement. *Polygyny* and *polyandry* are two basic forms of polygamy.

polygyny   The marriage of one man to two or more women.

restrictive parenting approach   Child-rearing approach emphasizing strict parent-child relations.

serial monogamy   A succession of partners through the process of marriage, divorce, remarriage, and so on.

single-parent family   A household in which one parent assumes the responsibility for raising biological or adopted children.

surrogate motherhood   Type of reproductive technology in which a chosen surrogate mother is artificially inseminated with the husband's sperm. The surrogate mother carries and bears the child, which is then given to the couple.

transactional-analysis theory   Child-rearing approach that takes into consideration three ego states (child, parent, and adult), and how they relate to overall communication.

voluntary childlessness   A conscious decision among couples not to have children.

Index

About the Author

Jeffrey Scott Turner is chairperson of the Human Development and Family Studies Department at Mitchell College in New London, Connecticut. Dr. Turner is the author of many college-level textbooks, among which are *Marriage and Family: Traditions and Transitions, Encyclopedia of Relationships Across the Lifespan, Lifespan Development, Contemporary Adulthood, Exploring Child Behavior,* and *Contemporary Human Sexuality.* He is also the author of various articles and studies and has received numerous awards and citations for his teaching and writing accomplishments.